Words to Measure a War

Words to Measure a War

Nine American Poets of World War II

DAVID K. VAUGHAN

McFarland & Company, Inc., Publishers
Jefferson, North Carolina, and London

ALSO OF INTEREST AND FROM MCFARLAND
Runway Visions: An American C-130 Pilot's Memoir of Combat Airlift Operations in Southeast Asia, 1967–1968, by David Kirk Vaughan (1998)
MiG Alley to Mu Ghia Pass: Memoirs of a Korean War Ace, by Cecil G. Foster with David K. Vaughan (2001)

LIBRARY OF CONGRESS CATALOGUING-IN-PUBLICATION DATA

Vaughan, David K.
 Words to measure a war : nine American poets of World War II / David K. Vaughan.
    p.   cm.
 Includes bibliographical references and index.

 ISBN 978-0-7864-4306-2
 softcover : 50# alkaline paper ∞

 1. American poetry—20th century—History and criticism.
 2. World War, 1939–1945—United States—Literature and the war.
 3. Soldier's writings, American—History and criticism. 4. War poetry, American—History and criticism. 5. Poets, American—20th century—Biography. 6. Soldiers—United States—Biography.
 I. Title.
 PS310.W68V38   2009
 811'.5209358—dc22   2009011915

British Library cataloguing data are available

©2009 David K. Vaughan. All rights reserved

No part of this book may be reproduced or transmitted in any form or by any means, electronic or mechanical, including photocopying or recording, or by any information storage and retrieval system, without permission in writing from the publisher.

On the cover: Marine dashes through Death Valley on Okinawa ©Corbis Images

Manufactured in the United States of America

McFarland & Company, Inc., Publishers
  Box 611, Jefferson, North Carolina 28640
  www.mcfarlandpub.com

Acknowledgments

"Conscription Camp," "Elegy for a Dead Soldier," "The Fly," "Full Moon: New Guinea," "Homecoming," "The Leg," "Lord, I Have Seen Too Much," "Nostalgia," "Recapitulations VIII," "Scyros," "Troop Train," and "V-Letter" from *Poems 1940–1953,* by Karl Shapiro copyright © Random House 1953. Reprinted by permission of the estate of Karl Shapiro, Robert Phillips, trustee.

"On Sending Home My Civilian Clothes," "Expendability," "Ritual for Singing Bat," "Elegy," "Elegy Just in Case," "Wafflebutt," "V-J Day," "Poem for My Twenty-Ninth Birthday," "On a Photo of Sgt. Ciardi a Year Later," "Two Songs for a Gunner," and "Massive Retaliation" from *The Collected Poems of John Ciardi,* ed. Edward M. Cifelli copyright © the University of Arkansas Press. "Suddenly Where Squadrons Turn," "Reflections While Oiling a Machine Gun," and "I Meet the Motion of Summer Thinking Guns," from *Other Skies* by John Ciardi copyright © 1947 estate of John Ciardi. Reprinted by permission of the estate of John Ciardi, John and Myra Ciardi, trustees. Excerpts from *Saipan,* by John Ciardi, copyright © 1988 by John Ciardi. Reprinted with the permission of the University of Arkansas Press, www.uapress.com.

"June: Dutch Harbor," "A Kodiak Poem," "Airman's Virtue," "In Memoriam Stratton Christensen," "Notes for an Elegy," "Envoi to *Ships and Other Figures,*" "Carrier," and "Transport" are reprinted from *Effort at Speech: New and Selected Poems* by William Meredith, published by TriQuarterly Books /Northwestern University Press in 1997. All rights reserved; used by permission of Northwestern University Press and the author. All other William Meredith poems used by permission of the author.

All poems by Howard Nemerov from *The Collected Poems of Howard Nemerov* and *War Stories: Poems about Long Ago and Now* by Howard Nemerov copyright © 1977 and 1987 the University of Chicago Press. Reprinted by permission of Margaret Nemerov.

Acknowledgments

Louis Simpson, excerpts from *The Owner of the House: New Collected Poems 1940-2001*. Copyright © 2003 by Louis Simpson. Reprinted with the permission of BOA Editions, Ltd., www.BOAEditions.org. Excerpts from *The Collected Prose of Louis Simpson* copyright © 1988 Louis Simpson, reprinted by permission of Louis Simpson.

"The Jewel," "The Enclosure," "The Performance," "The War Wound," "Confrontation of the Hero," "Reincarnation (II)," "The Firebombing," and "The Driver" by James Dickey from *The Whole Motion: Collected Poems, 1945-1992* (Wesleyan University Press, 1992) © 1992 by James Dickey and reprinted by permission of Wesleyan University Press.

All poems by Lincoln Kirstein from *Rhymes and More Rhymes of a Pfc*, copyright © 1964, 1966 by Lincoln Kirstein. Reprinted by permission of New Directions Publishing Corp.

Table of Contents

Acknowledgments v
Preface 1
Introduction 3

1. Karl Shapiro, U.S. Army	15
2. Randall Jarrell, U.S. Army Air Forces	32
3. John Ciardi, U.S. Army Air Forces	48
4. William Meredith, U.S. Navy	65
5. Howard Nemerov, U.S. Army Air Forces	82
6. Louis Simpson, U.S. Army	98
7. James Dickey, U.S. Army Air Forces	114
8. Richard Hugo, U.S. Army Air Forces	136
9. Lincoln Kirstein, U.S. Army	151
10. Conclusion	167

Chapter Notes 179
Bibliography 187
Index 191

Preface

This study considers the effects of wartime experiences on nine American poets who served in the American armed services during World War II: Karl Shapiro, Randall Jarrell, John Ciardi, William Meredith, Howard Nemerov, Louis Simpson, James Dickey, Richard Hugo, and Lincoln Kirstein. Three (Shapiro, Jarrell, Ciardi) were published poets who had begun to establish their reputations prior to their war service; in war they were challenged to adapt their poetic styles and themes to a harsher subject. One poet (Meredith) was able to publish his first volume of poetry during the war, and another (Nemerov) published some poems prior to and during his time in the service. For three (Dickey, Simpson, and Hugo), their war experience served as the impetus to become poets and provided the material for some of their early works. Kirstein is in a special category, because although he had published a volume of poetry before the war, that publication did not signal the beginning of a career as a poet; his most important achievements resulted from his work as a patron of American ballet, and his only major poetic work was his collection of poems about his progress through the war.

This study reviews the circumstances that brought these men into the war and examines the most important poems they wrote about the war through the perspective of their tasks, experiences, and attitudes. Finally, it attempts to compare the achievements of these men through an assessment of their overall success in representing the American wartime experience.

Some of the essays included here were presented in earlier versions at meetings of professional organizations. I presented a comparison of the World War II poetry of Randall Jarrell and John Ciardi at Interface '98, and I gave presentations of the war poetry of James Dickey, Richard Hugo, and Howard Nemerov at annual meetings of the Popular Culture/American Culture Associations. An earlier version of the essay on Lincoln

Kirstein appeared in *Visions of War: World War II in Popular Literature and Culture*, edited by Paul Holsinger and Mary Anne Schofield, published originally by the Bowling Green State University Popular Press, now under the editorial management of the University of Wisconsin Press. I thank the officials of those organizations, and especially Ray Browne of Bowling Green State University, for their support of preliminary versions of the essays included here.

I owe my thanks to many people and institutions for their involvement and assistance with this project, which otherwise would not have been successfully completed. For assistance with access to the military records of James Dickey, Howard Nemerov, and William Meredith, I would like to thank the following individuals and others in their respective Special Collections departments: Beverly Allen and the staff of the Woodruff Library of Emory University in Atlanta, Georgia; Sonya McDonald and her assistants in the John M. Olin Library at Washington University, St. Louis; and the Special Collections staff at the Charles E. Shain Library at Connecticut College.

I owe a special debt for the wonderful contributions made by the officers and civilians who enrolled in my *Literature of the Air Force Experience* course at the Air Force Institute of Technology (AFIT), Wright-Patterson Air Force Base, Dayton, Ohio, in which I included samples of the poetry of Jarrell, Hugo, Dickey, and Ciardi in course readings. I was continually surprised and pleased at the energy and insight these men and women displayed when they engaged with some of the most difficult poetry written by these important modern American poets who happened to spend some time in the United States Air Force (actually, the Army Air Forces when they were serving). I was delighted to see that these specialists in the areas of logistics, finance, maintenance, engineering, and yes, even pilots and navigators, had the desire and ability to solve a poem with the same determination and skills they used to solve problems in their engineering and management courses. Like all teachers of literature, I believe I learned more from my students than they did from me.

I would like to thank also Dr. Jan Muczyk, who, as Dean of the AFIT Graduate School of Systems and Logistics, lent his strong encouragement in support of literary enrichment for AFIT's graduate students.

Introduction

Karl Shapiro, the first of the American World War II poets to participate in the war and to be acknowledged as a war poet while serving in the war, has said:

> Our generation—the generation of Jarrell, Wilbur, myself, Roethke, Lowell, Schwartz, Bishop, Ciardi, Berryman, Kunitz, Nemerov, Whittemore ... lived through more history than most or maybe any. We lived through more history even than Stendahl, who fell, as he says, with Napoleon. We were reared as intellectuals and fought the Second World War before it happened and then again when it did happen. We witnessed the god that failed and then helped trip him up.[1]

The poets of Shapiro's generation experienced the most tumultuous period in American history, including the American Civil War. The period from 1939 to 1946 saw major philosophical debates, first about involvement in World War II, and then about the purposes and goals of Allied fighting forces. During this period there occurred the most dramatic and varied combat engagements seen yet by any fighting forces, on land, sea, and air. The events of this period had profound impacts on all artists living at the time, but especially on poets, whose task is to interpret the behaviors and beliefs of the members of the society of which they are a part. The impact on poetic response was even more profound on those poets who served in the armed forces of the United States during the war. Shapiro's comments invite consideration of the ways in which those poets who were directly involved in the war were affected by that participation: how they reacted to their wartime experiences and how they processed those experiences in poetic form.

For the British, French and Germans, World War II began in August of 1939, when Germany invaded Poland. The war in Europe had been under way for over two years before the Americans were brought irrevocably into the conflict with the attack on Pearl Harbor in December 1941.

For the English, there was little doubt about the rightness of the war. Americans, however, had participated vigorously in debates about the war, typified most notably by the arguments of Charles Lindbergh and the America First group, on one hand, and supporters of the Allied war effort on the other. By the time the Americans were brought into the war, the British had had ample opportunity to express their views on the war in prose and poetry, views that, for the most part, stated their distress over the fact of the war but accepted the cause for which they fought. The British soldiers had a well-established tradition of war poetry to use as the basis for their poetic interpretation of the horrors of war. Certainly the majority of university-educated British officers knew their Wilfred Owen, their Robert Graves, Siegfried Sassoon, and Edmund Blunden.

The generation of Englishmen who fought in World War I included a number of individuals who had described the trials and trauma of their combat experiences in a variety of poetic and prose forms during the twenty years that followed. These poets, who were mostly college-educated, established a literary dimension to the history of the war that was unknown in America. America had produced no World War I equivalents of Owen, Graves, or Sassoon. Not that Americans lacked sensitive artists capable of producing similar poems; America just had not had the equivalent experience: the Americans had had less than one year of hard fighting in the war compared to four and a half years for the British, French, Italians, and Germans, and they had experienced relatively little of the mind- and body-numbing conditions of combat life in the trenches. As Vernon Scannell points out, "the Great War was not, for those who fought under the Stars and Stripes, a war of attrition, of prolonged and almost intolerable anguish, of the brutal shattering of ideals, but a splendid surging forward to assured victory."[2]

While many Americans who participated in World War II knew something of the English literary heritage of the first war, this heritage had not molded their esthetic outlook as it had the outlook of the English soldiers. In his prefatory remarks to a collection of World War II poetry that he edited, Harvey Shapiro observes that "there are continuities but mostly strong discontinuities between the English poets of that war [World War I] and the American poets of this one [World War II]." Additionally, the American poets of World War I, he says, were "too few to constitute a group."[3] Against the earlier English poets of Owen, Graves, Sassoon, Blunden, and Rosenberg, Shapiro lists the American poets e. e. cummings, John Peale Bishop, Archibald MacLeish, and Alan Seeger. These men hardly constituted a battle-hardened group comparable to the British war poets. Instead of thinking of themselves as part of a brotherly tradition shared by earlier poets, the American poets of World War II saw themselves "caught in a giant machine."[4]

Karl Shapiro suggests that there was "a salient difference between our war poetry such as Jarrell's and that first great war poetry written in our father's war by Wilfrid Owen and Sassoon and Rosenberg and Blunden and so on. The British war poets who showed everyone how to write antiwar poetry were themselves all outstanding warriors and heroes. They cried out against war but were as conversant with blood as Lawrence of Arabia. None of my generation [of poets] were war heroes, that I remember, nor even outstanding soldiers.... In a sense we waited out the war in uniform."[5]

In the American perspective, the American combatants, lacking a body of war literature and war experiences comparable to the English, were experiencing the cruelties of full-scale war for the first time, without benefit of any literary indoctrination. Although many American families remembered ancestors who had fought and died in the American Civil War, that conflict had occurred a half-century earlier and utilized different modes of combat. The greater bulk of the poetry of the American Civil War was, for the most part, tainted by sentimental partisanship that shaded the carnage of combat. Forced to break out of their isolationist beliefs, which had prevented external wars from infringing on the national borders or national consciousness, Americans had little to draw on to prepare themselves for conflict in World War II, either from personal experience or literary description. Their immediate expressions were political, not poetic.

By the time America entered the war, the British combatants were intimately familiar with all aspects of conflict of World War II (with preliminary experiences in Spain) as well as with a large body of poetry, fiction, and non-fiction accounts of the first great war and even the early years of the current war. As a result, English soldiers carried with them a sense of literary tradition which reinforced their commitment and sense of sacrifice to the cause for which they fought. Americans, on the other hand, at first reluctant to enter a war that initially seemed remote to them, came finally into their war angry and in a state of shock, as the attack on Pearl Harbor surprised them into combat. When America entered the war, the men became part of a "fighting machine," a phrase heard everywhere in military training and endorsed by the government responsible for its operation.

For the most part, the American poets studied here had no comparable sense of a tradition of war poetry, although they acknowledged the influences of Whitman, Yeats, Auden, Eliot, Pound, and, in the case of Kirstein, Kipling, a poet not fully included in the English tradition of war poetry due to his perceived support of the imperialist goals and practices of the 19th century British Empire. Less familiar with the horrors of trench warfare, the Americans were perhaps not able to fully appreciate the disturbing accounts of Owen or Sassoon. The tradition or mode of the English Great War poets appears to have had little impact on their best poems, certainly those written during the war itself. Knowing relatively little of the hazards of trench warfare and of the terrific personal cost of ill-trained soldiers going "up the line to death," American poets instead developed their own tradition of war poetry after 1940, improvising voices and forms as the occasion required. Due partly to the fact that trench warfare of the World War I patterns seldom occurred in the fighting of World War II, the poems that the American combatants of World War II produced are less grim in that fatalistic perspective, and more varied in the settings and conditions of war.

M. L. Rosenthal observed that there were "at least two significant differences" between the World War I poets and Jarrell's generation of American war poets: "First, they felt a far greater initial detachment from official rhetoric and from the assumptions of the social system. And second, though there was a good deal of old-fashioned combat in the later war, the over-all organization and the far greater importance of the air forces and long range technology and communication made the involvement of most soldier-poets far less immediate than before."[6] Auden held a similar opinion; appraising the achievement of Lincoln Kirstein's *Rhymes of a Pfc* when it first appeared in 1964, he said: "It must be admitted, I think, that the Second World War has produced, so far at any rate, less literature of outstanding merit, whether in verse or prose, than the First." Auden gave three reasons for this result: first, fewer soldiers were directly involved in face-to-face combat. Second, because of more sophisticated assignment procedures, the men with greater literary potential were usually assigned to non-combat positions; and, finally, attitudes towards the war were different on both sides: while the First World War was an accident of political alliances, the Second World War was not.[7]

When the war became an inevitability for Americans after the Japanese attack on Pearl Harbor, it soon became evident that poets as well as non-poets would be called to serve, and that poets would be leaving their preferred habitats of lecture hall and coffee shop to venture into the less well-known world of barracks, mess halls, and firing ranges, not to mention the distressing realities of blitzkriegs and battlefields. It was natural, therefore, that where possible, some kind of communication system should be established to provide information, however tentative, for and about the recognized practitioners of the craft as they encountered this relatively unknown territory. The correspondence columns of *Poetry: A Magazine of*

Verse, the most important American publication devoted to the dissemination of new poetry and poetry criticism, soon were filled with news of poets in uniform. In the February 1943 issue, for instance, Corporal George Dillon wrote that he had met with "nothing but friendship and good humor since joining the army," and he had experienced a "community of interest" which "makes people very tolerable it seems—even when the common interest is nothing more than this efficient no-life, which we have to adopt now in order not to have it permanently."[8]

In the April 1943 issue Patrick Evans wrote that it was a "grand idea to turn over a page of *Poetry* to us [poets] who are in uniform," which he thought would help keep him "in touch." Evans said that "being in war is like living on an iceberg. Cut off from everything. Of course one has friends and companions. But for the things I care about there is no time, no spaciousness, no thought left to be devoted." In the same issue, Henry Rago agreed that receiving *Poetry* magazine was a "lifeline in an isolated army barracks." The community of affected poets included those living in England as well; a letter in the same issue from Keidrych Rhys in England reported on the hazards of war, as he mentioned the deaths of Timothy Corsellis, Nigel Weir, Gervase Stewart, and David Bourne, all pilots in the Royal Air Force. Rhys also reported on the military assignments of seventeen other poets, including Alun Lewis, Denyer Cox, G. S. Fraser, Lawrence Durrell, Roy Fuller, and John Manifold.[9] Throughout the war *Poetry* continually tracked the progress of its American poets; the February 1945 issue reported on the status of, among others, Karl Shapiro, John Ciardi, Stephen Stepanchev, William Meredith, William Jay Smith, Thomas McGrath, Edwin Honig, Stanley Kunitz, and Richard Eberhart.[10] That *Poetry* was important to John Ciardi is evident in his wartime correspondence with Peter De Vries and Marion Strobel, who were editors during the war years. *Poetry* was a strong supporter of Karl Shapiro's poetry during the war as well.

As individuals molded in their varied service patterns, the nine poets considered here were directly affected by impersonal bureaucracies that assigned them jobs on the basis of test scores and chance rather than individual merit or preference. They learned about the military, an institution about which most of these poets knew very little and in which few cared to distinguish themselves beyond the necessary challenges of minimum professional success and personal survival (Meredith is the exception). In terms of influences that would affect their poetic outlook, the war poems of Wilfred Owen probably made less of an impression on them than the occasional self-serving training noncommissioned officer or pompous superior officer to whom the military was a line of work to be taken seriously, even in peacetime.

Having fought their way through training, these poets then had to deal with their roles in war itself, which they soon began to see (those who found themselves in combat environments) could provide even greater hazards to long life than the unpleasantness of training programs. Their training programs, their combat experiences, and the military service in which they found themselves obligated to serve determined the forms and contents of their poetic outlook possibly as much as any received poetic tradition. As in all good poetry, experience precedes art. Few of them opted for the World War II equivalent of trench life, the life of an infantry soldier. In fact, it seems clear that almost all of them took determined steps to avoid such a life, seven of the nine volunteering initially for flying training programs that promised a more appealing and more romantic means of waging war. Or so they believed. (Of those seven, two were successful in becoming pilots, and three others flew in combat in other capacities.)

They all passed through periods of apprenticeship in which they experienced the services' attempts to eliminate individualism in favor of a group identity—the platoon, the flight, the ship—to which the self should sacrifice its autonomy. This is not the kind of experience that poets (or even nonpoets) generally enjoy. Having agreed to participate, however, they continued through their training programs with resignation if not determination, and certainly with a strong sense of detachment which they used to protect their artistic cores. It is not surprising to see resentment towards the system in many poems written about training or apprenticeship experiences.

In time of mass mobilization, the odds against successful selectivity in training programs and the urgencies of operational necessity militate against anything like a rational outcome for the individuals involved, and so what these men ended up doing in the war was perhaps much different from what they initially envisioned. Nevertheless, having passed through that process, they moved to their eventual position in the war, developing perspectives that could be little appreciated or understood by those who did not share their experiences. It is not surprising, then, that the visions presented in their poems, as well as the terminologies or duties, should be unique and occasionally difficult to comprehend. Not that those poems heavily invested with military languages and concepts cannot be understood and appreciated; some poets explained terminology and tactics, often giving detailed footnotes to explain the specific situation. Jarrell, for instance, was at pains to do this, as was Meredith, and Simpson provided prose commentaries which supplement his poetic versions of combat experience. Kirstein's footnote section to *Rhymes of a Pfc* could be thought of as a history of the (well-educated) support soldier's life. Several

(Shapiro, Ciardi, Simpson, Hugo) provided a variety of prose narratives that fill in some of the details of their operational tasks.

Clearly, to appreciate the accomplishments of the poets considered here, it is necessary to understand something of the conditions, training, and combat environments in which these men lived and worked. It is especially important in the case of those who were associated with aircraft, as each particular aircraft was unique in its interior configuration and combat role. It is essential to understand, for instance, the working conditions of a side gunner on a B-29 (as in the case of John Ciardi), or the radar observer's position in the P-61 (James Dickey), or the training environment for a celestial navigation instructor (Randall Jarrell), or the pilot's position in a navy observation aircraft (William Meredith), or the pilot's duties in a Royal Air Force Coastal Command patrol aircraft (Howard Nemerov), or the bombardier's duties in a B-24 (Richard Hugo). Even an infantryman like Simpson was affected by aircraft, as he was trained to jump out of them to enter combat. Only Shapiro and Kirstein, the first and last poets considered here, avoided direct association with aircraft, but although their experiences differed widely (Shapiro was a medical technician, Kirstein an administrative gadfly), they wrote poems about the hazardous effects of friendly or hostile aircraft.

The men who could call themselves poets before they joined the military service found themselves occupied with two large issues. The first was simply how to account for oneself as a poet wearing a uniform. The idea was best expressed by the English poet Henry Treece: "I volunteered for the Royal Air Force in order to fulfill a social duty: so that I should not be ashamed of myself as the years went on. As a poet, I was naturally cynical of such behaviour."[11] Those who were established poets had worked hard to establish their unique creative identities. They were not particularly pleased to find themselves in uniform, but they were not necessarily reluctant soldiers either. Although their poetic inclinations made them averse to almost everything the military stood for, they believed that the cause in which they had enlisted was just or at least necessary. But, as poets, they had begun to commit themselves to developing the poetic vision required of the person who would truly be known by the name of poet (even if they had not written significant numbers of poems). A poet, almost more than any other kind of artist, declares himself an independent agent of society with the creative task of depicting the strange, appalling, inconsistent, surprising, and occasionally inspiring behavior of larger or smaller segments of that society. How then, could these individuals justify—even to themselves—their function as part of one of the most highly regimented agencies of that society? They could do so, perhaps, on the basis that their actions were caused by a national emergency, the defense of their country, or to help defeat the spread of fascism and totalitarianism. But most good poets seldom worry about large political causes. Some of them were motivated by the appeal of a relatively new way of engaging in war, the war in the air, while others thought that their military duties were useful. But regardless of their motivation or the success of their efforts, they still found themselves part of the armed services, the most obvious and destructive agency of the *State* (with a capital S, a word Jarrell used extensively).

The second large issue was language, partly the use and misuse of familiar words, but more often the problem of creating or establishing vocabularies adequate to carry the meanings of the events and circumstances in which they found themselves. They found that words, the essential tools of the poet, were in some cases becoming increasingly unreliable and inappropriate, especially in the case of public rhetoric, or inadequate or insufficient, in the case of their new military experiences. As the war approached, and especially as it caught America up in the first months and years of conflict, many of society's agents—the government, the media, even other writers and poets—appropriated the language to present their particular political or social agendas. Early in the war, many writers employed language to create a positive perspective on troubling scenes or events. In an effort to bolster flagging public morale, many writers resorted to the language of advertising and propaganda to describe world events and the Allied response to the war. In response, the established poets, especially Shapiro and Jarrell, expressed suspicion of such language, pointing to the inaccuracies and false representations created by the rhetoric of wartime circumstances. They consciously tried to renew the words they used to present their individual, personal visions of their war experiences, unaffiliated with public patriotism or righteous indignation. Their efforts were also directed at manipulating the technical and tactical words of the military professions, giving them new meanings and interpretations.

One way the established poets attempted to react to these issues was to cast themselves in the role of philosophical and ethical commentators on the events of the war. Because they were part of the war effort, even if they were not involved in hostile fire, they nevertheless were much closer to the operation of the military services and could see for themselves the workings and outcomes of military actions. Their education and aesthetic outlook placed them in a privileged position to recognize both the practical requirements and the moral complexities of those actions. Thus they worked to create philosophical frameworks through which to view the events of the war, and then selected views of the war to interpret. Those located at the periphery of hostile action could more easily maintain a detached philosophic perspective. Those who were directly involved in combat activities found intellectual detachment less easy to achieve, and their poetry reflected their involvement as participants as well as artistic interpreters of the actions of the war-making machinery.

For the second and larger group of poets, the men who began to build their poetic reputations during and after the war, the issues were different. Not having achieved the status of poets before they entered the war, it was more difficult for them to claim that they were displaced persons operating in an unfriendly environment. Perhaps because more of the poets in the second group were engaged in combat activities (Simpson was in the infantry; Meredith and Nemerov were pilots; Dickey was a radar observer, Hugo a bombardier), their poetry, nearly all of it written well after the war ended, demonstrates narrower, more personal perspectives instead of broader philosophic frameworks. They did attempt to construct such frameworks, but their efforts to establish personal mythologies are based on the often hazardous events and conditions they experienced. Events first, then the framework: this is the pattern of these poets.

Like the first group, they are also concerned with the meanings of words. Unlike the first group, however, they are less concerned with the pre-war meanings of words than with their symbolic complexity. Because they were not yet established poets, and thus not yet part of a larger community devoted to interpreting life experiences, they were less concerned with the interpretation that society wanted to imprint on certain words, because they were more interested in the possibility of extending the meanings of words (which is after all one of the true purposes of a poet).

Thus we can see two kinds of poets writing poems about the war. The first group complains about the failure of societies to deal with the important problems of the world, causing dehumanization and bringing about the deaths of millions and the destruction of cultural landmarks. The second group focuses on individual survival and the creation of a myth which can explain survival in the face of that destruction. Kirstein is a special case, addressing individual actions with an overriding concern about the war's impact on art.

The three principal criteria used to select the poets discussed in this study include service in uniform during World War II in one of the branches of the armed services of the United States; publication of a significant body of poetry resulting from military service, typically in the form of volumes of poetry primarily about the war; and significant poetic achievement in the total body of published work and overall stature in the field of American poetry. Given the circumstances and cultural values and practices of the period, these criteria resulted in the selection of nine men with no women or minority representation. Of the nine poets considered here, three served in the ground army, five in the army air forces, and one in the navy. Their military assignments took them to varying locations: the northern Pacific, the southern Pacific, Australia, Europe, the United States. All were caught up in the war for most of the four years (from 1941 to 1945) that America was officially involved.

Karl Shapiro joined the army before the war started and served in the army's medical corps in the South Pacific–Australia area. William Meredith joined after the war started and flew patrol and reconnaissance aircraft in the Alaskan–Aleutian chain area and later in Hawaii. James Dickey joined the war effort late but flew in the Philippines and eventually over Okinawa and Japan before the war ended. Howard Nemerov flew coastal patrol aircraft with the Royal Air Force in England. Louis Simpson was an infantryman with the 101st Airborne Division; he fought in Europe during the last year of the war and saw service from the coasts of France to Bastogne. John Ciardi joined early, but delays kept him from participating in the war until he was assigned as a gunner on B-29s flying missions over Japan in the last year. Lincoln Kirstein served in a supporting role in the army in Europe, following the advancing front-line army. Richard Hugo served as a bombardier on B-24 bombers flying from Italy to targets in Germany and Austria during the winter of 1944-1945. And Randall Jarrell, the only one to remain in the United States for the duration of the war, trained air force navigators in celestial navigation techniques at a training field in Arizona. Thus the works of the poets considered here provide a broad cross-section of training experiences, geographical areas, operational activities, and chronological perspectives.

Three of the poets discussed here (Shapiro, Jarrell, Meredith) produced their war poems during the war or immediately after and wrote few, if any, war poems later. Five of the poets considered (Nemerov, Dickey, Simpson, Hugo, Kirstein) wrote their most important war poetry several years after the war ended. One (Ciardi) wrote significant numbers of war poems both during and after the war. As we will see, the poets considered in this study created a variety of poetic responses to the wartime situations they encountered, providing philosophical, natural, artistic, or personal perspectives with which to frame their experiences. They assessed their responses against the larger issues of national goals and wartime morality in a variety of ways, but all were unified in their knowledge of the significance of their efforts. Although they were speaking individually, they recognized as well that they were speaking for (or, at least, of) those around them who were sharing their responsibilities, burdens, and fates, many of whom were acknowledged or named in their poems.

A number of widely respected American poets who participated in the war are not considered in this study, including Stanley Kunitz, Richard Wilbur, Hayden Carruth, Richard Eberhart, and W. D. Snodgrass. Although all of these men produced a large body of poems, including some memorable poems about the war, their total numbers of war poems are relatively small compared to the others, and their poems do not display the full range and significance of the war experiences comparable to the depth and involvement demonstrated by the poets considered here. Stanley Kunitz, whose best-known war poems are "Careless Love" and "Reflection by a Mailbox," served three years with the Air Transport Command, in North Carolina and Washington D.C., in the Army Air Forces. A superb poet, he produced only a small body of war-related poetry, an understandable result of his essentially pacifist outlook.

Richard Wilbur initially started training in cryptography, a natural line of work for a poet. However, his college involvement with leftist organizations caused his removal from that field, and he was sent to Europe as a communications specialist with the 36th Signal Company of the 36th Infantry Division, seeing action in France and Germany in 1944 and 1945. He wrote several poems about his war experience; the most notable are "Mined Country" and "First Snow in Alsace." He also wrote an engaging and readable history of the signal company with which he served. However, his total output of war poems is relatively small.

Hayden Carruth also entered the military as a cryptographer but did most of his work as a public relations specialist for the 455th Heavy Bombardment Group in southern Italy. He "spent most of the war writing stupid 'features' for the newspapers back home, or interviewing GIs on disk for their hometown radio stations. It was dull work.... Only after the war did I read the poems of Jarrell and Shapiro and [Thomas] McGrath and see what I might have done in the army if I had been more aware of the possibilities."[12] Carruth's total number of war poems is small.

Richard Eberhart served in the U.S. Navy from 1942 until 1946, working as a naval gunnery instructor at Dam Neck, Virginia, for two years and then becoming Training Officer at the Naval Air Station at Wildwood, New Jersey. As the war ended he was reassigned to a naval station in California, where he remained until he left the service in the spring of 1946.[13] Eberhart's best-known war poem is "The Fury of Aerial Bombardment." "The Groundhog" is also considered by some to be one of his war poems, but its relation to specific circumstances or actions pertaining to World War II is remote at best.

W. D. Snodgrass served in the U.S. Navy, primarily at a naval facility at the island of Saipan, in the Pacific. His two best-known war poems are "Ten Days Leave" and "Return to Frisco, 1946," both about the difficulties of the serviceman adjusting to life at home after wartime service. It is likely that Snodgrass was on the island of Saipan at the same time that John Ciardi was assigned to Saipan as a gunner on B-29 bomber aircraft.

Late in 1944 the American poet and anthologist Oscar Williams requested contributions for an anthology, *The War Poets*, which included those poems which seemed to him to have been written with "an emotional comprehension of all that war implies" and which expressed no "sham patriotics."[14] This book, which appeared in the spring of 1945, was the most important volume of serious war poetry published in the United States during the war. Williams included poems written by poets of all English-speaking nationalities, civilians as well as soldiers. The soldier poets section included 57 men and one woman; of the poets in uniform in the anthology, there were 25 Americans, 29 British, two Canadians, one South African and one Australian. The list of British soldier poets included such well-known names as Timothy Corsellis, Gavin Ewart, Roy Fuller, Sidney Keyes, Alun Lewis, Emanuel Litvinoff, H. B. Mallalieu, John Manifold, John Pudney, Keidrych Rhys, Gervase Stewart, Julian Symons, Henry Treece, and Vernon Watkins. Included among the American soldier poets were Walter Benton, Hubert Creekmore, Richard Eberhart, Stanley Kunitz, Selden Rodman, William Jay Smith, Donald Stauffer, Dunstan Thompson, Edward Weismiller, and five of the nine poets discussed here: Randall Jarrell, Howard Nemerov, William Meredith, John Ciardi, and Karl Shapiro.

Over fifty years later another American war poem anthology appeared: *Poets of World War II*, edited by Harvey Shapiro, a volume in the American Poets project published as part of the Library of America series in 2003. This volume contains poems written by 62 American poets, of whom 40 had served in uniform, including all of the poets discussed here. The 37 poems of the nine poets considered in this study constitute approximately one-third of the poems in the volume (of the other American names included in the 1945 *The War Poets*, only three—Eberhart, Kunitz, and Smith—appear in *Poets of World War II*). These statistics give some idea of the enduring value of the war poems of the nine men considered in this study, which offers a discussion of the most important poems of these nine poets, taking into consideration not only the ideas in the poems, but the impact of the training and combat experiences of the poets who wrote them.

1

Karl Shapiro, U.S. Army

Of the poets studied here, Karl Shapiro was the first to enter military service, drafted into the army nine months before the attack on Pearl Harbor. Surprisingly, perhaps, he was not particularly unhappy about being drafted. He thought that spending a year in the army (which is how long he believed he would be required to serve) would take him out of his Baltimore neighborhood, give him some new experiences, and provide fresh ideas. His first book of poems had been published, though he didn't consider it an especially significant achievement, as he had published it with the help of family members. However, the publication of that volume gave him the moral authority to call himself a poet and encouraged him to pursue a poet's work, and he completed an increasingly large body of poems, many of which were published in respected poetry journals during his years in the army. The events he experienced while in the army gave him new and different subjects for his poetry, in which he demonstrated a variety of moods and styles.

After attempting unsuccessfully to determine a career path for himself—thinking of the academic life and the life of a librarian—he found his future determined by the arrival of a draft notice in March of 1941, when Shapiro was in his twenty-seventh year. He was sent for his initial army training to Fort Lee, in Petersburg, Virginia. Because he had writing skills, he was assigned as a clerk-typist in a hospital unit, of which many of his fellow conscripts, most of them like himself from Baltimore, became a part. His clerical duties gave him new subjects for his poems and time to write them. In the army, he said, "One can write because everyone writes in the Army. People who have never put pen to paper spend hours composing letters. I found I was in a Writer's Colony."[1]

Soon after he was drafted, he wrote one of the war poems for which he became known, "Scyros." This poem, he tells us, was based on Milton's "Nativity Ode" but filled with surrealistic images, one piled on top of another.² The first stanza is an impressionistic summary of his induction:

> The doctor punched my vein
> The captain called me Cain
> Upon my belly sat the sow of fear...

After three stanzas summarizing the war's preliminaries, Shapiro provides images of the destructiveness of the war:

> Thus in the classic sea
> Southeast from Thessaly
> The dynamited mermen washed ashore
> And tritons dressed in steel
> Trolled heads with rod and reel
> And dredged potatoes from the Aegean floor³

In his third-person autobiography, *The Younger Son*, Shapiro tells us that he chose Scyros as a symbolic island at the center of the poem's action because the World War I poet Rupert Brooke was buried there. Brooke was the author of an immensely popular poem, "The Soldier," which begins, "If I should die, think only this of me." The general public was fond of this poem, but the tone was antithetical to the mood and style of the great war poets like Owen, Sassoon, Blunden, Graves, and David Jones.

"Scyros" was not typical of Shapiro, and as he said, "only when he was extremely disturbed would he fall into this mode, or when he had something to hide but needed to express."⁴ The conflicting ideas in this statement (that "he had something to hide but needed to express") can be discovered in much of the poetry Shapiro wrote during the war (and in much poetry he wrote after the war): attacking the rigidities of the system (governmental, military, critical) while participating in and writing about (and thereby indicating approval of) its activities.

Because the United States was not yet at war, the poems Shapiro wrote while stationed at Fort Lee explored the typical activities of a peacetime army: the structured environment, the heritage, the nature of the men who were a part of it. "Conscription Camp," for instance, examined the emotional impact on the conscripts of the training programs and mass drill formations:

> Through the long day of school, absent in heart,
> Distant in every thought but self we tread,
> Wheeling in blocks like large expensive toys
> That never understand except through fun.⁵

In his third-person memoir, Shapiro describes "Conscription Camp" as a "savage antipatriotic poem"⁶; but although the poem suggests that the army's training program did not invariably produce the desired results—a perfectly trained soldier—only an already prejudiced reader would be likely to read it as "antipatriotic." By antipatriotic, Shapiro apparently meant he was writing a poem that did not clearly support the methods and goals of the United States Army, that did not suggest the training program would produce highly motivated soldiers who would defeat enemy forces in defense of the democratic ideals of their country. Whatever one's definition of patriotic, no one who experienced military training would doubt for an instant the truths of Shapiro's description.

The poem that Shapiro thought was his best, most typical pre-war "war poem" was "The Fly," which is less about killing flies on a hot afternoon in a Virginia army office than it is about the rage that overcomes individuals trained in the use of violence, caught up in what is believed to be a morally righteous cause, the elimination of the despised enemy by any possible means:

> But I, a man, must swat you with my hate,
> Slap you across the air and crush your flight,
> Must mangle with my shoe and smear your blood,
> Expose your little guts pasty and white....[7]

Shapiro apparently believed that discerning readers would see the point behind such outrageous carnage. He wrote later that this poem "was his war poem," describing "his rage, controlled rage, his banzai charge." He was surprised that no one ever saw what the poem was trying to do, even though it had been reprinted frequently.[8] His private joke was perhaps too well camouflaged, especially after the emotional surge of hatred against the Japanese generated by the attack at Pearl Harbor.

He did not, in general, find fault with the army as an institution nor with the men in it; they were in an unfortunate minority, subject to the orders given by those holding higher rank. Many of his civilian friends and fellow poets were suspicious of the government and especially of such a rigidly run institution as the army, but Shapiro, with his newly developed perspective as an insider, was not. He was dismayed and amused to discover the weaknesses, physical and mental, of many of his fellow soldiers, he was mostly sympathetic to their plight and unwilling to cast them in a harsh light in his poems. As John Updike comments, Shapiro's poems "do not wave the flag, nor do they mock it."[9]

He never saw himself as anything but a temporary soldier, a visitor to the world of the "old army," reasonably happy in doing the duties he had been given but always a detached participant, observing the world of the peacetime army, and himself in it, from a distance. He saw himself in his early months in the army not as a *patriot*, because "he was sitting there in uniform writing shamelessly antipatriotic poems," but as an American in uniform: "one was an American whether you liked it or not." And he "loved being an American."[10] As a result of this perspective, many of the poems he wrote while in the army, in peacetime and later in wartime, were supportive of the American effort, generally avoiding jingoistic or patriotic aspects. Notified that a number of his poems were to be published in an anthology with four other poets, he wrote an essay in which he "tried to wrestle with the inescapable problem of being not just a poet but an American poet," and he said that he wrote not about *America*, "the word that is the chief enemy of modern poetry," but about his own experience.[11] As he explained later, he did not like it when was called a "war poet": "He was no such thing, only a poet who happened into a war, and how could you write poetry and leave the war out?"[12]

In introductory comments to *V-Letter*, published in 1944, Shapiro wrote that "since the war began, I have tried to be on guard against becoming a 'war poet.'" Speaking of the poems in that volume, he said, "I have not written these poems to accord with any doctrine or system of thought or even a theory of composition. I have nothing to offer in the way of beliefs or challenges or prosody. I try to write freely, one day as a Christian, the next as a Jew, the next as a soldier who sees the gigantic slapstick of modern war."[13] The phrasing of these comments suggests that Shapiro developed a flexible, but probably not insincere, attitude towards the subjects about which he wrote his poems. However, his apparent willingness to adopt a variety of orientations suggests some ambiguity about his place in the army and the poems he wrote. Shapiro's political and poetic esthetics were constantly evolving, and to think that he was writing his poems only as the occasion and the mood suited would be facile; he was too serious a poet not to have had a serious vision of the philosophic and theoretical basis of his art. But the statement indicates something of the effects of his war service. Whether or not he was uncomfortable with his Jewish origin, he seems to have willingly accepted his role as a spokesman for all the men in the army—or at least that part of the army in which he was working. He seems to have been proud of the fact that he could speak from a variety of religious or philosophic perspectives. During the war he recognized that he had become a poetic "voice" speaking for the men with whom he was associated, locally, in the South Pacific, or globally, in any branch of the armed services. Though he might have liked to protect his ability to detach himself from the immediacy of the war, his success as a "war poet" had the opposite effect.

Shapiro's comments in *V-Letter* are similar to those he made in his autobiography published 45 years later: "The [soldier] poet must wear his uniform lightly, and unlike the general it is not part of his skin; ... it must not become his other skin, the tattoo of the professional soldier who has no other identity."[14] In this passage the soldier's uniform becomes "America," the symbol not just of the soldier's unit or military service. It symbolizes the entire country (at least as Shapiro saw it). If he saw himself in the dangerous situation of a poet doomed by his uniform to represent the country that made him wear it, in his poetry he would have to both recognize that fact and pretend it didn't exist. This was a difficult feat to accomplish, and one that required both an affirmation of the poet as authorized speaker and yet one who distanced himself from the events he described. As he admitted later,[15] his best poetry came from a sense of visual description, and this was (for the most part) the basis of his successful war poems. Suspicious of any attempt to write poems that might be tainted by "patriotism," Shapiro preferred instead to write about "what soldiering was like, what it did to the man, the soul, the poetry."[16]

Given the chance to attend officer training school three months before the Japanese attack on Pearl Harbor, he turned the opportunity down, because he was certain he would be leaving the army soon, when his period of enlistment expired. After the attack at Pearl Harbor, Shapiro was shocked to discover that he would be in the army indefinitely, and that he might well become associated with the more unpleasant aspects of military life; he was, as he says, "almost insane with fury" when he discovered that he was going to be shipped to Australia.[17] His anger was undoubtedly due to the fact that his plan to spend a quiet year in the army writing poems had been rudely interrupted by the onset of the war. It would seem that, even though he was a member of the army, he was incompletely motivated by any sense of necessity to resist the forces of fascism and totalitarianism.

Soon after the attack on Pearl Harbor, he and the other members of his medical unit were dispatched for the remote areas of the South Pacific. They were first sent to Fort Dix, New Jersey, and then to Boston, Massachusetts, where they boarded the liner *Queen Mary*. They reached Perth, Australia, by way of Rio de Janeiro and Cape Town, South Africa, in the spring of 1942.

Shapiro's mood before his arrival in Australia is suggested in "Nostalgia," which, according to the date indicated in *Person, Place, and Thing*, was written March 19, 1942, in the middle of the Indian Ocean. The poem describes the physical and emotional split between his body, now far removed from home, and his soul, which he envisions as his feminine component, referring to it as "her," remaining in his civilian environment, where it

> stands at the window of my room,
> And I ten thousand miles away;
> My days are filled with Ocean's sound of doom,
> Salt and cloud and the bitter spray.[18]

He recalls his self-centered youth, his expensive books, his plants in pots set along the edge of the window, as he considers his current situation where the body's night is now his soul's day, "my day her night," on the other side of the globe. He sees changes in the sun and the stars as his latitude and climate change, and even his clock is "hunted down the skies," as he must constantly change personal time to adopt the local time. He feels the loss of an essential part of himself, perhaps fatally split as he moves towards war, where, as the refrain chants, the wind blows and "many a man shall die." In this condition, the poem suggests, small incidents can prove disastrous to the sensitive individual, "a pin can make the memory bleed, A word explode the inward mind." The use of war-related terms like *bleed*, *explode*, *hunted* suggests the fragility of his state of mind and emphasizes the contrast between home and the approach to war and danger—the danger of physical as well as emotional destruction.

Shapiro recalls his home again in "Lord, I Have Seen Too Much," which opens with a statement that suggests he was much more comfortable in a naive life when he believed that essential knowledge came from books and that he could learn the important lessons about life from them:

> Lord, I have seen too much for one who sat
> In quiet at his window's luminous eye
> And puzzled over house and street and sky,
> Safe only in the narrowest habitat;
> Who studied peace as if the world were flat,
> The edge of nature linear and dry....

Forced to venture closer to the harsher world of armed conflict, he discovers that the lessons that war has to teach are like a "brilliant entity" drawn from some magician's hat. The onset of war, perhaps in an assault on the beaches of the South Pacific, for instance, may bring disturbing, even appalling, images:

> Lord, in a day the vacuum of Hell,
> The mouth of blood, the ocean's ragged jaw,
> More than embittered Adam ever saw
> When driven from Eden to the East to dwell,
> The lust of godhead hideously exposed![19]

After the *Queen Mary* docked in Perth, Shapiro and the other men in his unit boarded a train that carried them along the southern edge of the Australian continent to Melbourne. Shapiro used this experience in "Troop Train," in which the poet considers what the movement of the troop train means to the men riding inside and to the people who watch it pass, as it makes its way towards the war. "It stops the town we come through," the opening line puts it, suggesting that as the train stops, the people stop their daily routines to watch the men on it, the men hanging like "fruit of the world," "clustered on ourselves ... as from a cornucopia." The men hang out of the openings of the train as the inhabitants of the town—children, workers, businessmen, and especially women—try to understand the meaning of the moment.

> And on through crummy continents and days,
> Deliberate, grimy, slightly drunk we crawl,
> The good-bad boys of circumstance and chance,
> Whose bucket-helmets bang the empty wall
> Where twist the murdered bodies of our packs
> Next to the guns that only seem themselves.
> And distance, like a strap adjusted, shrinks,
> Tightens across the shoulder and holds firm.

The men carry with them their accoutrements of combat: packs, guns, helmets, the modifying phrases foreshadowing the inevitable outcome, packs described as "murdered bodies" twisting under the stress of movement. As the train leaves its departure station, it moves closer to its destination, war, and the shrinking distance tightens across the men like a strap.

The inevitable card game becomes an appropriate symbol for the wish that the chances of war, as well as the card game, will favor the skilled player:

> Out of this hand
> Dealer, deal me my luck, a pair of bulls,
> The right draw to a flush, the one-eyed jack.
> Diamonds and hearts are red but spades are black,
> And spades are spades and clubs are clovers—black.

In card games played in the context of eventual combat, the colors are significant—red for blood, black for death.

The final stanza carries the troop train closer to its inevitable destination, the hazard of war, as the train leads eventually to ships or trucks and marching at the end, all of which can lead to death. The final stanza repeats words signifying means of transport—*trains* (repeated five times), *ships* (four times), *trucks* (four times), and *march* (three times)—like a litany of the inevitable forward movement which will bring the men to *death* (repeated six times); "And death leads back to trucks and trains and ships," to bring the dead men back for eventual burial.

The last three lines of the poem appear to offer the hope of survival:

> But life leads to the march, O flag! at last
> The place of life found after trains and death
> —Nightfall of nations brilliant after war.[20]

But this hope ("nightfall of nations brilliant after war") offers an apocalyptic vision rather than an image of a safe haven, as carrying the tools of war works against a safe return.

After some delay in Melbourne and then Sydney, Shapiro's unit was dispatched to Brisbane, on the east coast of Australia, where Shapiro was designated a member of a temporary medical unit assigned to assist during beach landings. This duty required the medical team, of which Shapiro was an administrative assistant, to remain on the landing craft to give first aid to wounded soldiers in the attacking forces. The team left Brisbane on a Dutch freighter that took them first to islands in the New Guinea chain. There they were assigned to support a number of landings in the Trobriand Islands and New Britain. During this period Shapiro witnessed bombing and strafing attacks by Japanese aircraft at Finschhafen, and the medical team was called on to give treatment to the injured. The attacks were so intensive that the men they had just treated would often be immediately re-injured:

> The dead and wounded were carried into the little galley and sometimes carried out again after a word from one of the doctors, all four of whom were operating elbow to elbow. After an operation, even an amputation, the patient was carried out on deck to make room. A few times the just-operated-on-man would be struck again by flying shrapnel or a bullet, and would be brought back in.[21]

About this experience, this "night of death," Shapiro said he "could never write a poem,"[22] suggesting an aversion to the more unpleasant aspects of war, which could produce unsettling and disturbing images severely counterproductive to the poetic processes.

Yet Shapiro seems to have been fascinated by the personal destruction of war, as his poems explore the price the body pays as one implement among the tools of war. "The Leg," for instance, illustrates Shapiro's concern for the ultimate damage of the war—the disintegration of the individual as a result of its forces. In this poem Shapiro first describes the reactions of a soldier who regains consciousness in a hospital, thinking "*What have I lost?*"—the first thought of anyone who has been wounded in combat seriously enough to be placed in a hospital and subjected to intense medical treatment. The fear of not being whole, of having lost some essential part of the anatomy, overwhelms the soldier's recognition that he is still alive. In the first three stanzas we share the perspective of the soldier, as he thinks to himself, "*When will I look at it?*" Eventually "his fingers begin to explore the stump," and he "learns a shape that is comfortable and tucked in like a sock." Having examined his wound, the soldier considers that his situation

> has a sense of humor, this can despise
> The finest surgical limb, the dignity of limping,
> The nonsense of wheel-chairs. Now he smiles to the wall:
> The amputation becomes an acquisition.

The fourth stanza looks at the situation from the point of view of the leg:

> For the leg is wondering where he is (all is not lost)
> And surely he has a duty to the leg;
> He is its injury, the leg is his orphan,
> He must cultivate the mind of the leg,
> Pray for the part that is missing, pray for peace
> In the image of a man, pray, pray for its safety,
> And after a little while it will die quietly.

The unusual perspective of the leg thinking about the missing body may be logically disturbing until we recognize that the poem at this point is taking on an apocalyptic aspect, a doomsday vision of scattered bodies and parts of bodies rising at the last judgment to become reassembled, reunited in completeness. This aspect is at the heart of the final stanza of the poem, that considers the body as a symbol:

> The body, what is it, Father, but a sign
> To love the force that grows us, to give back
> What in Thy palm is senselessness and mud?
> Knead, knead the substance of our understanding
> Which must be beautiful in flesh to walk,
> That if Thou take me angrily in hand
> And hurl me to the shark, I shall not die![23]

The poetic persona understands that his body, like that of the soldier in the ward, may suffer grievous wounds in the hazardous conditions of war. It is important to believe that ultimately any loss suffered will be remedied or at least made comprehensible. This concluding stanza seems to be a deeply heartfelt expression of concern on the part of the poet, and not just a wartime platitude uttered on behalf of the combatants. The emphasis Shapiro places on the disintegration of the body, whether it has to do with amputation of arms and legs, or separation of the soul from the body, is part of an essential response to the personal hazards and costs of war. It is not surprising that a man who spends his wartime service in the medical field should employ metaphors and symbols of physical and spiritual wholeness; whether through environment or personal inclination, Shapiro clearly sees bodily integrity as the main focus of his poetic comments on the war.

"Full Moon: New Guinea" recognizes that enemy night bombing raids can cause casualties as easily as enemy bullets. The men "fear the aspects of the moon," for soon "The small burr of the bombers in our ear / Tickles our rest; we rise as from a nap" to seek the protection of trenches, where they "breathe and wait," hoping to avoid the bombs "falling darkly for our fate."[24] This vision of the experience, a night air raid by enemy bombers, captures the sense of fear and tenseness of the men on the ground, waiting in the trenches they have dug, which will be their protection from harm or their grave, depending on how closely the bombs strike. The men can do little except wait, breathe, and look up. The nighttime sky shows them the enemy bombers (compared to a form of deadly insect), perhaps caught by the defensive searchlights, appearing to burrow for safety in the bursts of high explosive from the anti-aircraft fire. They see also the constellations of Orion the hunter and the Southern Cross, symbolically used here to suggest the impartiality or possible hostility of higher powers. The reference to the bombers as insects is suggestive of the use Shapiro made of similar images, in "The Fly," to suggest the carnage of hostile military action. The classic sonnet form of the poem reminds us of the most appealing characteristics of the best sonnets, well-crafted but with a tension resulting from internal ambiguities, the most obvious of which is the final outcome of the action: will it be a "spectacle" or a "mishap"?

It was during this time that Shapiro wrote "Elegy for a Dead Soldier," his "most anthologized poem in after years."[25] This eleven-stanza poem was written about the death of a soldier killed not in combat but by accident; the man apparently shot himself while cleaning his M-1. It was possibly a suicide, but this aspect was not relevant to the poem's meaning, according to Shapiro: "Accident, suicide, battle casualty, it was neither here nor there." What was important for the poem was the fact that this was the first death Shapiro had witnessed at first hand: Shapiro "saw his first dying, first death, first funeral—at the age of thirty." In his autobiography Shapiro says that he "liked the poem, which used a kind of sonnet stanza which he invented." After establishing the setting, it leads to a "funeral oration about the unknown man and his sense of history, or lack of it, and led out again into the scene itself."[26]

The opening stanza describes a makeshift altar for the burial ceremony:

1. Karl Shapiro, U.S. Army   25

> A white sheet on the tail-gate of a truck
> Becomes an altar; two small candlesticks
> Sputter at each side of the crucifix....

The second and third stanzas consider the sentiments of those in attendance:

> Who has not wrapped himself in this same flag,
> Heard the light fall of dirt, his wound still fresh,
> Felt his eyes closed, and heard the distant brag
> Of the last volley of humanity?

The poem seems to be sympathetic to the death of the soldier, but the language, especially of the third stanza, blends sympathy with irony. The event is beginning to seem like an opportunity for the poet to demonstrate linguistic capabilities disturbingly inappropriate to the occasion. In the fourth stanza, however, the details of personal observation bring the poem into the present tense of the experience: "By chance I saw him die, stretched on the ground." The language of general experience is replaced by the details of the specific event; we see what the poet sees:

> By chance I saw him die, stretched on the ground,
> A tattooed arm lifted to take the blood
> Of someone else sealed in a tin. I stood
> During the last delirium that stays
> The intelligence a tiny moment more,
> And then the strangulation, the last sound.
> The end was sudden, like a foolish play,
> A stupid fool slamming a foolish door,
> The absurd catastrophe, half-prearranged
> And all the decisive things still left to say.
> So we disbanded, angrier and unchanged,
> Sick with the utter silence of dispraise.

Yet even in this scene the ambiguous stance of the poet is suggested: the death of the soldier is "stupid," "foolish," as any death associated with the activities of war must be. Shapiro's language theatricalizes the event, as if it is an unfinished scene, interrupted before giving way to a more satisfying, happier ending. On one hand, this is one way of showing that the unpredictable events of war will always interfere with normal living. On the other hand, the use of the drama comparison draws attention to the manipulation of events by the poet, shifting our attention from the dying man to the poet's art. And, in fact, the cause of death will make a difference: our response will be different if the death is caused by a suicide instead of a combat-related casualty. Does a suicide, a self-inflicted death, deserve to be considered on the same level of significance as the death of a soldier who died, even accidentally, while participating in, or preparing for, combat?

In the stanzas that follow, the poet describes the thoughts and beliefs of the man who has died. This poetic summary cannot be factual, since the poet, as he admits, did not know the man, and Shapiro uses the opportunity to generalize about what he may believe is the typical soldier's perspective on the world's institutions, based no doubt on thoughts similar to his own:

> I would not speak for him who could not speak
> Unless my fear were true: he was not wronged,
> He knew to which decision he belonged
> But let it choose itself....

Shapiro makes a creative leap at this point, assigning himself the responsibility and authority to characterize the mind-set and prejudices of the dead soldier. He is justified, perhaps, because, like the dead soldier, the Shapiro-poet persona made the same decisions that brought him to this location, to the side of the dead soldier. Even though the soldier "knew / Little of times and armies not his own," he "cast his vote, / Distrusting all the elected but not law." His "ideals were few and those there were not made / For conversation. He belonged to church / But never spoke of God."

> He hated other races, south or east,
> And shoved them to the margin of his mind.
> ....
> His ancestry was somewhere far behind
> And left him only his peculiar name....

The final stanza returns to the burial scene, where the ceremony concludes and the poem ends with an epitaph:

> Underneath this wooden cross there lies
> A Christian killed in battle. You who read
> Remember that this stranger died in pain;
> And passing here, if you can lift your eyes
> Upon a peace kept by the human creed,
> Know that one soldier has not died in vain.[27]

It is difficult to know how to react to this poem, with its vacillation between sincerity and irony. Shapiro acknowledges this quality in his autobiography, stating that the poem "was not a flag-waving poem and it was not an anti-flag waving poem, a hard balance which the poet always tried for, slipping from one side to the other while his balancing pole wavered."[28] This kind of comment is a constant refrain in his autobiography, that

Shapiro the poet consistently demonstrates an ambiguous (he uses the word often) attitude towards his subject.

If the poem is, as Shapiro says, one of his most anthologized, then readers apparently saw little of its irony. The form of the poem argues for a serious, unambiguous reading: its formal pattern, sonnet-like, with an iambic pentameter scarcely broken, seems made for declaration on solemn occasions. There are twelve lines in each stanza, twelve stanzas total (if we count the Epitaph as a stanza; it contains only six lines, however, and the rhyme scheme is different). The intricate end rhyme scheme (*abbcdaedfefc*) suggests an ornately embroidered carpet in which the lines are carefully woven. It would be the model of a perfect memorial poem if it were not for the fact that the subject occasionally disappears. Even in the fourth stanza, with its sharp return to real life, no blood is shed, with the result that the poem is in danger of becoming a kind of monument to sacrifice of life in times of war. Its cleverness as a poetic construct tends to draw attention to itself more than to the subject which occasioned it.[29]

The ambiguity of the poem's intent was apparently not recognized by the American public, who saw it as a meaningful and significant poem honoring the death of an American soldier. The response of the public to this and other poems led to growing popularity and a sort of fame for Shapiro. As a result, he attained great visibility during the war, becoming widely recognized as the poetic "voice" of fighting Americans. During the three years he was soldiering in the South Pacific, he saw not once but three books of poetry published to critical acclaim in the United States—*Person, Place, and Thing* (1942), *V-Letter and Other Poems* (1944), and *Essay on Rime* (1945)—and was included in *Five Young American Poets* published by New Directions in 1941. No wonder, then, that although he was in the army in an uncertain time, his poetic voice seemed strong and full of confidence; he had, as he said, "an ecstasy of confidence and pride."[30] His success in poetry gave him the voice of confidence which pervaded his war poems.

Another poem to which the public responded enthusiastically was "V-Letter" (the final poem in the collection of the same name), which describes the poet's feelings for his love, far away from the hazards of war which the poet faces. This poem was undoubtedly popular because it seemed to catch, as no other poem of the period did, the feelings of any man far away from a woman he loved. Shapiro's description of the woman waiting at home effectively captured the mood of thousands of soldiers, sailors, and airmen:

> You turn me from these days as from a scene
>   Out of an open window far
> Where lies the foreign city and the war.

> You are my home and in your spacious love
> I dream to march as under flaring flags
>   Until the door is gently shut.
> Give me the tearless lesson of your pride,
>   Teach me to live and die
> As one deserving anonymity,
> The mere devotion of a house to keep
>   A woman and a man.[31]

The poem concludes with the thought that even if the poet should die in his duties, he will die content because their "love is whole." Such sentiment was shared by both the men at war and, apparently, by the women at home.

Although Shapiro commented later about his intent in writing "Elegy for a Dead Soldier," he said nothing about "V-Letter," presumably because it was (for him) unabashedly sentimental, with no evident ironic twists. If he wrote it with his wife-to-be, Evalyn Katz, in mind, one is a little suspicious of its sincerity, given Shapiro's active relations with his women friends in Australia, which he reveals in some detail in *Younger Son*. However, the woman in the poem is not to be thought of as some real person in the inventory of Shapiro's acquaintances. Rather, she should be thought of, as Susan Schweik reminds us, as a projection, an idealized portrait, an emotional repository.[32] Shapiro creates a portrait of a woman whose characteristics all soldiers would agree are desirable: strong, dependable, understanding, tied specifically to the household environment. In the words of Schweik, Shapiro's image of a woman is "confined" by the language of the poem "to the position of silent but reassuring object" which provides "a stabilizing structure." Just as Shapiro attempted to create an idealized portrait of a dead soldier in "Elegy for a Dead Soldier," so did he attempt to create an idealized vision of the woman waiting at home in "V-Letter."

After his period of service on the north coasts of New Guinea, he was relocated to the south coast of New Guinea and then to Biak, an island in Dutch New Guinea, where his unit prepared to establish a hospital to treat injuries expected to result from the fighting in the Philippines. During his time in the South Pacific, Shapiro's reputation as a poet grew, partly as a result of the appearance of several volumes of his poetry, but mostly, it seemed, because he had become a "kind of phenomenon, a poet in the Battle Zone, which he had seen almost nothing of, who was serenely writing good poetry, ... supposedly dodging Jap bayonets every five minutes."[33] His reputation grew not only with the reading public, but with the higher-ranking officers in his unit as well. As he discovered after the war, the letters that he wrote to Evalyn Katz were thoroughly read by the officers in his unit, whose job was to censor the mail written by all enlisted men to ensure that no vital military information was revealed, or, in Shapiro's case, that no suspicious or un–American information was being transmitted. He saw, after he returned home, that his letters had been "cut to ribbons with deletions" and had been read by officers "all the way up to [General Douglas] MacArthur's headquarters."[34]

One poem that he had included in a letter to Evalyn Katz, "The Communist," caused an especially robust stir, because it seemed to encourage a sympathetic view of the communist philosophy. However, when asked to explain it to an immediate officer, he found it difficult to do so, for, typically, as he himself admitted, he "didn't know himself what it meant": the poem "flip-flopped on both sides." He had written it after hearing about the Russian defense at the Battle of Stalingrad and was motivated to celebrate what he considered as an important victory against the causes of fascism. However, he hadn't fully appreciated the effect of referring to members of the Red Army as "my comrades" might have on his superior officers.[35]

Finally, after three years in the South Pacific, Shapiro was notified that he was scheduled to return to the United States. He was relieved but filled with anxiety about his return. The poem that best captures Shapiro's thoughts upon return is "Homecoming," which juxtaposes Shapiro's worries about reaching home safely with the thought that he is on a ship that carries psychologically scarred soldiers (although he has supposedly not been scarred by the war, the poem suggests he is a fellow traveler in more ways than one):

> We bring no raw materials from the East
> But green-skinned men in blue-lit holds
> And lunatics impounded between-decks;
> The mighty ghoul ship that we ride exhales
> The sickly-sweet stench of humiliation....

His isolation, physically and mentally, from the men with whom he voyages suggests his efforts to distance himself from them. When the ship enters territorial waters, Shapiro senses a physical release from the pressures of the wartime experiences: "that convulsive terrible joy, more sudden / And brilliant than the explosion of a ship, / Shatter[s] the tensions of the heaven and sea" to liberate the "imprisoned souls of soldiers and of me."[36] This separation of the soldiers from the poet shows clearly how Shapiro attempted to maintain emotional if not physical distance between himself and those with whom he lived for three years. Although he was seen by the public as a soldier poet who wrote about the daily activities of soldiers in far-off areas of the world, his poetry repeatedly suggests that he never identified with them in any truly meaningful sense. Shapiro's attitude towards his subjects helps to make clear why many of his readers experienced ambiguous reactions to his poems.

Soon after his arrival in the United States, Shapiro married Evalyn Katz, in March of 1945. He ended his service days in comfortable circumstances, moving between New York City and Washington, D.C. Initially assigned to the Foreign Nationalities Section of the Office of Strategic Services, he was assigned to eavesdrop on phone calls of people designated suspicious. But he expressed his dislike for this work and was able to work with another poet on an anthology of poetry. When the war in Germany ended, Shapiro was out of the army, and when he heard the news, he "didn't feel anything, not even glad it was over, because he had become part of the war-state-of-mind and didn't think it was over and didn't think it would ever be over because nobody knows how not to make war."[37]

After the war ended, Shapiro allowed himself the luxury, in "Recapitulations VIII," of an unvarnished metrical postwar self-assessment:

> For four years stupefied by martial law
> The poet in khaki held his tongue. Coward
> Or Patriot or both, he learned the raw
> Truth of the life where only rifles flowered....[38]

Again, his tendency to demonstrate a tentative attitude towards his subject—in this case, himself ("Coward / Or Patriot or both")—is evident.

Although Shapiro held a reputation throughout the war as the most important American poet serving in the war, his best poetry was about the soldiers not directly involved in the fighting and about the army that he knew before America became involved in the war. While he wrote an exceptionally large number of poems and saw four books of poetry published while he was in the army, most of the poems in those publications were on topics other than military. One book, *Essay on Rime*, was a statement on poetic theory, and another, *Five American Poets*, published in 1941, contained pre-wartime poetry. *Person, Place, and Thing* contained many more "civilian" poems than military. (The military poems were based primarily on his experiences at Fort Lee, though some of the poems had been written on the way to Australia or shortly after arrival; the latest, "A Cut Flower," was dated July 20, 1942). Only *V-Letter*, of the books published during the war, contained poems written while he was serving in, or on his way to, the South Pacific area. The poems in this volume demonstrate Shapiro's "outsider" attitude towards his subjects: clever, perceptive, detached, and more about the landscape through which the soldiers travel than the events that have brought them so far from home.

Shapiro transitioned into civilian life as a renowned poet, serving initially as poetry consultant to the Library of Congress before becoming editor of *Poetry* magazine, the publication that had done so much to further his career during the war. Restless in his profession as well as in his poetry, he was affiliated with a variety of universities before his death in 2000 at the age of eighty-six.

2

Randall Jarrell, U.S. Army Air Forces

Randall Jarrell has generally been viewed as the most important of the American poets who wrote about the war. Vernon Scannell speaks for most readers when he states that Jarrell is "widely regarded as having written some of the most memorable poems of the Second World War."[1] According to Lorrie Goldensohn, Jarrell's war poems "are the largest and most singularly vivid group of American poems that we have on World War II."[2] Every reader of Jarrell's war poems would probably agree that no other American poet matched Jarrell's consistent intensity of vision; certainly no other poet developed, in his poetry, such a strong sense of overwhelming blind force exerted on the participants in the war by the various forces of the war. Jarrell's war poetry is *serious* with a capital S. Jarrell worked hard to achieve that effect.

Many readers assume that because Jarrell's poetry was so serious, and described many aspects of the air war—training, the European theater, the Pacific theater, prisoner of war camps—that he was an integral operational member of the air arm. Those who read "The Death of the Ball Turret Gunner" may assume that the horrific vision that the poem presents must have been written by someone who witnessed the event (cleaning the ball turret with a hose after the bloody, messy death of the gunner), someone who must have been flying the missions. Scannell, for instance, credits Jarrell as having been "a sergeant-pilot in the U.S.A.A.F, first operationally and subsequently as an instructor."[3] However, for all of his many poems' brutal combat imagery, Jarrell never flew as an aircrew member and never held any position other than that of a training specialist.

Although Goldensohn does not identify Jarrell as a combatant, she states that the force of his poetry "may well come from his position of suspension within the army and within the war but ... outside combat."[4] It is difficult to imagine, however, the exact status or perspective of someone who lives "within the war" while "outside combat," especially someone who takes as his topic the brutality of war. The fact is that Jarrell himself never got within two thousand miles of war. While this fact itself does not alter the effectiveness of the memorable images of many of his poems, it may affect our interpretation of them.

Jarrell had begun to establish his reputation as a poet with the publication of his first volume of poetry, *Blood for a Stranger*, which was completed in 1939 but which appeared, after some delay in finding a publisher, early in 1942, after he had accepted a position with the English department at the University of Texas in Austin. The Japanese attack at Pearl Harbor seems scarcely to have distracted his attention from his interest in literary matters, for he notes in an April 1942 letter to Edmund Wilson that the war had not had "an unusual effect here," adding, however, that a military camp would soon be developed near Austin.[5] If the war was not having a major effect, as Jarrell indicated, it is somewhat surprising to read, in his October 1942 letter to Amy Breyer de Blasio, that he was participating in an air force pilot training program, "sitting in a Trainer with the hood down trying to get the airspeed, altitude, and direction all right at the same time."[6]

One month later, he wrote to Edmund Wilson that he was in the Air Corps, and would soon begin flight training; he told Wilson that if he completed the ten-month training program he could become "a ferry pilot, flight instructor, or co-pilot on an airline."[7] The agenda of events Jarrell describes was established for those who enrolled in the Civilian Pilot Training Program, which was designed to provide the United States with a supply of pilots for the support, or non-combat, flying roles. For someone with so little inclination to become involved in political issues, and with a fondness for the literary life, his sudden decision to become involved in a highly technical military occupation seems completely out of character. It is possible that he joined the service to avoid the unpleasant consequences of the draft, but if that is the case, he says nothing about it in his letters.

It is immediately evident, however, that Jarrell is not comfortable with the routine aspects of flight training: in a section Jarrell added later to the same letter to Wilson in which he announced his entrance into the training program, he acknowledges that he is having difficulties in the program: "Flying is pretty dull and I'm bad at it."[8] In a January 1943 letter to Lambert Davis, he reports that he has been ordered to report to Sheppard Field, near Wichita Falls, Texas, because he "washed out" of the flight training program. Apparently he had caused the airplane which he was flying on an evaluation ride to inadvertently enter a spin, an uncontrolled sharply descending spiral turn, and the "chief pilot decided I wasn't a safe flyer." He adds that flying wasn't as romantic an occupation as he had imagined: "I thought flying about as thrilling, or romantic, as juggling three oranges,"[9] a reference to the complicated tasks involved in controlling an airplane in flight; one would be too busy managing the tasks of coordinated flight under the watchful eye of an instructor to devote much time to enjoying the sensation of flying. In a brief biographical note which he provided to Oscar Williams in connection with the inclusion of some of Jarrell's poems in Williams' 1945 anthology, Jarrell wrote that he had enlisted in October 1942 but "washed out after about thirty hours flying."[10]

If Jarrell thought that the flying life was disappointing, he soon discovered that the life of an army air force ground support enlisted man, which is the position to which his flying failure relegated him, was even less appealing. After his arrival at Sheppard Field, near Wichita Falls, Texas, he wrote that he was not at all happy about the kind of people with whom he had to associate while he awaited assignment to a new duty, and encouraged friends to "stay out of the army, *as enlisted men*" (Jarrell's emphasis).[11] In a letter to his wife Mackie, he complains: "I always talk in a good deal less cultivated way with uncultivated people; but these people are *so* uncultivated I never have the slightest tendency to do that—it would be ridiculous to try to seem even remotely as spotted as these creatures."[12] Jarrell must have had *some* tactful or ingratiating qualities about him; otherwise he could scarcely have avoided confrontations if he demonstrated such an attitude openly among his fellow soldiers.

Yet even as he complains of his circumstances, he still reveals flashes of excitement about the job opportunities for which he might be eligible; in another letter to Mackie, he lists three possibilities open to him: to go to cryptography school and be made a staff sergeant; to pass an Advanced Army Specialist Training Test and become an army psychologist and "almost certainly" become an officer; or to apply for Officer Candidate School (OCS) in Air Corps Administration, "practically the nicest branch of the army." "Doesn't it all sound wonderful?" he asks.[13] Unfortunately, none of these wonderful opportunities opened to him. Instead, after some delay, he was sent to Chanute Field, at Rantoul, Illinois, to train as a Link Trainer Operator.

The Link Trainer was an electronic flight simulator in which student pilots practiced their instrument flying on the ground. It was essentially a large covered box that contained a basic cockpit layout: seat, flight controls (control stick), a few simulated engine instruments, and attitude and directional indicators. It sat on a pedestal which provided a modest humming noise to suggest engine sound. In the trainer the student could simulate taking off, flying cross-country, and landing, all using simulated instrument references to electronic navigation aids, called automatic direction finder (ADF) beacons. Link trainers provided reasonably realistic flight simulation characteristics and were surprisingly effective in training instrument flight techniques and procedures. As a Link instructor, Jarrell would sit at a nearby desk and serve as a flight controller for the student, providing instructions and corrections through a headset like that worn by the student. Jarrell's Link trainer school ran for four months, from May through August of 1943. After completing this school, Jarrell learned that there were no Link Trainer positions available, and he decided to stay for six more weeks of training as a Celestial Navigation Trainer (CNT) instructor. After completing his CNT training, Jarrell was assigned to Davis-Monthan Army Air Field, at Tucson, Arizona, arriving in November 1943, a little more than one year after he entered military service.

The Celestial Navigation Trainer was an advanced, more sophisticated version of the Link Trainer; it relied on an artificial night sky placed around a simulated aircraft containing two or more crew members, pilots and navigators. Jarrell provided a description of his training tasks in a March 1945 letter to Allen Tate. As he had in the Link Trainer, he sat at a desk where he operated an elevated platform that simulated the cockpit of a large aircraft, in which the navigators could practice celestial navigation by reference to artificially generated images of the sun and stars. In the CNT the navigator could use his navigational sextants to practice sighting on the imitation stars on the ceiling of the dome as the operators mechanically advanced the rotation of the stars. Jarrell and the training staff communicated with the crew members, giving commands over the radio just as radio stations on the ground would during actual flight.[14] The navigators would locate their aircraft positions by using sextants to establish lines of position of the sun, moon, planets, and stars. His training facility was like a large planetarium, in which he could accelerate the movements of the stars by moving the star projection machine, advancing the apparent positions of the heavens in a few minutes instead of the hours required by an aircraft in flight. The celestial navigation trainer thus saved training time and reduced the costs of aircraft maintenance and fuel. It is clear in his letters that, as much as he disliked the army, he nevertheless took pride in his job.

Although Jarrell experienced periods of waiting and boredom between intense training activities, he still managed to find time to write poems, often doing so to maintain his emotional balance in an environment of (to him) futility and inflexibility; he later wrote to Allen Tate that the atmosphere he encountered in the service was "entirely one of lying, meaningless brutality and officiousness, stupidity not beyond belief but beyond conception—the one word for everything in the army is petty."[15]

Whether his sense of frustration or some other factor was the cause, while he was at Chanute Field, for instance, Jarrell finished thirteen poems, including "The Emancipators," "The Soldier," "The Soldier Walks Under the Trees of the University," "Soldier [T.P.]," "A Girl in a Library," "The Carnegie Library, Juvenile Division," "Children Selecting Books in a Library," "The Sick Nought," "Prisoners," "Come to the Stone...," "The Difficult Resolution," "The Boyg, Peer Gynt," and "Mother, Said the Child."[16] At Davis-Monthan he completed the remainder of the 33 poems included in *Little Friend, Little Friend*, his first volume of war poetry, and at least eight of the thirty-one poems in *Losses*, his second. While Jarrell's war years constituted a time of personal dissatisfaction and distress, they nevertheless provided him with one of the two greatest inspirational occasions in his creative life (the other was his postwar trip to Europe in 1948).

Possibly frustrated in his attempts to be a more integral part of the war effort, in his poetry Jarrell seems to have projected himself imaginatively into some of its hardest actions, describing the carnage of war and judging its effects. Writing about those scenes and events of the war, he employed a rhetorical stance in which the poet speaks as an authority on the facts of the war of which he is not really a part. Typically the central figure of his war poems is a young, confused, and inexperienced soldier. Feelings of frustration and powerlessness are evident in almost every poem he wrote during this period. This aspect may have been an early manifestation of his impatience with less than a perfect performance on the part of anyone entrusted with meaningful tasks, whether fighting a war, playing tennis (his favorite sport), or writing poetry.

Jarrell himself acknowledged his distanced attitude: writing to Robert Lowell shortly before he left military service, he stated that the majority of the soldiers he had seen were "ignorant of the nature and conditions of the choices they make," adding that they "usually do not have the information and training to make it possible for them to make a really reasonable decision" about their actions in the army, decisions that would be made for them by the "State," which had already given them "as much misleading determining information as it could": "Whether you're a gunner or a clerk, safe or dead, is random so far as the state is concerned, and completely determined for you so far as you're concerned."[17] Jarrell must have realized that he was speaking about himself as well. Jarrell concludes by telling Lowell what most readers of the poems have observed, that he never wrote a war poem in which he was personally present: "Unless you're vain or silly you realize that you, except insofar as you're in exactly the same boat as the others, aren't the primary subject of any sensible writing about the war." This statement may be true for Jarrell in his training environment, but once an individual enters a combat situation, it would certainly be difficult to write meaningfully about any other individual than oneself. Distanced from the war by job, geography, and temperament, Jarrell might have changed his outlook as well as his poetic stance if he had ever had the opportunity to participate personally in combat.

His comments to Lowell summarize the main ideas of Jarrell's war poems: the individual experience does not count, except as evidence of the inevitable operation of the impersonal, destructive machinery of the State. Jarrell acknowledged that he had turned to philosophy to provide the themes of his war poems; he wrote to Lowell in August of 1945 that an article he was writing about Auden contained an extended discussion of religious philosophers. He added that for an extended period of months he had been reading "almost nothing but theology, the most gigantic quantities of it you can imagine."[18] Reading theology in time of war would normally have been a civilian and not a military pre-occupation.

For the full time of the war, Jarrell never left the United States. Yet in his poetry he was imaginatively in nearly every theater of the war. *Little Friend, Little Friend*, his first volume of postwar poetry, was published in 1945, the last year of the war. It is difficult to imagine that *Little Friend* could have been published earlier in the war, for few American readers with family members involved in the war effort would have been able to appreciate these hard, sardonic, ungenerous poems, with their insistent messages of waste and futility. The poems in *Little Friend* can be described as poems about guilt, the guilt of the individuals described in them but also the guilt felt by the readers. That this was part of Jarrell's intent can be surmised from the "About the Author" description (probably written by Jarrell) on the dust jacket of *Little Friend*, which reminds the reader what *Time* magazine had said of Jarrell's previous book of poems, *Blood for a Stranger*, that the lyrics of that book "register the pain of human guilt as it has seldom been registered in American poetry." Noting this characteristic (as well as Jarrell's technique), Karl Shapiro said later that *Little Friend* was a "thematic book, a war book in which the poet is personally absent.... The anguish of the soldier is shown less in his anonymity, his exile from the human race, than in his emotional, sentimental desperation."[19]

The poems of *Little Friend* are filled with discomfort, depicting those associated with the war effort as victims, destroyed by the actions of war regardless of which side they support. There certainly is no false patriotism in these poems, no poems sentimentally celebrating the efforts of the combatants. Instead, there are expressions of destruction and loss, focusing for the most part on the little people of the war, the soldier, the combatant, and often, the "prisoners" of the war, figuratively as well as literally, prisoners of the systems that they helped to support and maintain. The figures of the poems are suppressed, used, and discarded by the system which establishes their duties. In these poems the words *death, dead, dying, grave, pain, dream, fire, burning* are repeated in a litany of distress and loss. The main ideas depict life as a dream from which the soldier will never awaken, in which the soldier is a tool to be worn down by war, and the State is a monolithic, impersonal force that grinds all beings as grist in its mill of operation.

Jarrell's war poetry addresses issues of judgment, and speaks to an external voice of insight beyond the sphere of the wartime activity. The narrator of Jarrell's poetry can scarcely be imagined as Jarrell himself, a man looking at events of which he may be a part. His poetry most often utilizes personas, characters with wide ranges of experiences and backgrounds, mostly military, but civilian as well, representing a variety of speaking voices and personalities. In many of these poems it is as if Jarrell is imitating a grim, humorless, dazed narrator from a Robert Browning poem. The narrators are detached, separate from the events they describe, emotionally remote from the disturbing scenes on which they report.

Jarrell perceived a continuity between the events of World Wars I and II, and saw in the pattern of World War I a model that was perpetuated in World War II. In "The Soldier," for instance, the narrator suggests that that war is the result of an excess of nationalism, patriotism, and economic greed. Jarrell repeatedly emphasizes *Trade* as the reason for the war.[20] Jarrell places the blame for the development of the control of the State on the effects of such historic figures as Galileo and Newton, "The Emancipators," who brought advances in science and technology to produce weapons of war. The final lines of "The Emancipators" echo this sentiment, that the most important desire of men is for Trade.[21] Even the wounded B-29 gunner Siegfried, recovering from the loss of a leg as a result of wounds received while flying in combat, is described as reading about war news and business news in the papers. In Jarrell's war poems, Trade is linked directly to the State, an impersonal, blind force that absorbs and destroys everything and everyone with which it comes in contact, including the people who operate and maintain it, as well as the opposing forces it is intended to resist.

The poem entitled "The State" describes the effects of the State's actions on one of its members/victims who has to bear the costs of supporting its practices. First the speaker's mother is killed to serve the needs of the State, and then his sister is drafted. Finally, after even his cat is conscripted into the service of the State, the poet is moved almost tears by the injustice of such events. The narrator is depicted as an unproductive member of society, passively allowing the State to appropriate his family members and even his pet for some Better Good of Society, rationalizing their disappearances from his life, showing emotion only at the loss of his cat. In Jarrell's wartime world the State takes the most unreasonable and inhumane actions with the full consent of its members. This image of the State is consistently maintained throughout the poems in *Little Friend*, as in "Soldier [T.P.]" (T.P. is, as Jarrell explains in a note, an abbreviation for Title Pending, an indication that the soldier does not yet have an army specialty task assigned). The poem describes a situation in which the soldier's fate depends on the outcome of an impersonalized bureaucratic mechanism: the soldier has no options, his future path through the destructiveness of war controlled by the actions of the State. Jarrell's fierce attitude towards the ill effects of the State is perhaps best illustrated in "The Difficult Resolution," which reiterates the powerlessness of the individual within the forces of the State; accepting that situation *is* the "difficult resolution."[22]

Against such a monolithic force, individual human effort seems pitifully small and ineffective, an impression that Jarrell cultivates in many of the poems in *Little Friends*. The central characters appear diminutive and foolish, almost ludicrous, in their efforts to assess the value of their lives in this hard situation of war. Jarrell gives a roll call of such individuals, beginning with the soldiers in "2nd Air Force," who move like unquestioning animals; a gunner stumbles as he walks to his barracks in a dreamlike frame of mind, and the observant mother wonders about the impact of their unthinking conditioned responses on these men. Or the "Pilot from the Carrier," who jumps from his burning plane, only to become the target of an enemy aircraft. Other examples include the dying airmen in the rescue boat in "The Dream of Waking," and "The Sick Nought," a simple soldier whose desire to live, to stay alive, is doomed to failure as a result of years of acceptance of the actions of the State. Jarrell's heartless, semicomic depiction of the "Gunner" shows another who dies a wasted death, whose medals are sent home to his cat. This poem illustrates Jarrell's poetic gift at its best, as the juxtaposition of unlike nouns—fighter, tracer, *rabbits*; pension, medals, *cat*—emphasizes the terrible unreality of illogical events that the world has come not only to accept, but even to take for granted.

The only poem in *Little Friends in* which Jarrell casts himself (or someone clearly like himself) as a central figure, "Absent with Official Leave," shows the individual as a victim of the system: the central figure, a soldier, lies in his bed, withdrawing into himself as the other men talk before falling asleep. In this simple yet complex poem Jarrell describes a transition from sleeping soldier into a youthful character in a dream of hunters, awaking to find himself become that youthful character, who wakes to see himself surrounded by men who will share his unknown fate. In this poem the ideas of entrapment, dream and death—the central subjects of other poems—are repeated as well.

Jarrell's most extended depiction of the doomed warrior trapped in the confines of the State is "Siegfried," his updated version of the traditional warrior whose death is supposed to be significant, leading to entry into Valhalla. In Jarrell's version, however, such is not the case. His Siegfried is a gunner (yet another version of Jarrell's basic type of combatant), in this instance a crew member on a B-29 bomber aircraft over Japan, who faces the threat of death from the attacking fighters and the random bursts of flak. The gunner's fire is designed to be statistically accurate against enemy fighters just as the enemy's flak—ground fire against the bombers—is also statistically effective. The gunner's hope that he will be safe, that no damage will occur on this mission, is unfortunately denied, for this mission brings him serious injury, after the bomber's bombs have been released. His damaged body is carried back to the base, where he will wake to find that he has lost a leg. In this case, the gunner does not die but survives, after the surgeons remove his shattered leg. Instead of Valhalla, the gunner must live in a reduced world, a world where Trade and the State govern.

The best known of Jarrell's wartime poems, the often-anthologized "Death of the Ball Turret Gunner" summarizes the short, desperate life of Jarrell's best-known figure, another gunner/victim, the ball turret gunner. Jarrell's position as a celestial navigation instructor for bomber crews at Davis-Monthan Army Air Base, a bomber training base, must have given him ample opportunity to observe the configurations of the two important bomber aircraft in the air force inventory, the B-17 and the B-24, the later models of which featured a defensive modification added to the aircraft structures: the ball turret, a small spherical glass and metal gun configuration attached to the bottom of the aircraft's fuselage. The ball turret, when fully lowered beneath the aircraft, allowed its gunner (necessarily small, ideally no taller than five feet) to fire his guns in all directions through the combination of its revolving and rotational movement. The B-17 was capable of reaching the altitude (six miles high, or 30,000 feet) at which Jarrell's gunner lives and dies.

The gunner's brief life begins and ends in wombs; from the womb of his mother he moves instantaneously into the womb of the "State," represented by the ball turret of the bomber, the epitome of the State's war-making machine. The womb-like environment is reinforced by the recognition that the gunner is forced to fire his guns in the turret by assuming something like a fetal position (also a position much like that of a woman giving birth), placing his feet in stirrups at the sides of the turret and firing his guns by controlling mechanisms and switches and looking out of the turret through a window located between his legs. His wet fur is the newborn's hair which scarcely has time to dry before he dies, as it becomes the fur of his flight suit which he wears to protect himself from the cold. In the bomber he is "loosed" from the dream of life as it might be lived on the surface of the earth away from combat or war. In the wartime environment, memories of peace and home could well seem like a dream. In the bomber he is awakened by the enemy's bursting anti-aircraft fire and by the attacking enemy aircraft which are attempting to shoot his bomber down. But his waking state is unpleasant, for he is pursued by the "nightmare" fighters, which would give him nightmares if he were to survive the mission. He is literally a child of War, whose fate is death.

The gunner's bloody remains are cleaned out of the turret by a hose producing a high-pressure stream of water (as Jarrell clarifies in a "note" to the poem, to make sure we understand the technical details).[23] Such a cleaning can occur only after the aircraft returns to its home base, which means that most of the crew members on his aircraft returned safely, even if the ball turret gunner did not. But the ball turret gunner is clearly not among the living, as he tells us in his first-person voice of the clean-up activities necessary to wash his remains out of the turret. The speaking voice is doubly disturbing because it is the voice of a dead man and because the events it describes are related in an impersonal and matter-of-fact manner. This is the kind of story that might have been told by a character in Edgar Lee Masters' *Spoon River Anthology*, which established the pattern, at least for most American readers, of first-person voices speaking briefly of the key moments of their lives and the causes of their deaths. Jarrell's account inverts the symbolic effect of Masters' poems, for those rural citizens were little noticed by their community and the people among whom they lived, while the ball turret gunner was a tool made by the State to be used in the war. Those who actively participated in the war as gunners soon came to realize this uncomfortable fact, as John Ciardi did. Only Jarrell, however, could have phrased it so coldly. This poem certainly would not have been much appreciated by the families of the aircrew members who faced these risks. The poem is indicative of the kind of stance Jarrell assumed in his war poetry, casting a dispassionate, analytical eye on the people and situations that the forces of the war created, commenting on the war of which he was a part in an arm of the State in which he worked cooperatively but with more than a little intellectual disquiet.

"The Death of the Ball Turret Gunner" is characterized by a disturbing coldness in the factual representation of a messy death that is hardly to be overcome by the merit of its interconnected metaphors (the mother's womb and the belly of the State; the dream of life and the nightmare of war). The poet speaking as the dead gunner adds thematic resonance to the recognition of a traumatically shortened life, but there is a sense of disturbed decorum, of a visceral attack upon the sensibilities. This is evident even in the title: it is not a poem about the death of *a* ball turret gunner, anonymous, representative; it is a poem about the death of *the* ball turret gunner. It is about all ball turret gunners.

This poem, perhaps more obviously than any other that Jarrell wrote during the war, illustrates the validity of Richard Flynn's thesis that many of Jarrell's wartime poems reflect his concern about the "lost world of childhood," a childhood missed by the soldiers and airmen who appear in his poems (reflecting, according to Flynn, Jarrell's own lost childhood). As Flynn says, Jarrell's war poems, especially the poems of *Little Friend, Little Friend*, describe soldiers who "are forced to become adults before they have been able to understand their childhoods," who "seem forced into adulthood unprepared."[24] The emphasis on the symbolic roles of children and women, as well as powerless men, is identified also by Adam Kirsch.[25] Jarrell frequently returns to the theme of the soldier as a young victim, a theme resulting from his evident anger and distress about the treatment of the young soldiers in his poems. Those readers who are sympathetic with Jarrell's pessimistic view of what happens to any state when a major war effort is begun will find much to admire in his poems describing gunners as victims. But those readers who do not share Jarrell's pessimistic vision may find these poems too relentless in their condemnation of the actions of the society of which they feel themselves a part.

In an October 1944 letter to Amy Breyer de Blasio, Jarrell writes that the two subjects of the poems he is writing are "bombing Hamburg and bombing crews—I feel sympathetic and sorry for both of them."[26] Three of Jarrell's most important poems about these two subjects combine religious imagery with wartime scenes to raise the issue of moral judgments of the results of war: "Angels at Hamburg," "Burning the Letters," and "Eighth Air Force." These poems show most clearly the effects of Jarrell's reading of the philosophers and church fathers, for each poem consists of a tightly woven mesh of military action placed against a background of religious and philosophical assessment. In "Angels at Hamburg," Jarrell depicts the coastal trade city of Hamburg in fiery turmoil as a result of the repeated aerial bombardment by American and British bombers. In the fire and smoke, the citizens of Hamburg are unable to distinguish between day and night, and, more importantly, between good and evil. The destructive effects of war have caused all considerations of morality to be set aside for the basic necessity of survival. The citizens find themselves in a kind of hell caused by the repeated dropping of bombs, where the "judges [have] come to judge man in the night."[27] In such a place, "human values disappear and justice as a concept is void," as Suzanne Ferguson says; the poem states clearly "Jarrell's general view of the war," that "all humans, civilians and soldiers alike, are morally annihilated as they are brutalized—conditioned—into accepting warfare as a normal, acceptable state of being."[28]

In "Burning the Letters," according to a note Jarrell provides, "a wife of a pilot killed in the Pacific is speaking several years after his death. She was once a Christian, a Protestant." The poem is balanced between images of fire (the flames of the destroyed aircraft carrier and planes, and the letters she is burning) and water (the sea that holds the dead ships and bodies of the dead men). Her images of the dead husband become mixed with images of religious symbolism until the body of the husband is surrounded by apocalyptic fire, his identifying dog tags fused to his bones in his fiery death.

In an October 1945 letter to Margaret Marshall of *The Nation*, Jarrell gave a detailed explication of his intent in the poem. According to Jarrell, the woman in the poem is remembering her own Protestant religious thoughts, based on the words of Saint Paul, comparing them to the images she creates in her own mind about the death of her husband. The woman compares the thoughts of early Christians to her own thoughts of the purpose of the death of her husband and others like him: "she thinks that he and they literally died for her (and that her life came out of their deaths) just as Christ is supposed to have died for her; it's because of this that I used 'it is finished' for the climax of what she says." Like Christ and the early Christians, they died for the sins of others, "atoning not for their sins [because they were too young to have had time to sin], but for ours."[29]

While this information may help to clarify the image sequences in the poem and to confirm some of the impressions an initial reading may give, it also confirms that the poem is carrying a heavy load of meaning, perhaps too heavy to hold together successfully. The unpleasant images of death suggest the apocalyptic vision that Jarrell must certainly have intended, in which the pilot's identification tags (referred to by all soldiers as "dog tags" in recognition of their reduced status) become welded to his breastbone wreathed in fire. The poem is strangely distanced from the human costs of war, a vision of wrath too strong for grief. One who had fought the fires of a doomed carrier would hardly have written such a poem, because he would have known too many men who died. Richard Fein suggests that the human situation of the woman in the poem is overwhelmed by the judgmental ideas Jarrell inserts: "they are imposed from above rather than coming from within the poem, from within the woman's consciousness." According to Fein, the effect of Jarrell's poem is to "replace or dominate the consciousness of the character who is thereby deprived, in some basic sense, of a will or life of her own." The result is that the individuals in the poem are "equipped only with the understanding that Jarrell perceives," adding that Jarrell "incites and defeats his characters."[30] While the images in the poem reinforce the idea of the victims' inability to react against an external controlling force, it becomes increasingly evident that it is Jarrell who is doing the controlling, not the State.[31] Another reader, William Pritchard, has observed that "these are poems which in their reiterated insistence never let up, but purchase their intensity at the cost, perhaps, of wearing out the reader."[32]

In contrast to the intense apocalyptic visions of "Angels at Hamburg" and "Burning the Letters," "Eighth Air Force" is much more successful in placing wartime actions within a religious context. This poem best illustrates and addresses the tension that can result when the poet as a man in the service of his country comments on the morality of war. "Eighth Air Force" is the most admired of his war poems, which Cleanth Brooks accurately describes as "intricate and rich."[33] The Eighth Air Force consisted of those components of the Army Air Forces which were located in England; they had the task of conducting the air war against enemy targets in France and Germany. Even though many different flying units were attached to the Eighth Air Force—fighters, reconnaissance, and cargo units, for instance—the poem focuses exclusively on the activities of the bomber crews, the men who were flying B-17s and B-24s and who were dropping bombs on cities in northern Europe.

The first stanza begins by describing the apparently innocent actions of the off-duty enlisted crew members of a bomber crew. The vision presented in the first two stanzas is of men at rest, playing cards, one asleep, one trying to sleep before his final mission, one shaving after having had too much to drink, a puppy drinking water. The tension of the poem is evident even in the first word, "If," suggesting that what the poet will tell us is hypothetical, not real. In the opening stanza the poet asks whether he can say that men are as wolves to other men. The reference is to an old Roman proverb by Plautus referring to the inhuman treatment of some men by other men. *If* this is the scene (of average men trying to pass the time before flying in combat), *can* the poet say that man is as men have said: a wolf to man? It is in a way as much a test of logic as a tentative beginning to the poem. The "if/then" framework asks us to consider the validity (or truth) of the proposition: can such men really be murderers, feeding themselves on other men?[34]

The poet intentionally complicates our reaction by introducing, in the second stanza, the word *murderers*, who enter yawning, and then offers a vision of the men attempting to rest before flying a mission. Just as we begin to develop sympathy for the men he again accuses them of being murderers in the final lines of the stanza. We are intentionally disoriented in each of the first two stanzas so that we cannot easily answer the question of morality the poem asks: Is it a morally justifiable act to bomb the populations of the enemy from the air? Although the locale is never specifically identified, the clues provided by the poem (hutments, puppies, counting the last mission) suggest an English base and combat in the European theater, with bombs to be dropped on German cities.

The final two stanzas seem designed to answer the moral proposition raised in the first two, especially as the final line of the second stanza proposes to indicate such inhuman actions can occur. The images of the poem suggest a much more complex process of how murder might be justified than simply to describe the effects of a bombing raid. In fact, the war is replaced by another kind of conflict. The first image the poem gives us is of the "murderers" going off to be killed on their bombing mission in an innocent state like that of the puppies with which they have been playing. But as soon as they are sent off to their probable deaths on their bombing mission, the poet becomes an integral part of the events of the poem, explaining that he has done as these men have done but did not die.

Before we can move very far with the idea that the poet may possibly be recognizing himself as a fellow serviceman (as Jarrell would have been during the war), we recognize that the poet has taken on the persona of the New Testament Pilate. Like Pilate, he will "give up these to them": he will give up the criminal crew members to the citizens who are demanding justice for the crimes they are thought to have committed. This is the language of the roman governor when he gave up Christ instead of the convicted murderer Barabbas to the people, because the people wanted their own justice. So if the crew members are murderers, they are also Christ-like in their innocence, in sacrificing themselves for the ultimate good of their society. This is clearly Jarrell's intent, for he says in a note to the poem that "the phrases from the Gospels compare such criminals and scapegoats as these [airmen] with that earlier and criminal scapegoat [Jesus] about whom the Gospels were written."[35]

The judgmental perspective of the poet is compromised by our recognition of his historical withdrawal from the issues raised by the case; he/Pilate states that he can "find no fault in this just man." The poet as Pilate has put the case to us and then has withdrawn from participation, leaving us to decide, with the recognition that the most impartial or the most severe critic is himself a part of the moral argument. The ambiguity of the phrase "just man" seems evident: the men are "just" in being *only* men, as they have the capacity to be *fair* men. The language says: these men were doing their work for us, the readers. We (as citizens of the State) made them murderers and condemned them to die while in the act of committing the murder we directed them to do. They are doing the best job (of killing others) that they can do.

It should be noted that Jarrell's "murderers" would not, technically, be the primary agents responsible for killing the people on the ground: that role would more accurately belong to the officers on the bomber crew: the pilots, navigator, bombardier, the men responsible for maneuvering the aircraft over the target and dropping the bombs. But the officers are not in the poem. Instead, the blame is carried by the enlisted men, the gunners, Jarrell's primary agents in all of his war poems: side gunners, tail gunners, ball turret gunners; their tasks are accomplished in support of the actions of the officers, the privileged members of the State.

The stanza form and rhyme scheme add to the blending of images of the modern aircrew members with the New Testament figures, as the repeated, simple end rhymes—"man," "can,"—and the similar sound of "one," "done," link the involved individuals thematically. The unusual stanza form—four verses of five lines each—bonds the two images through balanced representation of the new with the old, as the wartime vision is overlaid with images of the New Testament story.

What is Jarrell's position in this poem, finally? Are we to think of him as Pilate, unwilling to become more involved in the morally confusing situation than he needs to be? Or should we see him as Pilate's wife, who suffers, "in a dream," because of the situation? The poet–Pilate admits that he has been lying and could also be accused of manipulating events and responses. Only in this poem, of all that he wrote during the war, does Jarrell seem to recognize his precarious position as commentator when he speaks with the voice of higher moral authority in poems describing the actions of men like himself, wearing the military uniform of the government of the United States. The men who bombed the cities of Europe and Japan were able to do so only as the result of the training given to them by men like Jarrell, who never came near the hazardous arena of combat. In this poem especially, Jarrell leads the reader to the uncomfortable edge of the recognition of the great moral cost of the war to the men who participated in it and the public who supported them in their wartime activities. This poem, of all that Jarrell wrote about the war, best shows that his physical and emotional distance from the war could allow him to create poems that intensely engaged in the moral issues associated with its meaning and destruction.

When the war ended, Jarrell served for a time as literary editor of *The Nation* and taught briefly at Sarah Lawrence College before moving to the Women's College of the University of North Carolina at Greensboro, where he taught for many years. But never in his subsequent poetry did he revisit the war as a topic, and his career never quite fulfilled the expectations created by the achievement of his wartime poetry.

3

John Ciardi, U.S. Army Air Forces

Unlike Randall Jarrell, who wrote poems about action in a number of areas of the war from a detached and impersonal perspective, John Ciardi wrote poems directly linked to his personal training and operational experiences. As an integral aircrew member of a heavy bomber in the operational army air forces, Ciardi was intimately familiar with the jargon of the airmen and the military bureaucracy. The poems that he wrote during his wartime service have the knowledgeable language and hard surface of someone immersed in the daily details of the life of an aircrew member. Most of his poems about the war first appeared in *Other Skies*, published by Atlantic Monthly Press in 1947, although many other poems about the war appeared in later volumes of poetry. In *Other Skies* Ciardi wrote about himself as the central figure in many of the poems, such as "On Sending Home My Civilian Clothes," "Letter from an Island," "Elegy Just in Case," "I Ponder the Studious Dead," "First Summer after a War," "I Meet the Motion of Summer Thinking Guns," "On a Photo of Sgt. Ciardi a Year Later," and especially his birthday poems: "Night Piece for My Twenty-seventh Birthday," "Reveille for My Twenty-eighth Birthday," "Poem for My Twenty-Ninth Birthday," and "Poem for My Thirtieth Birthday." For Ciardi, his personal relationship to the events of the war was the most appropriate subject for his poems.

Born in Boston to Italian immigrant parents, Ciardi graduated *magna cum laude* from Tufts University in 1938. He went to the University of Michigan to write poetry under the tutelage of Roy Cowden, where he submitted a manuscript that won a Hopwood Award and became the basis for his first book of poetry, *Homeward to America*, published in 1940. He taught at the University of Kansas City until 1942, and then, terrified that he "might be drafted into the infantry and be made to sleep in foxholes," he entered the aviation cadet program.[1] He wanted to become a pilot, but after ten weeks of testing in Nashville, Tennessee, he was assigned to navigator training, which he began, early in 1943, at Selman Field, Louisiana. For the first few months he was successful in the navigation training program, but he was eliminated from the program on 3 September and reduced to the rank of private.

There are conflicting stories about the reasons for his elimination from the program. Ciardi stated that it was the result of the findings of the Dies Committee, which investigated possible un–American activities on the part of men about to be commissioned. He believed that his activities with a communist-sympathizing organization on the University of Michigan campus, where he had taught before the war, might have brought about his dismissal.[2] However, Ciardi may have contributed to his elimination in a number of other ways: showing disrespect to superiors, demonstrating substandard military performance, going absent without leave (AWOL) to visit his girlfriend, and fighting with an officer.[3] Although at the time Ciardi might have resented the administrative decision that removed him from a useful aircrew position for which he had trained, he later considered it a "lucky break" for him, after he learned that all forty-three navigators with whom he trained had been sent to the Eighth Air Force in England where they became casualties within a year's time.[4]

By the end of September 1943 he was attending a twelve-week course in gunnery training at Lowry Field in Denver, and by April of 1944 he was at Walker Army Air Base, Kansas, where he received specialized training as a gunner on B-29 aircraft, newly developed by the Air Forces as an improved high altitude bomber which could fly higher, faster, and farther than the B-17s and B-24s prominent in the aerial attacks on Germany. At Walker, Ciardi met the other members of his crew and flew with them to the Pacific theater in late 1944. There were typically nine other men on the crew: pilot, co-pilot, navigator, bombardier, flight engineer, radar operator, and two other gunners. Ciardi's position in the aircraft was on the right side of the aircraft, behind the right wing, where his seat in a bubble-shaped window allowed him to observe and respond to any enemy fighter attacks approaching the right side of the aircraft. Unlike the B-17, on which each gunner directly handled and fired his own machine gun, the B-29 was a pressurized aircraft, and the guns were externally mounted and operated by remote control. After receiving enemy aircraft position input from the gunners, a computer calculated the appropriate firing angles for the external guns. This was a new and complex system which worked reasonably well once the inevitable problems of a new weapons system were solved.

By the time he completed gunnery training, he was twenty-eight years old, the oldest man on his crew. He later reported that, as much as possible, he neither took an order nor gave one.[5] Like Jarrell, Ciardi focused on the gunner as the key individual in his poems, the central figure whom most of his poems describe. Unlike Jarrell, however, he had good reason to choose the gunner as a central figure: he *was* one. While Jarrell looked on the gunner from the detached perspective of an outside observer, Ciardi was trained in the use of guns and fired them in combat. Ciardi's recognition of the centrality of the role of the gunner began long before he became one. In "On Sending Home My Civilian Clothes," Ciardi describes his transition from civilian to military member: to "moth balls" the poet consigns his "civil colors, fit, and line." The poet sets aside his *civil* qualities: moderation, cooperation, the ability to resolve conflicts peacefully in the hope of advancing societies or civilizations of the world. By setting aside his former clothing and wearing the clothing of the military services (which represent the "Law"), he is transformed from a self with modest autonomy to a self which operates as part of a structured system:

> By a change of place and Law
> I am the stalker whose name is Claw.
> In olive drab and three-pound shoes
> I trample down the hills of Choose.
> And all the transformation done,
> My map is Do, my hand, a gun.

The poet declares that in his new self he has

> clamped badges to my coat
> And hung a number round my throat
> And set an engine on my will
> To measure, pity, stalk, and kill.[6]

The stance the poet assumes in the poem—that of someone who will become a trained gunner—is similar to that evident in later poems, a mixture of grim humor and cruelty. Even in this early poem, we wonder if Ciardi wants us to take his poetic persona seriously: does he truly wish to suggest that he is really capable of, or is capable in his imagination of, the kind of anger, determination, and grim heartless action suggested in the poem? Ciardi combines belligerency with wit, evident in the cleverness of a line in which his "three-pound shoes" trample "the hills of Choose." However, Ciardi's wittiness is combined with the stark imagery of an automated soldier whose "map is Do," whose "hand is Gun," and whose will is to "measure, pity, stalk, and kill."

Ciardi the poet is too clever to be the single-minded agent of the military the poem describes, but in the early poems he may be closer to that figure than we might like to think. As a result of his own extended training experiences, he certainly understood the discipline and training required to create such a person, the kind of stolidly determined individual the time and circumstances require. Perhaps Ciardi never quite became that individual while he was in the military service, but he approached it closely. He was a gunner, after all, and if he was nearly as good a gunner as he was a poet, even in 1943 and 1944, he must have been very skilled at his trade. His autobiographical poem "Reveille for My Twenty-Eighth Birthday" is filled with references to the mechanisms of the gunner's trade he was learning in 1944:

> Journeyman expert in the trades of kill,
> Scholar of bomb and fuse, and the controls
> Of wireless stars and the starred wire that pulls
> The turrets to their edict—dressed in such skill,
> Am I that burning angel whose wild stance
> Bore other features across distance?[7]

The change of character, from free agent to an agent of the state, whose actions are controlled by a system larger than the men who comprise it, is reflected also in the poem that introduces the war service section of *Other Skies*, "Suddenly Where Squadrons Turn": "Here across the iron sky / Iron squadrons simplify: / We must stay alive."[8] In contrast to Jarrell's gunners, who are simple, naïve victims of the system, the figure of Ciardi's gunner is competent, well-trained, self-aware, and supremely confident.

Nowhere is this attitude more evident than in "Reflections While Oiling a Machine Gun."[9] In this poem, probably written during his stateside training, Ciardi combines ideas and images from philosophy, history, and common experience in a setting to be found only in the military environment. In the poem, the poet reflects on scenes from his previous life as a student and precepts taught him as a traditional scholar while he concentrates on the smooth and efficient operation of his gun in his wartime schooling as a gunner. The opening line of the poem, "I think of Plato in a schoolroom dusk," establishes the central thematic figure in the poem: Plato, whose allegory of the cave set the timeless model for human learning. The poet says that while in school, the notes he took "resolved" and "pigeonholed" Plato's ideas; as a student the poet mastered the book definition of Plato. But, as subsequent allusions in the poem reveal, Plato's lesson (at least as it is expressed in the *Gorgias*: that we do not see clearly until we escape from the cave of our daily living into the larger light of truth) is translated into another world, the world of military activity.

According to the poem, the poet's teacher thought of Plato as "Shelley's father, / A sort of third-vice-resident-prime-mover, / Wearing a beard and the Order of the Garter," a part of the social establishment, a combination of distinguished philosopher and statesman. Like the poet's teacher, the figure of Plato provides a "shining image of *ding-an-sich*" for the "burgher," the poem's representative of political authority.

> Patently
> The body of the body politic
> Prefers its legend to its history.

No longer a student of history, the poet has become a student of armed conflict, with his hand

> on the thousandth of an inch
> Between the sear and firing pin, pin and wish,
> And who will die before or after lunch?

The student, taught his history by the authorized representative of the state ("teacher"), has now become an armed representative of the state's military force. The result of his new learning is not to understand and perhaps practice the higher truths of the allegory of the cave, but to serve as an automatic and highly trained instrument of the state, one of its high-tech guardians. The result of Ciardi's training as a gunner (the task he was finally assigned) is not enlightened behavior for the benefit of society, but harm and destruction of the individuals and machines who oppose the state. Ciardi's job was to defend his B-29 bomber against attacks by enemy aircraft, and he does not quibble about the job's realities; on the other hand, he never offers those realities as a defense for his actions or his poetic outlook in these poems.

As an armed member of a bomber crew, he takes responsibility for the destructiveness produced by the crew's actions. The bullets he fires in defense of his aircraft's progress are like the bombs the bombardier drops. Even if he kills only appropriately designated members of the enemy's armed forces, every man he kills or wounds is a representative of an opposing, but similarly structured, society. The person Ciardi may kill in the line of duty (following the "Law," to use his repeated phrase), the man who dies "before or after lunch," may be "buried in the usuries of a wreath" and "not hear the burgher's oratory praise / Teacher and God." The poem concludes with a chilling image of the results of wartime education:

> Scholar in oil and steel and numbered parts,
> I have poor teacher's error at my thumb,
> And would request good voters of all sorts
> To lay less emphasis on Kingdom Come.

One reader, seeing in these lines a "flippant, irreverent, socially critical attitude," charges that the poem demonstrates a "lack of sufficient seriousness" and that we, as readers, "simply do not want wit and cleverness on some subjects, especially in wartime."[10] While it is true that Ciardi is nothing if not an ironist, to say that these lines are too clever to convey important wartime truths is to miss the point of the poem: the mechanisms of state educational and political processes can lead, in a state focused on grim goals, to unimaginable and profoundly unsettling results. Ciardi's apparent pleasure at pointing out this unfortunate condition reinforces the sense of distress this poem (and others like it) can create in the sensitive reader.

The setting in which the poet reflects on the cultural implications of learning about the operation of guns in a wartime environment is familiar—one need think only of Henry Reed's "Naming of Parts" and Richard Eberhart's "Fury of Aerial Bombardment," for instance—but Ciardi's poem is more complex, more disturbing. In the poems of Reed and Eberhart, the poet is a detached observer. But for Ciardi, the gun is his. Not only does he know how to operate it, he knows why he is using it. His motivation has as much to do with the failure of Western philosophy as it does with enemy acts of aggression. Certainly his *Saipan* diary entries suggest that he knew how to handle and maintain guns and knew the gunners' technologies.

One entry from his wartime diary, for instance, reveals his pride in his knowledge of his weapons and in his ability to repair them. Departing Saipan for a bombing run over Tokyo, a crew member reports a "jam on the outside right gun of the upper forward turret." This is how Ciardi describes his subsequent actions as he moves through the cramped pressurized tunnel at the top of the fuselage that connected the gunners' compartment behind the wing to the main crew compartment:

> I dragged my tool kit out of the radar room and crawled down the tunnel on all fours for the fairly exhausting job of stripping the gun down in the air. In our [B-29] system the guns are in pressure-sealed turrets. A man needs to be part eel to reach things inside. With luck, however, things went my way and I had it sweated clear sooner than I could have hoped. (The links jammed in the link chutes, a round had jammed between the face of the bolt and the trunnion block, and the oil buffer had come out of adjustment.)[11]

Not only does Ciardi know how to fix the gun jam, he knows the words for the key parts, and he believes that information is important enough to record in his diary.

Ciardi and his crew arrived on the Pacific island of Saipan around the 20th of November 1944 and were assigned to the 882nd Bomb

Squadron, one of the squadrons in the 500th Bomb Group, 73rd Bomb Wing. The 73rd flew its first mission over Tokyo four days after Ciardi's crew arrived, on 24 November. Over 100 B-29s, fully loaded with fuel and bombs, took off from the recently completed runway at Isley Field, Saipan. Bad weather over the target restricted bombing success. The wing flew a second mission on 27 November; while the aircraft were bombing Tokyo, Japanese fighters from Iwo Jima attacked the field at Saipan, an attack which Ciardi vividly describes in his diary.[12] The third Tokyo mission was a night mission with limited success. Ciardi's crew had yet to fly a combat mission. On the first of December Ciardi noted in his diary that, tired of doing nothing, he would like "to get over a target—even Tokio."[13] Two days later, on 3 December, he got his wish, as he and his crew flew their first combat mission as part of the Wing's third daylight mission over Japan. Fortunately, their aircraft completed the flight successfully and without suffering any damage from enemy attacks.

Initially enthusiastic about the missions they were flying and the crew he was flying with, after their first mission Ciardi wrote in his diary about the pride he felt in the kinds of tasks he and the others were doing: "I was cockeyed proud of the crew. Not a rattle in the bunch.... Every man was functioning calmly and well and it was a proud thing to know."[14] Ciardi's excitement about flying the mission is evident in the fact that he devotes seven pages of his diary (in the published version) to recording the details of the mission. After a mission over Iwo Jima on 8 December, Ciardi and his crew flew a second mission over Japan on 16 December, and it's clear that excitement is being replaced by anxiety: when he learns of the mission (to Nagoya), "suddenly I dreaded it"; his anxiety disappears once he is in the plane, going through his assigned tasks. But he admits that he had a "sleepless night" prior to the mission.[15] On the next mission over Nagoya, Ciardi is terribly frustrated when his guns refuse to fire at an attacking Japanese fighter. After their safe return to Saipan, Ciardi checks the lower aft gun turret and discovers mechanical problems he thought should have been detected in the preflight but weren't, and he expresses his anger at one of his fellow gunners for not completing his preflight inspection properly.[16]

Ciardi's enthusiasm for combat soon began to wane. The automated firing system did not always work as it was intended, and the guns sometimes became inoperative even before the aircraft began the bomb run. In addition, it must have soon occurred to him that he was filling one of the least challenging positions on the crew. As a side gunner, he directly controlled only one of the four gun turrets on the aircraft, the lower aft turret; actually, he shared control of the turret with the side gunner on the other side of the aircraft, control switching to whichever side was experiencing the most direct threat from an attacking aircraft. In an emergency, the side gunners could also take control of the two forward turrets, upper and lower. In fact, however, their forward visibility was significantly limited, and control of the forward turrets was normally handled by the bombardier, who had a clear view forward. The long, thirteen-hour flights to Japan and back over the endless waters of the Pacific Ocean disturbed him, especially when engines malfunctioned and as some of the men he knew were being shot down over Japan or disappearing after ditching in the Pacific. Even his technical competence began to erode; during a mission on 14 January 1945, he noted that he had "committed an error in gross negligence" by making a mistake in assembling his firing mechanism in one of his guns, an "inexcusable error."[17]

But the major factor that caused him increasing concern was the arrival of a new commanding officer, a young general named Curtis LeMay, who replaced Haywood Hansell as commanding general of 20th Bomber Command about the 20th of January, less than two months after the command began its bomb runs over Japan. LeMay was tasked with improving the bombing accuracy and results of the B-29 aircrews. The B-29s had been designed to fly at high altitude, well above the flak and service ceilings of the attacking fighters. However, at those high altitudes, over 30,000 feet, the winds of the jet stream the bombers encountered in the skies over Japan interfered with the trajectories of the bombs as they fell through six miles of sky, scattering bombs wide of the intended targets. One of LeMay's first changes was to send the bombers in at lower altitudes, at or below 25,000 feet, so that the winds would interfere less. However, at the lower altitudes, flak and enemy fighters became a much greater problem. LeMay, who had seen the appalling conditions in which the B-17 crews flew on their early missions to Germany, believed that the risks to the B-29 crews were much less severe than those experienced by the B-17 crews. But this viewpoint was not necessarily shared by the men on the B-29s.

Ciardi was sensitive to the fact that the element that determined who would survive and who would not was usually chance. Which aircraft would be hit by flak, which crewman would be hit by the bullets of an attacking aircraft, could not be predicted. Ciardi expresses this idea clearly when he describes the loss of an aircraft next to the one his crew was flying in a mission over Japan:

> The plane on our right took a hit and began to smoke and fall out of formation, the Zeroes waiting to swarm on it once it was away from our covering fire. I was at the right blister as it passed under us. There was a boy in the top blister of the stricken plane. I was probably the only man in his direct line of

sight. He waved to me, and I waved back. A least exchange forever. He waved there at the end of his luck, I waved and went home, and nothing either of us had ever done had any voice in deciding which of us was which.[18]

The recognition that his position as a well-trained gunner did not necessarily protect his ability to stay alive is reflected in his postwar two-stanza poem, "Two Songs for a Gunner." In the first stanza, as a gunner firing at other planes, he is "dangerous," firing tracers "at the zodiac / Falling how-many-colored to sea-dark / Of the world's body under." In the second stanza, when he is "Being Fired At," he is "danger's" object, as "the tracers' endless / Jeweled cobra struck at my running tomb / In a cloud." He describes his vulnerable situation:

> How chaste and sweet a womb
> I cowered in to praise its luminous
> Waver and fall from power. And as it fell,
> How deep an egg I curled in very well.[19]

His recognition that the odds were coldly, mathematically calculated for the success of any mission, with statistical consideration of the human cost, is shown in these lines from "Expendability":

> I beg of chance the green and living day.
> I wheedle numbers, plot new averages,
> Alchemize probabilities (a play
> Of superstition tarred by our dark ages—
> That numbers have a ghost to give,
> Proof is a chart)[20]

The poems he wrote while he was on Saipan were less often about his role as a gunner, and increasingly about the gunners he had known who had not returned from their missions, as in "Ritual for Singing Bat":

> "One part Indian, one part Tennessee,"
> He said his first day in. We saw him dive,
> His feather dress of flame ceremoniously
> Prompt to the ritual of the pyre-borne dove.[21]

Or his "Elegy" for Kurt Porjescz, one of the Jewish crew members in the unit, who was reported missing in action 1 April 1945: "The boys are flowers: they strew themselves in seed."[22] And he wrote his own "Elegy Just in Case":

> Here lie Ciardi's pearly bones
> In their ripe organic mess.
> Jungle blown, his chromosomes
> Breed to a new address.
> . . . .

3. John Ciardi, U.S. Army Air Forces 57

> File the papers, pack the clothes,
> Send the coded word through air—
> "We regret and no one knows
> Where the sgt. goes from here."[23]

Ciardi began to brood more and more over the effects of LeMay's new orders to fly at lower altitudes:

> My civilian reaction to the general's order was what everyone I knew felt. "This man I have never seen will very likely be what kills me," I thought. I felt it was a far darker certainty when the next semi-official rumor followed. "The targets will be hit and wiped out. If the bombardiers cannot hit them from 25,000 [feet], the missions will be run at 20,000, and if they cannot hit them at 20,000 they will go in at 15,000 but the targets will be hit."[24]

It was only after he heard that information that Ciardi sat down to write "a letter home to be mailed in case I didn't come back."[25] Ciardi must have believed that his odds of survival were significantly reduced as a result of LeMay's new bombing policy. A skilled craps player, he recognized that you had to know the odds if you hoped to win the game. Also, Ciardi increasingly believed that his skill with words was more important than his questionable value in an airplane whose defensive fire capabilities were largely automated, as he found himself less an active combatant and more a passenger along for a very long and unpleasant ride. As he noted in his diary, referring to himself in the third person, "Ciardi seems to be having combat nerves.... I find myself thinking that it's foolish to stick my neck out over Japan when my real usefulness and capability as a person and as a unit of society is in writing what needs to be written well."[26] His waning motivation is clearly indicated by the fact that his diary entries ended a few days later.

Fortunately, someone at headquarters learned that Ciardi's poems were being published in *Atlantic* and *Poetry* magazines, and he was invited to transfer to the headquarters staff, where skilled writers were in demand. As Ciardi later related the incident to Studs Terkel, "I received orders to report to headquarters. The colonel in charge of awards and decorations said, 'We need somebody with combat crew experience who can write. You've taught college English, you've published a book. You're now working for me.'"[27] Having flown at least nine missions, Ciardi accepted the offer with mixed feelings of gratitude and guilt and became an administrative specialist in the office of General Emmett "Rosie" O'Donnell, commanding officer of the 73rd Bomb Wing, in the spring of 1945. The primary tasks in Ciardi's new job were to prepare award recommendations for crew members and to prepare letters of condolence for the families of the dead or missing. His old crew continued to fly missions with a new gunner. On their third mission after Ciardi moved to his headquarters position, the aircraft of the crew with which he had been flying exploded in flight. It was the last crew in the squadron to be lost in combat.

In his administrative position, Ciardi continued to write poems dipped in the language of the military service. "Wafflebutt" expresses his complex attitude towards his new duties; the title is taken from the imprint left on the seat of his pants as a result of sitting all day on the criss-cross pattern of the cane seats in the office chairs. A "wafflebutt" is the identifiable mark of one who can enjoy the safe life of a support worker while others fly hazardous combat missions. The opening lines at first suggest that the poem will be amusingly self-mocking:

> Reveille rung on telephones awakes
> The opening movement of an opening day.
> Alphabets in mosaics,
> Reports and rosters weigh
> Some who came through, some pending,

But even before the first stanza ends, the harsh realities of the duties of an administrative clerk in a combat unit are evident:

> some who died,
> And some delayed while oceans wait outside.[28]

The poem describes the paperwork of administrative tasks: measuring the life and death results of the daily bombing missions: preparing rosters of new men arriving, rosters of men awaiting assignments to crews, rosters of those who are missing or confirmed dead. Because Ciardi had had the experience of having flown combat missions, he was able to visualize only too clearly the unpleasant conditions that produced the lists of casualties. Unlike the men on the bomber crews, whose productivity is measured by their ability to destroy targets, the productivity of an administrative clerk is measured by the speed with which he processes the paperwork:

> One minute now, one paperclip to pin
> On one regret to tabulate and file
>   A finished lifetime in
>   (Not mine). One fraction while
> The silver bubbles rise, the corpses sink—
> In one more minute I will stop and think...

The poet imagines the progress of an aircraft on a bombing run, as the poem offers a series of visions of the experiences of the aircrews: flak bursting around the plane, then bombs and crewmen dropping out of the stricken aircraft. In a parenthetical stanza in the middle of the poem, the poetic persona speaks not as an administrative clerk but as a crewman who sees "our bombs" fall "like Phallic comets," and the vision of falling airmen is framed in a flowery analogy:

> Across the flowerfall of the tumbling chutes
> That bloomed hydrangeas where
> The dead in fancy suits
> All flowered in flame, heaved from the flaming ground,
> And settled back like seed pods—black and round.

In this apocalyptic vision, men in their flying suits dead before they hit the ground are denied burial because their bombs are exploding around them. The force and fire of the explosions turns them into hard dark objects, seed pods unlikely to germinate. Against the fiery heat of bombardment and aerial combat, Ciardi offers the contrasting image of the water that surrounds and isolates the men on Saipan, "the other side this surf."

For the men on the island and for the family members far away, the poem suggests that the kinds of visions described will result in emotions like "nostalgias" and "fear never put away" that

> Demanded and recalled and churned our sleep
> With a lead-gutted terror, dreamed and deep.

In the final stanza, Ciardi returns from his apocalyptic visions to the daily and weekly routine of clerk work, and the never-ending paper-processing tasks, tasks that deprive him of any sense of personal satisfaction or safety he might have:

> To file by rank and name (no longer ours),
> Insured in triplicate, indorsed, and signed
>   Six days a week in office hours.
>   But oh the telephone is mined,
> And boredom booby-traps desk, file, and wall
> Where day and day destroys us after all.

By the time the war ended, Ciardi could say truthfully that he had witnessed the full range of the ways in which the air force waged war, from the operational perspective gathered in the hazardous skies over Japan to the administrative perspective learned in the offices of 20th Bomber Command headquarters. Ciardi had earned his Air Medal for flying combat missions and had written awards for Air Medals for others. He had seen men in planes fade from view in the skies over Japan and he had typed lists of casualties for notification of next of kin. He knew the language of the operational and administrative air force. It is not surprising that both perspectives appear in the poem he wrote about the end of the war, "V-J Day."

"V-J Day" imagines the reactions of the B-29 crews on their way to bomb Japan when they learn that the war has ended. Hearing this news, they release their bomb loads into the sea and return home. No longer required to observe radio silence while en route to the target, they chatter over the airwaves like schoolboys out of school. The day when the war ends is the "tallest day in time," for reasons the poem makes clear:

> On the tallest day in time the dead came back.
> Clouds met us in the pastures past a world.
> By short wave the releases of a rack
> Exploded on the interphone's new word.[29]

The "interphone's new word," *peace*, frees the crews to release their bombs from their racks inside the aircraft, and to be released from their personal torture racks of duty and hazard. The released bombs "spring a frolic fountain daintily / Out of the blue metallic seas of doom." The image of the bombs striking the hard surface of the sea suggests the pleasure that the crews would have taken at their attempts to bomb the sea, to strike back at one of the aspects of the missions to Japan they feared almost as much as they feared attacks by Japanese fighter aircraft: the extremely remote chances of surviving a ditching at sea and the equally remote chances (at least early in the war) of being rescued after ditching.

They no longer have to worry about flak ("No fire-shot cloud pursued us going home") or doing harm to the people on the ground ("No cities cringed and wallowed in the flame"), but, the poem suggests, now that the survivors have survived the war, they face the challenge of learning from their experiences:

> Far out to sea a blank millennium
> Changed us alive, and left us still the same.

"Lightened" of their bomb load, physically and emotionally, the large, four-engine aircraft "banked like jays, antennae squawking." The voices a crew member can hear over the interphone, the radio system that connects the men in the aircraft to each other and allows them to hear conversations among other aircraft and the command posts on the ground, are generating "Abracadabra to the cumulus tops." The coded language of flight operations could seem like an unknown tongue to non-specialists. In the context of the prospect of peace, however, Ciardi suggests that the operational language of the aircrews now has something of a magical quality to it, as if it could create special effects:

> Dreamboat three-one to Yearsend—loud and clear,
> Angels one-two, on course at one-six-nine.
> Magellan to Balboa. Propwash to Century.
> How do you read me? Bombay to Valentine.

"Dreamboat three-one" is the call sign of a specific aircraft, perhaps one of the aircraft Ciardi flew. "Dreamboat" in fact was the generic call sign for the B-29, considered a dream to fly because it was modern and filled with the latest high-technology systems. "Yearsend" could be the call sign for the aircraft leading or monitoring the flight of bombers. Because the end of the war has just been announced, the idea of a year's end is linked to the end of the millennium. "Loud and clear" is the standard radio check terminology, transmitted to show that the radio operator can both hear and transmit successfully. "Angels one-two" indicates that the aircraft is flying at an altitude of twelve thousand feet, on a heading of "one-six-nine," or just east of south, the heading an aircraft would need to fly if it were returning from Japan over Iwo Jima to Saipan.

But then the radio language becomes increasingly allusive. "Magellan" and "Balboa" may be ground control stations; but they were also explorers of the Pacific who failed to return from their explorations. "Propwash" is the wind force generated by the propellers of the B-29, and four propellers could generate a good deal of propwash, propelling the men who flew it into a new time frame. "Century" is the middle term of the time framework Ciardi is establishing: first the millennium, then the year, now the century. Ciardi's calendar is not the Julian calendar; it is the calendar of the era of war. When the war with Japan ended, World War II ended, and even though the poem doesn't mention it, the war ended as a result of the effects of the atomic bomb, which all readers of the poem would know. An important page of history turned, Ciardi implies, when the war ended, and the events of the war, technical as well as personal, changed the lives of everyone involved. "Bombay" is a city in India, of course, but it also is the phrase for the part of the aircraft that dropped the bombs— the bomb bay—which, now that it is permanently closed, can signify friendlier aspects. Instead of the hatred of war, we can think of love, of a "valentine."

The poem concludes not with a vision of peace and prosperity, however, but with another of Ciardi's apocalyptic visions:

> Fading and out. And all the dead were homing.
> (*Wisecrack to Halfmast. Doom to Memory.*)

The concluding image shows that "all the dead were homing," and the call signs change appropriately: "Wisecrack" was normal GI speech. Wisecracking was the code of the soldier, a way of talking about the events and activities of war and of duty that acknowledged the necessity of obedience yet preserved the illusion of independence. But when the war ends and duty is done, wisecracking is obsolete. "Halfmast" is the universal military gesture of homage to the dead: the flag flies halfway up (or down) the flag pole. "Doom" communicates with "Memory" to ensure the final apocalyptic image remains vividly fixed in our minds:

> On the tallest day in time we saw them coming,
> Wheels jammed and flaming on a metal sea.

The men who died in the line of duty are reappearing from their fiery or watery ends, given new life after death. The poem suggests that these dead aircrews, in planes bathed in flame, are fated to fly forever, because their wheels are "jammed." Jammed wheels cannot be lowered for a safe landing.[30]

The other lines of the poem seem to celebrate the survival of the living crew members, released from the constraints of a difficult duty, not those who died in the line of duty. However, the end of the poem suggests that all crew members, living as well as dead, are in a condition of death, because the war has caused such a profound change in their behavior and outlook that they are no longer the kind of men they used to be.

When news that the fighting might stop reached the B-29 units, no bombing missions were scheduled. All major offensive operations were postponed while the authorities waited to see how the Japanese would respond to the dropping of the second atomic bomb. There was, in fact, no recall of a mission to Japan of the kind described in the poem. The mission described in the poem is Ciardi's way of suggesting what such a profound change would mean to the men in the unit, both practically and symbolically. In the actions and language of release shown in the poem, Ciardi implies the hardnesses of the war effort as it had been flown by the men in the bombers during the months preceding. The images of heavy, four-motored bomber aircraft banking "like jays" with antennae "squawking" effectively suggest the sense of release felt by those who flew.

"Poem for My Twenty-Ninth Birthday" (June 1945) contains images of the combat units with which Ciardi had, until very recently, been flying: "Now I have named another year of time / Learning to count not mine but a world's age." Ciardi's sad pessimism over the destruction the bomber crews are causing is evident in this poem, as he compares the "darkness" of a Saipan island native to theirs:

> His is the simplest darkness, our grotesque
> Of straps and buckles, parachutes and guns,
> Our gear of kit and cartridge, helmet, mask,
> Life vest, rations, and the elegance
> Of all our conscious gestures and our gum,
> Darken us further than his guess can come.[31]

It is instructive to compare the poems Ciardi wrote before he flew in combat to those he wrote after he returned from the war. His postwar poems are filled with a haunted sense of loss and futility, even despair, not hinted at in his pre-war poems. Of course, the war modified his outlook. But these later poems reverberate with a sense of loss and a depth of feeling only hinted at in his earlier poems.

"I Meet the Motion of Summer Thinking Guns" serves as a counterbalance to the poem he wrote early in his military career, "Reflections While Oiling a Machine Gun." In this poem, he is now a civilian again, but finds he cannot look at the objects of the natural world with the same perspective he used to have. Now he sees them through gunner's eyes:

> I meet the motion of summer thinking guns,
> Thinking the flowerless dead, who, siphoned on
> The protein circuits of the dandelions
> Rest motionless beneath our quickening motion.
>
> I am dark, hungry, blind, absurd
> At every opening motion of a rose.
> I am the cartridge that admires the bird
> By metal sights until my triggers close.[32]

It is not difficult to see in the poems in the final section of *Other Skies* the kind of adjustments that all veterans of all wars have had to make: the sense of strangeness and displacement upon returning home, the awareness of the disappearance of the unique wartime experience, partly terrible and horrifying, disturbing to the soul and to the spirit, but still valuable for having been experienced. Perhaps these poems served to make Ciardi's postwar adjustment easier, in allowing him to purge himself of the disturbing and unsatisfying lessons of the war.

Ciardi sums up the difference between his war and not-war selves most effectively in "On a Photo of Sgt. Ciardi a Year Later." Looking at a photo taken at the time he was a gunner on a bomber crew, the poet sees that

> The sgt. stands so fluently in leather,
> So poster-holstered and so newsreel-jawed
> As death's costumed and fashionable brother,
> My civil memory is overawed.
> . . . .
> He leans on gun sights, doesn't give a damn
> For dice or stripes, and waits to see the fun.[33]

The poet now acknowledges that the photo misrepresented the truth:

> The leather was living tissue in its own dimension,
> The holsters held Benzedrine tablets, the guns were no use.

The poem concludes with the statement that "the camera always lies" and "the camera photographs the cameraman": the camera takes the picture the viewer wants to see. In time of war, the public wants to see an image of the professional who appears to know what he is doing. So, perhaps, does the participant: he dresses for the part appropriately, wearing the necessary clothing and carrying the necessary tools. But, says the poet, what is shown is a lie: the man in the photograph was not a professional, not a soldier. There is a mild quibble here, of course; the subject (Ciardi's war self) did dress the part, and was attempting to fulfill the role as competent crew member:

> The careful slouch and dangling cigarette
> Were always superstitious as Amen.

The Ciardi postwar self, however, finds it difficult to recognize the man in the photograph. He is now nothing like that man; his experience has changed him. The photograph has to be a lie. Ciardi no longer identifies with, does not accept, the values and actions associated with the man in the photograph. In a way, the poems in *Other Skies* demonstrate the story of Ciardi's progress towards denial of that photograph. Even the title indicates that the activities of the Ciardi war self took place in another world.

The impact of his war experiences concerned him for many years, as shown in the significant number of war-related poems he wrote after the war ended. In "Massive Retaliation," written well after the war ended, a formation of B-29 bombers circling over an island checkpoint before commencing a bomb run becomes a vivid vision of the complex human responsibility of waging war:

> It was a thousand of ourselves we saw.
> A thousand theorems spiraled from the sun
> to some proof statelier than the thing done.
> A sky-wide silver of the coming of the Law.
> . . . .
> I gaped for all good men at what we were,
> dressed in such bridals, spilling from the sun,
> stuffed with such thunderbolts, and come
> so far from home, almost beyond return.[34]

After the war, Ciardi taught at Harvard and Rutgers and published several volumes of poetry. He is perhaps best remembered for his translation of Dante's *Divine Comedy* and his lively commentaries on American poetry and life as poetry editor of the *Saturday Review of Literature* from 1956 to 1977. Of the poets considered in this study, none matches Ciardi for profound analysis of the person and the poet, in combat and outside it, in wartime.

4
William Meredith, U.S. Navy

Unlike Shapiro, Jarrell, and Ciardi, William Meredith did not enter the war as an established poet. His first volume of poetry, *Love Letter from an Impossible Land*, which included several poems written after he joined the navy, was published while he was serving on active duty. For Meredith, poetry proved to be a means for dealing with and responding to the unusual circumstances to which the war brought him.

His war experiences helped him to discover his first poetic voice; as a consequence, the war-based poems in *Love Letter* are among his best and most intriguing.

Meredith graduated from Princeton University *magna cum laude* and worked for a time as a copy boy and reporter for *The New York Times*. In the summer of 1941 he was inducted into the army and served for eight months as a non-commissioned officer in Army Air Forces public relations before being discharged from the army to join the Naval Aviation program. He entered the naval flight training program on 17 January 1942 and began pre-flight training at a naval reserve base in Robertson, Missouri, in February 1942. In May he began flight training as an aviation cadet at the Corpus Christi Naval Air Station, Texas. He received his navy wings and commission in October of 1942.

Meredith was initially assigned to Scouting Squadron 49 (VS-49) at the Naval Station at Kodiak Island, Alaska, located at the southwest Alaskan coast, not far from the Aleutian chain. Meredith was assigned to VS-49 from December of 1942 through all of 1943. Significant military activity was occurring in the Aleutian chain during the time he was stationed there. Early in 1942, for instance, the Japanese had bombed the town of Dutch Harbor. (This bombing was eventually determined to be an attempt to draw American war resources away from the Midway Island area of the Pacific, where the Japanese were planning an attack.) Later the Japanese captured the islands of Attu and Kiska. During the spring and summer of 1943, units of the American army and navy dislodged Japanese forces from Attu, in some heavy fighting, and Kiska was recaptured soon after without a fight; the Japanese forces had left undetected. By the time Meredith arrived in the area, the Japanese threat to Dutch Harbor had largely been dissipated, but the need for defensive readiness remained high. As part of his patrol duties, he flew to a number of remote fields stretching along the Aleutian chain, including Afognak Island, Sand Point, Otter Point, and Dutch Harbor on Unalaska Island. Other satellite fields were located farther out the Aleutians, at Atka and Adak.

The Aleutian Islands made a striking impression on the American soldiers and sailors who served there. During the war years of the early 1940s, thousands of army and navy personnel came to the Aleutians, and they agreed that it was visually unlike any place they had ever seen before. One such visitor was Corey Ford, a professional writer who wrote for the Army Air Forces during World War II, and like the others, he found it difficult to describe:

> Nothing seems quite real, as a matter of fact, in this far-off and fabulous archipelago stretching west of Alaska.... It is a region as remote as Mars and almost as uninhabitable. Active volcanoes smoke ceaselessly against the sky; soot-smeared glaciers hug their craters.... Along the sandy beaches, purple with volcanic ash, seals and sea-lions snort and plunge in the pounding surf. The wind howls day and night with a steady banshee wail, driving the scudding rain before it.... The bare treeless hills are as unreal as the other side of the moon.[1]

The famous mystery writer Dashiell Hammett, assigned as a public relations specialist in the Aleutians, acknowledged in a letter to Lillian Hellman that the unreal strangeness of the place appealed to him: "I'm still having more or less of a love affair with this country. Once on a boat with islands looming up half-real in fog and rain I suddenly thought how nice it would have been to have been born on one of them and to be coming home to it."[2]

In addition to these ground-based views of the Aleutians, Meredith had the advantage of an airborne perspective. The Aleutian Islands were created by volcanic activity in an arc stretching to the southwest hundreds of miles long. They contained numerous active volcanoes producing smoke and ash, reducing visibility but simultaneously providing unique visual experiences.

The primary aircraft flown by the pilots of VS-49 was the Vought OS2U Kingfisher, a two-place patrol plane mounted on floats that featured a 450-horsepower engine with a top speed of 150 miles per hour. Never intended as a combat plane, the Kingfisher was designed to fly observation and rescue missions. The aircraft was well suited for observation missions, as the cockpit, positioned well above the low wing of the aircraft, included numerous plexiglass panels which provided excellent visibility in all directions. A gunner's position was located in a rear cockpit behind the pilot. Flying along the Aleutian chain of islands in this aircraft gave Meredith ample opportunity to observe the unusual geography of the area at close range. The low-powered, lightly armed Kingfisher was susceptible to the unpredictable and unpleasant weather of the Gulf of Alaska and was eventually phased out, but not until after Meredith left the unit. Meredith flew patrol and support missions with VS-49 for over a year.

In May 1943 the patrol activities in the Kodiak Island area were taken over by another Scouting Squadron, VS-70, and VS-49 was assigned to patrol duties farther out, on the westerly section of the Aleutian chain. Probably in connection with the changes associated with the squadron's new duties, in that same month Meredith was granted leave and visited his parents in Connecticut. Although there is no evidence that Meredith was directly involved in combat missions against Japanese forces, there were hazards enough in normal operational flying. On June 16, 1943, shortly after he returned from leave, Meredith and three other pilots were assigned a ferry flight, from Dutch Harbor to Adak, a distance of some 750 miles, to the distant end of the Aleutians. Meredith and a second pilot were assigned to fly Kingfishers, while a third pilot was assigned to fly an SNJ (the navy version of the North American Texan, a training aircraft). A fourth pilot, flying a Grumman Goose amphibious aircraft, was designated to accompany the other three aircraft and provide navigation and emergency assistance. Such precautions were prudent, because none of the four aircraft was a high performance aircraft, and they were flying along a string of small, barren, rocky islands, in a location where the strong winds and harsh weather could cause flying conditions to deteriorate quickly. An excerpt from the operations order suggests that the ferry flight was not a simple undertaking:

> In case a plane is forced down and lands in the water, the JRF [Grumman Goose] will land and recover the pilot and passenger and then demolish the plane to insure that it sinks (in case it is the SNJ [which was not a float plane]); if one of the float planes is forced to land on the water, the JRF will recover the pilot and passenger and do all practicable to secure the grounded plane for possible salvage.[3]

The ferry mission evidently concluded successfully.

According to a unit history, the primary activities of the squadron consisted of searching for enemy submarines and missing U.S. aircraft, as the following excerpts from the squadron log (during the time Meredith was assigned to the squadron) indicate:

> Kodiak, 30 April 1943: Enemy submarine sighted in vicinity of Seward, Alaska. Two planes were sent to search the area, remained overnight, searched the following day and returned. Results negative.
>
> Dutch Harbor, 11 June 1943: Searched for Army transport reported lost. Results negative.
>
> Otter Point, 19 June 1943: Searched for crashed B-24. Negative results.
>
> Dutch Harbor, 6 October 1943: Two planes searched for enemy submarine reported by transport plane. Results negative.[4]

In October 1943 Meredith was promoted from the rank of ensign to the rank of lieutenant (junior grade) and two months later he was transferred from the Alaskan area, eventually being assigned to Hawaii. During the time of his transition, *Love Letter from an Impossible Land* was published by Yale University Press as part of its New Poets series, and the geographical and emotional strangeness of the locale became the central idea informing its poems.

Like Ford and Hammett, Meredith thought that the Aleutians were strangely unreal, an "impossible land." For Meredith the phrase was literally true, capturing all the hazards of life in a location where rain, wind, fog, and clouds sometimes confounded not just military flying operations but subsistence itself. Adding to the difficulty, of course, was the possibility of encountering the Japanese forces. In the introduction to the volume, Archibald MacLeish, newly appointed series editor, stated that the later poems in the book, the poems "about the war,"

> give the sense of having *seen*, of having been present, which a man's face sometimes gives, returning. They have the quality of reticence and yet of communication, almost unwilling communication, which the words of soldiers have after a difficult and dangerous campaign. And because the experience of this war, fought with new weapons in remote and unimaginable places, is an experience strange to most of us, the communication itself is unfamiliar... . The account of the experience is oblique—seen from the corner of the eye like the movement of danger at night.[5]

In the title poem, Meredith indicates that the "impossible land" consists primarily of the islands of the Aleutian chain, "the exile islands of the mind," "Combed by the cold seas, the Bering and Pacific." The rugged, inhospitable coastlines, the steep, volcanic mountains, and the challenging flying conditions must certainly have made an immediate and profound impression on the young pilot, who had never seen anything remotely similar to this impressive but hazardous environment. The phrase "exile islands of the mind" suggests that no written account can catch their true essence:

> All the charts and history you can muster
> Will not make them real as the fog is real
> Or crystal as a certain hour is clear.

These islands are "impossible" because they are exceptional; their characteristics are unlike normal locations; they "shake and change and finally enchant," giving the poet "singular strange visions," as in his view of two local volcanoes, Shishaldin and Pavlof:

> One was, in the orange time of morning,
> The smoking peak Shishaldin in a glory
> . . . .
>
> Pavlof, the black volcano, throwing flame
> At night, to seaward when beacons were forbidden.
>
> And when I put a wing across the cone
> (Snowy and striking deeply at the memory),
> It drew me, too, driven and weary
> What with the war, and those foolish citizens my thoughts.[6]

This complex image is composed of the favorite elements of most poets, water and fire, directly joined—a volcano out of the ocean—as they could seldom be. A volcano would draw any aviator to investigate it, especially one "driven and weary" by thoughts of difficult flying in times of war.

Striking landmarks in Meredith's "impossible land," the volcanic peaks Shishaldin and Pavlof are as unusual as they are unknown. Shishaldin Volcano, located near the center of Unimak Island, halfway along the Aleutian chain, is a symmetrical volcanic cone a little over 15 kilometers in diameter at the base. The mountain, which rises to a height of 8500 feet above sea level, is the highest peak in the Aleutian Islands and is topped with a small summit crater from which a steady cloud of steam is emitted. The surface of the volcano above 3000 feet is almost entirely covered by perennial snow and ice. Shishaldin is less than 10,000 years old, one of the more recently developed volcanoes on the surface of the earth. The volcano Pavlof (there is also another immediately next to it, Sister Pavlof) is located to the northeast of Shishaldin, on the end of the Alaskan Peninsula. It is equally impressive in appearance if slightly lower in altitude. Even Dashiell Hammett was taken with the vision of these two volcanoes; in a letter to Lillian Hellman, he wrote how he "was in love with a volcano named Pavlov." In the early morning he could see Pavlov "smoking against the sky," its base "hidden by mist that was glowing white in the sun" as "two long thin cloud streaks cut shiny white cross-sections out of the volcano. The puffs of smoke were very dark against all this bright gray and white. It was lovely—two dimensional and as unreal as fairyland." Hammett mentions that he also saw Shishaldin but that Pavlov remained his favorite of the two: "I stayed pretty faithful to it."[7]

Meredith sees the familiar vision of the moon strangely altered in this new land, "With streamers of snow dancing in the moon at the summits, / An ageless dance with the peculiar rhythm of zero, / And the wind creaking like a green floe." Against these unusual natural visions the poet places the wartime activity:

> Twenty-four blue sailors anticipate
> Orders of drill that drift up on the wind.
> And stiff on the apron are the pretty planes
> That waddle to the water and drum away,
> Leaving me stammerer, inept to say
> Why in their simple duty there is pain.

Meredith's most important poetic theme has been described as "the efforts of imagination and intellect to order the chaos of the self and of the world, to overcome the resistance of life and experience to significance and form."[8] The shift of viewpoint occasioned by Meredith's transition from Princeton undergraduate to navy pilot, and the experience of flying an underpowered floatplane in a world dominated by sea, sky, strong winds, and rugged mountains, provided him an altered aesthetic perspective available to few practicing or potential poets.

Flying along the Aleutian chain, the poet sees a kind of "providence" in the contrast of the wilderness lands and the wartime activities, in which he will "salvage these parts of a loud land / For symbols of war," its "simple wraths and duties." In a place where

> Sleep for us here is a leaping down safely in silk
> From the flaming bull's-eye plane of day,
> Stricken ship that twists and thirsts for the metal sea

the strongly primitive elements of nature become the appropriate setting for the scenario of war. If war is by its nature a strange and unusual activity, there could be no more appropriate place to conduct it than a location which possesses "a mystery beyond the mist of mountains / Ornate beyond the ritual of snow."

The images in the poem depict what MacLeish called "unimaginable places." On the basis of the evidence in this poem alone, we can understand what Meredith meant when he said, years later, that during the war "I found myself relying on my writing to make sense of an experience and a world for which nothing in a protected and rather unobservant childhood had prepared me."⁹ The experience and the world: both unusual, strange, contrasting yet not conflicting.

The strangeness of the natural environment of the Aleutian Islands is noted by another naval officer, Courtland Matthews, whose *Aleutian Interval* (1949) provided another glimpse of the unusual landscape, in this case, of the area near Dutch Harbor. In the poem Matthews describes how, in peaceful moments between periods of harsh weather, the men on the island could see the bay full of warships and the airplanes arriving and departing on their wartime missions. At such moments, when the williwaws and snow showers did not blow across the island, the land seemed

> Unreal as something we had dreamed,
> Like a country found on another star.¹⁰

Meredith's "June: Dutch Harbor" continues the contrast of the uncommon natural environment with uncommon wartime activities. The poem begins with a description of the vibrancy of the natural environment responding to the onset of summer, and the "turf slides" of the island "grow to an emerald green," a "neon green":

> Where the snow streams crease the fields darkly
> The rite of flowers is observed, and because it is a new land
> There is no great regard to precedent: ...

The poem catalogs the flowers that bloom in abundance: violets, anemones, lupine, wild geranium, flag, cranberry, buttercups. Birds arrive to perch on the accoutrements of war: "In the morning sandpipers stumble on the steel mats, / Sparrows sing on the gun."¹¹ The poet describes the irony of flying (in wartime) over the green ocean in an area that is both bird sanctuary and air space restricted to authorized military aircraft. The poet is repeatedly confounded by the strange juxtaposition of natural forces and the forces of war: "Fly just above the always-griping sea / That bitches at the bitter rock the mountains throw to it." The aircraft carries the pilot past the harsh land modified for human use in the form of runways to land on, and the significance of the task of the pilot fades in comparison to the environment:

> Though you are drawn by a thousand remarkable horses
> On fat silver wings with a factor of safety of four,
> And are sutured with steel below and behind and before,
> And can know with your fingers the slightest unbalance of forces,
> Your mission is smaller than Siegfried's, lighter than Tristan's,
> And there is about it a certain undignified haste.

Finally, almost as an afterthought, the death of a fellow flier is mentioned:

> The one who knew all about birds spun in that month.
> It is hard to keep your mind on war, with all that green.

The bitter irony of the death of a pilot who "knew all about birds" falling to his death by "spinning in" could hardly be greater: that the one who possesses expert knowledge of the birds who live in the islands should lose control of his own vehicle of flight and fall to his death is unnaturally inappropriate. The word picture that Meredith paints is terribly impossible: in the forefront are the huge, bright flowers: violets, anemones, lupine. In the background, birds flying, and beyond them an airplane, spinning slowly into the ocean. The image suggests the pastoral landscape of Brueghel's *Fall of Icarus*.

A third Aleutian poem, "A Kodiak Poem," continues the word picture of the Aleutian Islands, as on Kodiak "Precipitous is the shape and stance of the spruce / Pressed against the mountains in gestures of height." The poet contrasts the hazardous mountains of Kodiak with "fonder mountains" which "Surely curl around your homeland, / Fondle the home farms with a warmer green." Though the natives who live on Kodiak are now fishermen, they were once fierce hunters:

> Fire-needing, they buried their dead with faggots,
> And when a man went to their hell, he froze.[12]

As in all these Aleutian poems, there is the constant reference to "you," the poet's "Love," the reader, who has an important role to play in the effect of these poems. The reader faces the challenge of developing an understanding of what the poet is attempting to describe: an environment hazardous, strange, difficult to survive in, and appropriate somehow for the war effort that has to be made. It is this challenge that Meredith poses to the reader, especially in these poems that MacLeish has in mind when he says the later poems "have the quality of reticence and yet of communication."

In contrast to the vivid energy of the Aleutian poems, in which the sea and land combine and conflict to create a backdrop of vital tension for the wartime activities of the naval flight patrols, there are the other poems, such as "Altitude: 15,000," in which the poet flies above the water, isolated by clouds, which form a new kind of landscape, whose shapes suggest images of the interior mind:

> The chill and stillness of the landscape here
> Edged with these rare and regular white towers,
> Reminds, oh, reminds of the faded passageway
> Down which we were smuggled as children, barely saved.

The cloud-lined environment at 15,000 feet recalls to the poet youthful days of playful escape and domestic safety. He wishes now for the possibility of safe return to that childhood place, where one

> looks at last for a passage leading out
> To domesticity again and love and doubt,
> Where a long cloud makes a corridor to earth.[13]

Meredith's war-related poetry consistently reflects the idea that life in the air creates a special sensitivity that provides enhanced ways of seeing the world from a magical but hazardous perspective. In "Airman's Virtue," for instance, the poet suggests that it is the "virtue" of an airman (possessed of an "outward-aching soul") which can overcome the tendency of his plane, the clouds, even the aerial environment itself, to bring about the fatal fall of the flier.[14] Meredith is surely thinking of the meaning of virtue in its earliest form, a quality of moral goodness. It is not the goodness of the airman's thought that will save him, but the strength of his desire. Even when an airman falls—the occasion for the elegy "In Memoriam Stratton Christensen," written to commemorate the death of a friend who died in flight school—Meredith translates the circumstances of the flier's death from the training area to an "impossible land," which could be reached only by someone driven by a "single angry curiosity / Savoring fear and faith and speckled foam."[15] The poem, in the traditional sonnet form, contains numerous internal rhymes and alliterations, much of its language suggestive of an Old English poem, carrying a sense of the struggle against the inevitability of death.

Meredith's "Notes for an Elegy" proposes that although the hazards of flight are significant, and men know there is a possibility of death in the air, "in practice the martyrdom has been quiet, statistical, / A fair price. This is what airmen believe." In the specific occasion of the poem, the poet recalls the death of a pilot who crashed into a stand of woods near an airfield. The accident could not have been caused by the engine, which was working until the end; nor by the wings, which still held the plane aloft. The cause must have rested with the pilot himself, or, as it would be known today, pilot error. Somehow the trees ("bronze and terrible"), the forces of nature ("they") spoke to him:

> How they at last convinced him is not known:
> ....
>   No, the invitation
> Must have been sent to the aviator in person:
> Perhaps a sly suggestion of carelessness,
> A whispered invitation perhaps to death.
> Death.[16]

Meredith as poet, singing for his fellow fliers, lost in their efforts of the war, provides the voice that can allow the mute others to become "articulate at last." Meredith appeared to realize that his position as a pilot-poet brought with it a special obligation to speak about the conditions and challenges fliers faced. He consciously identifies himself as a poet charged with a duty to speak to the non-flying readers about the life of fliers.

In January 1944 Meredith was reassigned to Scouting Squadron 46 (VS-46), at Roosevelt Field, San Pedro, California, where he participated in various administrative and ferry flights. In May of 1944 he was again reassigned, this time to Scouting Squadron 69 (VS-69), which was located in the Hawaiian Islands. Here he received training in anti-submarine warfare, conducted at Kaneohe Bay, Hawaii, in July of 1944. While he was with VS-69 Meredith flew the Douglass Dauntless and the Curtiss Helldiver. The Helldiver, which was being produced in sufficient numbers to supply flying squadrons in 1944, was a much larger, more rugged, and more powerful aircraft than the Kingfisher he had flown in Alaska. It was powered by a 1900 horsepower engine with almost four times the power of the 450 horsepower engine in the Kingfisher. And it could carry a much heavier load of bombs and armament, if required. As in the Kingfisher, the cockpit configuration (which included a gunner's position as well) provided excellent visibility for the pilot.

Meredith must have flown a number of anti-submarine patrols and observation patrols around the Hawaiian Islands but apparently engaged in no combat activity.

Love Letter from an Impossible Land was published as Meredith was transferred to the Hawaiian Islands; the poems he wrote while on duty in Hawaii appeared in his second book of poetry, *Ships and Other Figures*, published in 1948. Of the 29 poems in *Ships*, over half are about the war. As in *Love Letter from an Impossible Land*, the best poems in *Ships and Other Figures* are about the unusual perspective of the natural world available to the flier. In *Ships* there is less emphasis on poems about flight and more emphasis on ships and other traditional navy topics as well as the war itself, especially political aspects.

Meredith's fascination with the natural world, especially as seen from the cockpit of an aircraft, can be seen in several of the poems in *Ships*. Certainly his new aircraft, the more modern, larger Curtiss Helldiver, offered him greater operational flexibility, with a more powerful engine and the capability to fly higher and farther than in his previous aircraft. He reports on the different kinds of natural scenes he has witnessed; in "Lines Written but Never Mailed from Hawaii," for instance, he notes

> the things I could tell you about sunrise in the islands,
> About the sense of summer troubling the cane,
> Of flight as smooth as love above the sea at night....[17]

Even though he has "looked at the ocean in the moonlight for a long time," the meaning of such a vision is "no more than death's meaning," suggesting that the sea continues to represent the same ambiguous force as it did in the Aleutians: out of the sea come the islands that fascinate those who fly over them, but it is into the sea that some will fall, whether from planes or ships.

The clouds in the Hawaiian area continue to provide an airborne landscape of symbolic significance to the flier, as shown in "The Impressment":

> Days like today we are the clouds' men
> And what they do all day is our concern.[18]

The clouds are a force whose motions, according to the poem, it is the job of the fliers to follow:

> Taken with their success and clean-edged march
> Against the sky in rout, we join up

The aviators follow the clouds as if joining a military action against a fleeing foe ("the sky in rout"). But later, the poet suggests that he and his fellow fliers would like to be free from the tasking to join the clouds' forces, "seeing the cause false and us poorly led"; there can be little human understanding of the forces responsible for the movement of the clouds, the clouds' maneuvers "pieced out by espionage," their military secrets "useless data / For secrecy's sake kept, for an air of mystery."

The reason for disillusionment with cloud behavior is clear in the final lines of the poem, when the poet states that clouds are not governed by human responsibilities, as the fliers are:

> clouds do not take into account the mixed duties
> To anyone's invalid father, troth to a cripple,
> Or an old borrowing, kept in peacetime mind
> And asking payment....

The routine tasks of life or war have to be completed regardless of human preoccupations or bad weather, "when anyone wakes to the sky blank blue or grey." The fliers have been "impressed," forced into the service of the clouds, whose motivations they cannot understand, as their daily flying missions require their continued service.

Although the striking contrasts of human efforts set against a rugged natural environment are not as evident in *Ships* as in *Love Letter*, they appear occasionally, as in "Against Excess of Sea or Sun or Reason":

> The sea that comes to the beach now softly
> Like a woman giving a gift,
> Has taken at night whole fields, and in winter
> Has pitted the sentry cliffs.[19]

"Civil Twilight" describes a pleasant sunset, framed in clouds and giving a "long light on the lawn" in the near-tropic climate of the Hawaiian Islands, suggesting the strong contrast between the calming vision of a sunset seen in the midst of war and the war effort itself:

> This truce of dark might settle once for all
> The differences between the parts of earth.[20]

The pleasant atmosphere of life in the Hawaiian Islands allowed a less demanding life than Meredith experienced in Alaska; fewer poems in *Ships* written from the flier's perspective match the sharpness of vision of the war poems in his first book. It is as if, removed from the harsh beauty of the Aleutians and living now in the tropical lushness of Hawaii, his rugged inspiration waned in a land of relative luxury and fertility. However, the poems in *Ships* contain the same elements of nature as the backdrop against which the war effort moves, presented with the same juxtaposition of natural scenery and literary reference. As well as a variety of standard poetic forms, poets and poetic influence are constant references in *Ships*, more so than in *Love Letter*: the names of Yeats, Wordsworth, Milton, Shakespeare, Auden, Spender, even Homer, appear regularly, serving as reminders of the literary context against which Meredith views his unique visual and metaphorical constructs.

The title (*Ships and Other Figures*) draws attention to the poems it contains as literary constructs to be read primarily as such, and only secondarily, therefore, as word pictures of naval operations. The "Envoi" which begins the volume states that his "little book" should

> Tell how the comeliness I can't take in
> Of ships and other figures of content
> Compels me still until I give them names....[21]

This is the same idea found in *Love Letter from an Impossible Land*, that the poet is burdened with the task of relating the efforts of others to those who cannot easily appreciate the special circumstances of the poet's wartime environment. Acknowledging a literary as well as a cultural tradition in adopting this stance, Meredith begins with a short series of exercises, or figures, in which he describes three kinds of ships—carriers, battleships, transports—using natural comparisons.

The first poem, "Carrier," illustrates Meredith's concept nicely; its model is a sonnet in the classic form, with fourteen lines and a fairly regular rhyme scheme. But the rhyme scheme occasionally alters and the lines are uneven; yet its goal, of describing the strength and function of an aircraft carrier is effectively achieved:

> On the streaked sea at dawn she stands to the streaks
>   And when her way and the wind have made her long,
> The planes rise heavy from her whining deck.
> Then the bomb's luck, the gun's poise and chattering,
>   The far-off dying, are her near affair;
> With her spring creatures become weak or strong
> She watches them down the sky and disappear,
> Heart-gone, sea-bound, committed all to air.[22]

The carrier is compared to a large sea bird, teaching the young to fly, concerned for the safety and well-being, "committed all to air," an image that conveys the meaning more effectively than a dry technical description. Meredith provides notes to make sure we completely understand the idea of the poem: "A carrier normally launches her planes only when she is under way and proceeding upwind, so that both her motion (or 'way') and the motion of the wind have the effect of increasing the length of the take-off run down the flight deck. The wind makes streaks in the direction of its movement upon open water."[23]

In "Transport," sea birds follow behind and suggest a "new myth" involving certain old men, while "Battlewagon" addresses the idea of camouflage covering the destructiveness contained within the ship. Meredith's note to this poem tells us the "the purpose of camouflage of large ships is not primarily to make them difficult to see, but rather so to obscure their characteristic structural features in profile as to make them difficult to identify as to type and number."[24]

In these three poems Meredith gives us two versions of the same idea for each ship, one poetic, one practical: how carriers head into the wind to launch their aircraft; how transports survive in spite of their slowness and vulnerability; and how to read the profile of a battleship. Meredith provides detailed footnotes not only to explain technical details but to serve as a plain language word picture of these ships, a prose contrast to the creative interpretation of the poem. There are no explanatory notes in *Love Letter from an Impossible Land*; there we are left to our own resources to interpret the meanings.

An example of the literary self-referencing at work in the volume is in "Middle Flight," with its echo of Milton's "advent'rous song / That with no middle flight intends to soar / Above th' Aonian mount":

> The loneliest place I know of nowadays
> Is a cumulo-nimbus cloud I seem to find
> As I often fly; I went there first
> When the sky and a war were new, but memories now
> Are as heavy in its belly as a squall.[25]

In case we were not reminded of Milton in reading this passage, Meredith adds a detailed footnote with instructions: "A connotation that the writer would like this title to convey, but is too remote, is the negative of Milton's grandiose phrase in the invocation to *Paradise Lost*." (Perhaps Meredith is also thinking of the phrase "rend the middle air," from Milton's "Hymn on the Morning of Christ's Nativity.") The cumulo-nimbus cloud opened "to imprecision, at the base to rain, / And the hope that it held five years ago is spilt"; the early hope of a promising end to the war is, for undefined reasons, not to be forthcoming. Instead, it has been replaced by a sense of isolation, and a nagging sense of failure:

> But what I mean about the cloud
> And its forlorn vicinity where gather
> Vapors of doubt that not our lonely day
> Shall see precipitate, is that even here
> Nobody goes alone who knows so much
> As one human love; so much I know,
> Whence hope, if any, in the covered sky,
> Choir in this uncompanionable air.

The poem's mixture of modern language ("what I mean about the cloud," "nobody goes alone who knows so much") and Miltonic ("where gather / vapors of doubt," "our lonely day shall see precipitate") tasks us to think of the war Milton described in *Paradise Lost* as somehow comparable to actions in the Pacific theater (which it certainly was, at least by those who were participating in it). Although Meredith's footnote informs us that he has in mind Milton's "grandiose phrase" in the Invocation to *Paradise Lost*, Meredith, of course, has in mind a different kind of "middle air" than Milton had: the main feature of "middle air" is typically characterized by cumulo-nimbus clouds caused by the rising of warm air, with rain and strong winds the result. Pilots might like to fly near them, but never through them. Thunderstorms in any region, but especially in the tropics, are especially violent and dangerous.

Meredith's practice of using notes to explain technical details of a poem, which is itself a poetic exercise, is carried further in "Homeric Simile," an extended account of a flight of aircraft through bad weather to reach a strategic target. The title of "Homeric Simile" seems to suggest that it will consist of a poetic exercise linked to the standard similes found in the *Iliad* or the *Odyssey*. But instead, we read:

> As when a heavy bomber in the cloud
> Having made some minutes good an unknown track;
> Although the dead-reckoner triangulates
> Departure and the stations he can fix,
> Counting the thinness of the chilly air,
> The winds aloft, the readings of the clocks;
> And the radarman sees the green snakes dance
> Continually before him in attest
> That the hostile sought terrain runs on below....[26]

Like Odysseus' crew in the *Odyssey*, the men on the navy bomber are challenged by the forces of nature to reach their target, a task made especially difficult by the vast emptiness of the ocean over which they fly. The bomber aircraft, having arrived safely over its target on a remote island, finds the city below marked in fire as the enemy gunners try to capture the attacking ships in their searchlights. At the point of bomb release, according to the poet,

> in this fierce discovery is something found
> More than release from waiting or of bombs,
> Greater than all the Germanies of hate,
> Some penetration of the overcast
> We make through, hour upon uncounted hour,
> All this life, fuel low, instruments all tumbled,
> And uncrewed.

The point of the poem—the basis of the simile—is that the achievement itself is its own "fierce discovery," the achievement of the crew members to travel such distances through difficult territory under trying circumstances, in an aircraft barely functional through hard use or enemy action. The act of reaching the target is a more meaningful achievement than dropping bombs once there; the struggle with the environment is more difficult than the struggle with opposing forces. The use of the word "Homeric" suggests that the efforts of the bomber crew members are comparable to those of the crew of Ulysses (of course, Ulysses and his men are trying to return home, their war-fighting days supposedly over). Once again, Meredith wants the reader to comprehend his technical vocabulary, as he explains in his notes that "clocks" mean aircraft flight instruments, that "uncounted" refers to the importance of keeping accurate time, that "blips" are images on the radar screen, and that "tumbled" instruments means flight instruments that lose their ability to reflect the true condition of the aircraft as a result of a series of violent maneuvers.[27] The technical details of the poem should not hide the fact, however, that the simile *is* the poem.

Just as in *Love Letter from an Impossible Land* there are poems describing the transition into war, so in *Ships and Other Figures* there are poems depicting the movement out of the war, poems addressing social and cultural concerns, like "Reconversion Sonnet," which questions whether the fundamental truths over which the war was fought have been understood. One of the more prescient poems is "'Do Not Embrace Your Mind's New Negro Friend,'" which cautions the reader to proceed with moderation towards a more enlightened attitude towards acceptance of cultural and racial differences, not because the impulse is wrong but because there is a process of guilt to be worked through, a struggle as great, Meredith suggests, as the war that is just concluding.

Later, twenty-five years after the appearance of *Love Letter* and *Ships*, Meredith provided an enlightening personal perspective on his poems of that period, in a poetic introduction to his war poems ("Reading my poems from World War II") included in *Earth Walk: New and Selected Poems*. Looking at these poems from a distance of a quarter of a century, he creatively but accurately summarizes their design and effect. Describing his war poems as a group of inter-related scenes on a broad tapestry about the war, Meredith suggests that they were united by the elements of composition ("mountains and landscapes") and theme ("a stylized chase"). The ships in these poems "course through a blue meadow / like hounds," and the airplanes, "like shoals of tropical fish, / swim in a thin upper sea." Describing the hazards as well as the local environment of war, he acknowledges the deaths that occurred in training or on operational missions, the "clumsy ones / spinning earthward like sparks." The poem confirms that the earlier poems are "not narrative," that is, they don't tell a complete story, and the reader never finds out "how they end"; nevertheless, the poems seem "impelled" by a "moral purpose."[28] It is as if Meredith recognized the special importance of his war poems, not just because they marked the clear line between poetic apprenticeship and mastery, but because they spoke from a tense period of time that combined operational stress and poetic insight.

In February of 1945 Meredith requested reassignment to Instrument Flight Instructors School at the Naval Air Station in Atlanta, Georgia. His reasons for requesting reassignment included his desire for experience in twin- and multi-engine aircraft. However, this request was apparently denied, for Meredith remained with Scouting Squadron 69 and was in fact appointed commanding officer of the squadron briefly, in September of 1945, after the war with Japan had concluded. In October he was reassigned to the office of the Chief of Naval Operations, Navy Department, Washington, D.C., for further duties. Although he requested to be continued on active duty for the purpose of transferring to the regular navy from the naval reserve, his request was not approved, and he was released from the service on 20 February 1946, after serving over four and a half years. After the war Meredith taught English at Princeton University, the University of Hawaii, and finally at Connecticut College. He was recalled into military service during the Korean War and flew anti-submarine patrols from the naval aircraft carrier USS *Valley Forge*. But his subsequent flying duties produced few poems to match the intensity of his unique poetic vision in *Love Letter from an Impossible Land*.

5

Howard Nemerov, U.S. Army Air Forces

Howard Nemerov was educated at Harvard, graduating in 1941. He applied for pilot training in the United States Army but was eliminated from the training program because he was slow in picking up the points of instruction. Undeterred (and possibly motivated) by his failure in the United States, he applied for and was accepted into the flight training program in the Royal Canadian Air Force in October 1941. He attended Number 2 Service School, in Uplands, near Ottawa, during the winter months of 1942 and 1943, when the temperatures were so cold that his moustache "froze white with instant age ... on the dawn walk down from barracks to flight line." According to Nemerov, the life of the aviation cadet "curiously combined military savagery (lacking only the enemy, who came later) with the coddling environment of a moderately nice nursing home."[1] After a day of flying and ground school classes, Nemerov had time to maintain his interest in literary study that he had begun at Harvard. A favorite aunt sent him a copy of Proust's *Remembrance of Things Past*, which he read lying in his upper bunk, "just under one of perhaps only half a dozen ceiling lights. Had I been put in a lower bunk, I couldn't possibly have read for two or three hours a night without ruining the eyesight indispensable for flying, and my life twenty and forty years later on would have been other than it has been, and poorer."[2]

After completing his training in Canada in March of 1943 he was sent to England, arriving in June. In England he flew anti-submarine and anti-shipping patrols for the Royal Air Force (RAF) Coastal Command over the North Atlantic and the North Sea. He flew with the RAF as an officer of the RCAF until January of 1944, when he received a commission in the United States Army Air Forces. Although he had become an Army Air Forces officer, he remained attached to the RAF until he completed his tour of duty in April of 1945, when he returned to the United States. During his duty with the RAF he accumulated a total of 750 hours of flying time, including 200 combat hours. He flew 57 missions, eventually flying as a squadron lead, a position of responsibility assigned to only the most competent and experienced pilots. Although Nemerov's writings never mention the specific type of aircraft he flew, one of his poems does identify his flying unit as 236 Squadron of Coastal Command. The aircraft flown by the members of 236 Squadron was the Bristol Beaufighter, a high-powered twin engine aircraft; this aircraft occupies a central position in his later poems, which describe the kinds of flying activities associated with the coastal patrol missions. Nemerov acknowledged that as a youth he had had a "passion for flying," which was inspired by Lindbergh's flight across the Atlantic when Nemerov was seven.[3]

Nemerov wrote relatively few early poems about his war experiences. With the exception of two or three poems relating directly to his flying experience in his first volume of poetry, *The Image and the Law*, Nemerov wrote about the war almost as if he had been a civilian. Ross Labrie observes that the war poems in *The Image and the Law*—published in 1947, two years after the war ended—are "surprisingly restrained." Labrie suggests that this is a "confirmation of Nemerov's later conviction that he did not grasp the significance of the war until it was well behind him."[4] While effective and clever, many of his early war poems lack the unique ironic but earnest tone indicative of Nemerov's direct personal involvement in the events the poems describe. In the final years of his career, however, his poetry of the war became more personal and compelling.

Most of Nemerov's early war-related poems address ideas of soldering generally, often echoing the sentiments of the World War I poets who wrote of the impersonal destructiveness and dehumanizing effects of war. This aspect is evident in the widely anthologized poem "Redeployment," which suggests that though the action of combat may have ended, the effects linger indefinitely:

> They say the war is over. But water still
> Comes bloody from the taps, and my pet cat
> In his disorder vomits worms....[5]

"The Old Soldiers' Home" could be mistaken for a Sassoon poem, as the Old Soldier recalls

> How trumpet and drum paraded before
> The marching young men, how they led
> Us, green and dumb, where the war
>   Opened his mouth to be fed.[6]

"Armistice," written about the day celebrating the anniversary of the end of World War I, depicts the American Legion's legionnaires selling poppies. Nemerov emphasizes the soporific effects of the poppy, linking its opiate effects to the sleep of the war dead:

> His name is Legion, and with a red eye
> Gay as a gander's he offers me
> The paper opiate of this poppy
> Twisted on a green wire stem.
>
> Remember who died for you. They sleep
> In Flanders, in the poppy beds,
> The real, narcotic and forbidden
> Beds of huddled buddies dead.[7]

The poem's mention of poppies is a witty, ironic reference to John McCrae's "In Flanders Fields": "In Flanders fields the poppies blow / Between the crosses, row on row." The poppies of the fields of Flanders have become transformed (and reduced) into paper representations handed out by members of the American Legion. Nemerov continues his ironic assessment of the returned soldiers in "Grand Central, with Soldiers, Early in the Morning," in which the poet expresses the view that the soldiers "may go in stealth and leave no trace, / In early morning before business starts."[8]

In "Instructions for Use of this Toy," Nemerov describes a situation that must reflect his own involvement with training related to technological devices. This wonderfully ironic, clever poem mechanically rattles off the method of operation of a potentially dangerous mechanism, something like a gun,[9] perhaps representing an instance from his wartime training experiences:

> ... is worked this way. Release the striking arm
> (marked A on diagram) by means of the
> End ratchet on the cylinder marked B.
> Slight humming noises should not cause alarm,
> But if explosions, or loud coughing sounds,
> Seem to be coming from the diaphragm,
> It might be well to disengage the cam
> Before examining the guard for grounds.
> So far so good. The automatic trail
> Guide bracket post should be secured against
> Vibration of the flange, but do not fail
> At any time to keep the wire tensed
> That in the event of fire throws the switch
> (marked Jettison) that breaks the circuit which....[10]

The comic tone of the poem results from the undercutting effect of qualifying cautions inserted into an otherwise supremely confident voice of instruction. The rhetorical quality and use of ellipses at the beginning and close of the poem disguise the classic sonnet form.

In "A Day on the Big Branch," Nemerov shows that thoughts of the war are never far away although many years have passed. The poem depicts the poet, in the company of a group of men with similar backgrounds, on an outing in the wilderness, climbing up a stream bed after a night of card playing and drinking. As they attempt to return to nature, visiting a particularly striking location on the stream bed, they focus their thoughts on the important issues of living. Eventually they think about how their war experiences might have affected their outlooks on life:

> After a time we talked about the War,
> about what we had done in the War, and how near
> some of us had been to being drowned, and burned,
> and shot, and how many people we knew
> who had been drowned, or burned, or shot;
> and would it have been better to have died
> in the War, the peaceful old War, where we were young?[11]

The men, but especially the poet, seem to be longing for earlier days when the courses of their lives were determined more by the impersonal forces of the war and less by imperfect actions of their own volition, even if the war resulted in their deaths. This poem shows the shift in Nemerov's perspective about the war in relation to his poetry; up to this point he has seen the war as a subject for ironic commentary about the effects of the war on the men who participated in it. Now, however, he is beginning to think about what the war meant to him personally, about his role in it and how his experiences have molded his outlook, not only about war, but about the way in which he lives his life. Although most of the poems which reflect his experiences in the war have yet to be written, this poem shows a change in his perspective.

"An Old Warplane," written many years after the end of World War II, illustrates the further development of Nemerov's empathy for his wartime occupation, as the poem recalls the destructiveness of an aging warplane, once used for combat and now used for training. Looking at an aircraft like the one he flew during the war, Nemerov assesses the impact the aircraft had on the men who flew it.

> Even a thing like this takes pathos
> After the years; rust flaking the paint
> And oil stains streaked as if by speed
> Along the fairing aft of the engines.[12]

Only a flier could use such accurate (British) language of aviation technology.

> Not now the young men lost she hurts,
> Who mastered her weapons and her ways
> And dove her into seven dead seas:
> Their blood is thin as water. But
>
> We live whom she endangers now.
> Pity reddens beneath the paint
> As all our future rusts inside
> The bright invention of the war....

This poem was first published in 1953, when the Korean War was ending. The aircraft Nemerov is describing was possibly a B-25, a medium twin-engine bomber used during World War II (it is the aircraft which carries Yossarian over the cities of Italy in *Catch-22*) for a variety of attack and bombing missions. After the war it was used as a training aircraft for pilots assigned to fly multi-engine aircraft. Whether Nemerov ever flew the B-25 or not, it surely would have reminded him of the twin-engine aircraft he had flown during the war.

After 1955, Nemerov wrote few war poems for a twenty-year period. He returned to the subject in *The Western Approaches* (1975). Although the title of this volume of poetry is derived from his World War II flying experiences, only two poems in this volume are directly about the war, "The Western Approaches" and "A Memory of the War." The phrase "Western Approaches" refers to the World War II convoy route from Iceland to Liverpool over which Nemerov occasionally flew. Nemerov flew the eastern half of this route along a path that would have taken him past the Skerries, a group of rocky islands off the coast of the Hebrides. "The Western Approaches" is an evocative account of his inability to fully appreciate the significance or value of his wartime experiences during the war. The poem begins with a statement about how the mind processes the events of war:

> But looking back on life it is as if
> Our Book of Changes never let us change.[13]

The poem then gives the personal example which serves as the basis for the lesson:

> When I was young I flew past Skerryvore
> Where the Nine Maidens still grind Hamlet's meal,
> The salt and granite grain of bitter earth,
> But knew it not for twenty years and more.
>
> Stories already told a time ago
> Were waiting for us down the road, our lives
> But filled them out....

The literary allusions associated with the geography over which he flew, but did not recognize at the time, suggest that Nemerov was beginning to realize that he had not reflected appropriately on an important part of his life (his war and flying years), and that he would do so in the future. At the time of his flights, the cultural value of his experiences was lost in the danger and the routine activities of flying operations.

Nemerov's personal experiences as a pilot rarely appeared in his early poetry, but as the number of his war poems increased, their effect was to eventually modify his normal ironic pose. At the midpoint of his writing career Nemerov acknowledged the symbolic and emotional significance of his flying experience: in *Journal of the Fictive Life*, for instance, Nemerov occasionally acknowledged the complex aspects of his flying environment:

> "Hard to get into because so high off the ground." In a dream about flying, ... these words must have to do with the airplane I flew during the war, which they describe accurately; one entered and left it through a hatch in the belly, and the door, which swung down to permit this, had a stirrup-like step. Even then, I thought of getting out of the airplane, after a mission, as being born.[14]

One of his first war poems in *The Image and the Law* is addressed to his Coastal Command squadron, "For the Squadron (236th Coastal, Royal Air Force)." It gives us some insight into his operational experience:

> We fought the war
> From places called North Coates and
> Skegness, and saw the Danish coast
> And Heligoland like a gunboat
> On the shallow sea.[15]

The 236th Squadron was stationed at bases near North Coates and Skegness for most of 1943 and 1944, when Nemerov was assigned to the unit. North Coates was located in Lincolnshire, along the east coast of England, just east of York. By the time Nemerov reported to the unit, the squadron had transitioned from the slower Bristol Blenheim aircraft to the much more powerful Bristol Beaufighter. The airfield at North Coates featured one long concrete runway and a larger, wider grassy area at right angles to the runway. The wider grass field gave pilots greater flexibility in adjusting to the powerful Beaufighter, which often tended to swing on takeoff.[16]

According to one member of the unit, the men who came into the squadron in early 1943 were joining one of the "squadrons on the east coast [of England] which had suffered heavy losses [during the Battle of Britain] while operating over the North Sea and along the Frisian Islands."[17] The 236th Squadron was one of three (the other two were 143 and 254 Squadrons) which constituted a "strike wing" designed to attack German shipping in the North Sea. All three squadrons carried out their own and joint exercises; in April 1943 they jointly attacked a large German convoy off of the Dutch coast.[18] Old and experienced, 236 Squadron had suffered heavy losses of men. Of the men who served in 236 Squadron during the Battle of Britain, for instance (before Nemerov arrived in the squadron), at least 38 died before the war was over.

If the operational life in the air was hazardous, life on the ground had its compensations, and the crew members agreed that North Coates was a reasonably pleasant installation to fly out of. Perhaps one reason for that was the fact that the squadron flew consistently from that location from several months and as a result did not have to experience the unpleasant aspects of moving and reestablishing itself at other airfields.

"For the Squadron" begins and ends in water, the water of the East River and the sea, which is linked to the salt blood that runs in the bodies of the aviators:

> The water in every ocean, like
> The blood in one body, ever
> Equalizing pressure and level.
> Of Middlemas and Prince, then
> . . . .
> Resting forever behind their
> Four smashed and rusting guns.

As in Eberhart's "Fury of Aerial Bombardment," the listing of the names of men who died changes the poem from an abstract meditation to a personal vision of the war. The emphasis on water is logical given the mission of the unit, to patrol the coastal waters and attack enemy shipping.

In "For W—, Who Commanded Well," Nemerov considers the death of one of the squadron's pilots, who died in the course of the war:

> You try to fix your mind upon his death,
> Which seemed it might, somehow, be relevant
> To something you once thought....[19]

According to the position of the higher authorities, individual deaths can be justified to some extent if some progress in the course of the war can be associated with the death of the combatant. The poet, reflecting on this wartime practice, decides (ironically) that

> Death is paying for itself: and so
> It does not seem that anything was lost.

One of the main ideas that consistently appears in Nemerov's later poetry about the war—his distrust of the judgments and motivations of the leadership—is evident here, along with the ironic stance: it "does not seem" that any kind of loss occurred.

If Nemerov wrote relatively few poems about his war experiences for the first forty years of his academic life, he made up for the deficit in *War Stories*, a collection of poems about war and specifically about his own war-related experiences as a pilot, published in 1987. It is as if Nemerov, reluctant to generate poetry about himself in the war, had been holding back these poems until the end. Nemerov's final poems offer direct commentary on the role of the airman in the war and the complex reactions to the situations of aerial operations. The title of the book (and of the section of the book in which his war-related poems are to be found) carries the suggestion that these poems could be the embellished reminiscences of an old veteran, telling self-enhancing stories to a younger, naively credulous audience; the title suggests that readers should be on the alert for exaggerated stories possibly glorifying or romanticizing the poet's life as a pilot during the war. But the poems do not have this effect. Instead, the poet as pilot is seldom a central figure; in the poems directly about flying the poet is on the periphery, relating aspects that affected all who might have been involved.

The first poem in the "War in the Air" section, "Models," illustrates the progress of the pilot from youthful model-maker to seasoned veteran:

> Sanding the parts, glueing and lacquering
> And pasting on the crosses and the rings
> The brave identities of Fokker and Spad
> That fought, only a little before his birth,
>
> That primitive, original war in the air
> He made in miniature and flew by hand
> In clumsy combat, simulated buzz:
> A decade away from being there himself....[20]

The poem describes the progression of symbolic ideas, crosses and rings, first marking the national identities of the German and the Allied aircraft models the poet built in his youth, then merging (the cross within the ring) to become the gunsight used to fire at a target when it is his turn, a decade later, to participate in the war in the air. The final stanza shows the price paid by the survivors of the war, shown in their faces, the innocence of the novice contrasting with the habitual scowl of the veteran, who believes that the novice, even if he survives, can never know the particular soul-changing truth of combat which the veteran has paid a high emotional price to learn:

> Where the survivors, by their likenesses
> Before and after, aged decades in a year,

> Cruel-mouthed and harsh, and thought the young recruit
> Not worth their welcome, as unlike to last.

This aspect is illustrated also in "The War in the Air," the poem that lends this section its name (and perhaps is the inspiration for the other sections—War in the Streets, War in the Heavens—that make up the book).

> For a saving grace, we didn't see our dead,
> Who rarely bothered coming home to die
> But simply stayed away out there
> In the clean air, the war in the air.[21]

The poem is based on the familiar idea that the men who died in aerial combat died in isolated situations. Whether over sea or over land, when they crashed, there were no survivors to bring them back to the men with whom they had flown, as could be the case in ground combat. This disturbing aspect of the war in the air is recognized by others who flew as well—Ciardi, for instance, or Joseph Heller, in his play *We Bombed in New Haven*, where dead crew members remain offstage and the remaining actors rebel against being required to move offstage (supposedly to fly a mission), fearing that they will not be allowed to come back onstage, the equivalent of failing to return from a mission.

Thus the living members of the unit never see their dead or even the enemy dead, for they deliver their bombs or fire their guns at an altitude above the earth. The poet refers to this aspect as "a saving grace," one of the most heavily ironic lines of a poet known for his irony, as if there were anything "saving," in a religious sense, about the results of their combat actions. The war of which they were a part had become known as a "good war," the title of Studs Terkel's popular book and a line often repeated before and after, as if the line between good and evil or even less good were clearly known. Nemerov's intent is again clearly ironic, especially when he acknowledges the contributions of the "losers" who "helped" the survivors win the war, the "losers" referring not only to the enemy dead but also their fellow aviators who died in the "clean air," "losers" because, due to some error of their own making, perhaps, they did not return safely.

In "Night Operations, Coastal Command RAF," the speaker describes the normal hazards of flying that could kill the crew members before they reached the combat area:

> Remembering that war, I'd near believe
> We didn't need the enemy, with whom
> Our dark encounters were confused and few
> And quickly done, so many of our lot
> Did for themselves in folly and misfortune.

5. Howard Nemerov, U.S. Army Air Forces 91

> Some hit our own barrage balloons, and some
> Tripped over power lines, coming in low;
> Some swung on takeoff, others overshot,
> And two or three forgot to lower their wheels.[22]

The title suggests that the poem will describe the desolation of flying long distances over a hard sea in the dark and gloom, but it does not: instead, the poem is about accidents occurring on takeoff or landing and about the odds against safe survival due to bad luck or the pilot's inattention or incompetence. Those who died when they "swung on takeoff," for instance, killed themselves through their inability to control the powerful engines of the aircraft.

The aircraft flown by the men in the unit, the Bristol Beaufighter, was a twin-engine aircraft with a crew of two: pilot and observer-navigator. Each engine delivered over 1600 horsepower; it was an especially powerful, high-performance aircraft that could fly at a top speed of almost 300 miles per hour. According to one pilot:

> The Beaufighter layout consisted of a roomy pilot's cockpit in the snub nose with an unexcelled forward view, and an observer's cupola in the dorsal position with a good view aft. Pilot and observer were not in direct sight communication if the pilot's armored doors were closed. The fuselage between pilot and observer was largely occupied by four cannons and their magazines which held 250 rounds per gun. The observer was navigator, wireless operator, and rear gunner. Primary entry for both positions was by hatch doors with ladders that folded flush with the belly when closed.[23]

Another pilot recalled:

> The view from the pilot's position was superb. The helmeted head would have been just a few inches below the perpex top hatch when sitting on a parachute pack. On either side [of the pilot's compartment], the great Hercules ... engines jutted forward, emphasizing the brute strength of the aircraft.[24]

The entry ladders for the Beaufighter featured the "stirrup-like step" that Nemerov remembered using to climb into the aircraft in *Journal of the Fictive Life*.

There was general consensus among pilots that flying the Beaufighter could be a challenging task, especially due to the forward positioning of the powerful engines, which could adversely affect controllability during takeoffs and landings. Another pilot reported, for instance:

> Flying Beaus was no piece of cake: their reputation for being hard to handle was deserved. The great torque generated by the powerful engines, connected to large, three-bladed propellers, tended to create wild swings on takeoff. Also the high wing-loading dropped you out of the sky like a brick on landing.

Furthermore in the air there was no hands-off flying because Beaufighters were relatively unstable: they needed constant trimming and had no auto pilots.[25]

One 236 Squadron pilot reported his lack of success with handling the aircraft during a check-out ride: "After two successful takeoff and landings, the third one ended in a ground loop as after touch down the aircraft swung violently to the left collapsing the port undercarriage. I had not been told by the instructor that the aircraft had a tendency to swing to the left on takeoff and landing."[26] The challenge of flying at night or in bad weather while trying to control this high-powered aircraft is readily apparent in Nemerov's poems describing his flying experiences.

This idea of the hazards of flying a typical combat mission at the request of those in higher authority is shown in "IFF" (a footnote to the poem explains that IFF is an acronym for "Identification Friend or Foe, a signaling device carried on aircraft for that purpose").

> Hate Hitler? No, I spared him hardly a thought.
> But Corporal Irmin, first, and later on
> The O.C. (Flying), Wing Commander Briggs,
> And the station C.O. Group Captain Ormery—
> Now there were men were objects fit to hate,
> Hitler a moustache and a little curl
> In the middle of his forehead, whereas these
> Bastards were bastards in your daily life,
> With Power in their pleasure, smile or frown.
>
> Not to forget my navigator Bert,
> Who shyly explained to me that the Jews
> Were ruining England
> . . . .
> All the above were friends. And then the foe.[27]

One of the greatest tragedies of war occurs when combatants are killed by "friendly fire," by shots fired by one's fellow soldiers. If "friends" can create obstacles to personal survival, how much worse can the enemy's threats be? Nemerov's ironic use of the title "IFF," a form of technology designed to protect the aircraft as it flies, suggests that the aircrew needed to be on their guard against other forces inside and outside the aircraft, which challenge the powers of discrimination to protect against personal and professional harm.

One squadron pilot recalled the importance of IFF when returning from a night mission: "On our way back we would climb to 1000 feet and make sure that Identification Friend or Foe (IFF) was on the right channel so that the home radar could identify us. Also if we spotted a Royal Navy vessel near the English coast the observer would flash the letter of the day quickly, as the navy shot first and asked questions afterwards."[28] However, the point of this poem is that while the electronic instrumentation of IFF is important to safe return, the real impediments to doing one's job in normal military life include the self-serving training NCOs and superior officers, impressed with their own rank and position; a crew member who reveals an appalling prejudice; and friendly gunners who fire at their own aircraft, mistakenly, perhaps, but with deadly results nevertheless.

Nemerov's identification of his navigator as someone who distrusts the Jews in England (and therefore might not have trusted Nemerov—a Jew—as pilot) partly explains this anecdote recorded years earlier (in *Journal of the Fictive Life*) in which he remembers a "probably shameful scene" he made the night before leaving his squadron after finishing his tour: "Terribly drunk, I think I made a great fuss before the Wing Commander Flying about my navigator's receiving the Croix de Guerre while I, who drove him around [as pilot of the aircraft], got nothing."[29] Nemerov is describing an extremely unusual situation: one wonders how the staff would have known about the navigator's "heroism" if Nemerov—the pilot—hadn't told them. And if the navigator deserved an award, surely the pilot did too. It is not surprising that Nemerov was angry, if the facts are true. The frustration that Nemerov experienced can be more fully appreciated by recognizing that there were only two crew members in the Beaufighter: the pilot, Nemerov, who sat in front and flew the aircraft, and the observer-navigator, "Bert," who sat farther back, in the interior of the aircraft.

Nemerov's poetic representation of the kind of direct combat action typically performed by an aircraft of the RAF coastal squadron, an attack on a ship, is told in the third person, as the poet relates the ambiguous tale of another flier, in "Double Negative," a poem presented as a story told by one of the participants:

> "You start your cannons going going in,
> Though far too far away to count, because
> The bullets going out are a guarantee
> Of sorts against the bullets coming in.
> . . . .
>
> "Nor don't you imagine, when during your dive,
> As it's almost bound to happen, one of your chaps
> Crosses his aircraft over in front of yours
> Between your gunsight and the sitting ship
> —plenty adrenalin then, instead of fear—,
> You won't keep pressing your pale-knuckled thumb
> Down on that button. I know it for a fact,
> And sank the ship that day, and got my gong"[30]

The double negative construction in the poem, "Nor don't you imagine ... You won't keep pressing," translated literally means "you realize you must keep pressing" the firing button; the pilot will keep his thumb on the firing button—whether necessary or not—because his fear and determination will drive him to keep firing at the ship even though he very likely will shoot down one of his own planes which is also diving to attack. The grammatical double negative identifies a thematic double negative in which the effects of his fear could cause the destruction of a friend as well as the enemy ship.

The situation described in this poem can best be understood by comparing its details with an account provided by one of the pilots in Nemerov's squadron, describing the procedures the squadron aircraft followed during an attack on a German convoy of ships:

> One strike that I remember illustrates the general idea. It was ... against a very large well protected [German] convoy.... The whole wing took off in the order as given at the briefing, formed up and set course for Coltishal where we rendezvoused with the fighter escort of twelve Spitfires and the whole force set out for the target. When the convoy was sighted the fighters went overland to intercept any German fighters that may interfere, while the wing also turned overland so as to attack from the landward side and, losing height, it went into the attack, each pilot knowing what his target was. The object is for the cannon-firing Beaus [236 Squadron] to attack the escorts [escorting ships] and draw their attention away from the torpedo boys who had to fly at a predetermined height and speed before releasing the torpedo [at the protected German ships]. The gunfire from the escorts was always considerable and included machine gun and cannon and very often the multi-barreled "Pom Pom" [gun] which was recognizable from the winking lights as each barrel fired in turn. Tracer bullets were used which appeared to be going away from you only to suddenly veer towards you and one instinctively ducked as silly as it is. Barrage balloons were often encountered and were a hazard. After the attack each pilot made his way back to the base and after landing would be interviewed, together with his observer, by an intelligence officer to get their version of the attack and the results seen.[31]

The idea that the costs of war are high and death is impartial, and that those who participated in the war, especially the war in the air, were neither heroes nor hoodlums, but somewhere between, is expressed in "The Faith," a poem ostensibly about those, as the Kenneth Burke epigraph informs us, "for whom war is a vocation." In this poem Nemerov considers the difference between "heroes" and the "duty-bound," or those who served in the war because that was what they were required to do. But in Nemerov's poem, the heroes are the dead, and the survivors are the "duty-bound." He recalls two pilots, "a strange pair," who "behaved the same / In combat, coldly reckless and extreme." One was "mild / and moderate, but the other cantankerous."

> One aimed his aircraft at a battle cruiser
> (it turned out one of ours) and was blown away;
> The other signalled from behind the Frisians
> That he and his crew were hit and going down,
> ....
>
> They were the heroes, we others carried the spears
> In the war that in the last place had been won
> By the duty-bound, the neither more nor less.
> And now I can't remember which was which.[32]

In his description of the events, the "heroes" have little claim to heroic status other than the fact that they died, that their aircraft were among those which "failed to return." Certainly the death of the first flier reflected no significant achievement, because he was attacking a friendly battle cruiser, and the other flier may have been lost through some personal failing: bad pilotage, perhaps, or an unfortunate inability to defend his aircraft against enemy attack.

Nemerov gives a humorously ironic portrait of himself as a pilot in "D-Day + All the Years," in which he appears to be answering the standard question a young child (perhaps his young daughter) might ask: "What did you do during the war, Daddy?"

> He led the squadron out before first light
> Over the Channel as far as Cap Gris Nez
> And turned to port along the Frisian shores
> Up past Den Helder and Terschelling where
> We had lost a few, and so on up as far
> As the Bight of Heligoland and distant Denmark
> Where Hamlet and the others used to live,
> And so wheeled homeward on a parallel track
> To land at Manston in Kent for an early lunch.[33]

Here Nemerov gives us a clearly defined route of flight; the details could have come from a diary he might have kept. Departing the east coast of England, he and the other planes in his flight flew across to Cap Gris Nez, on the north coast of France, then northeast along the Netherlands coast, past the Frisian Islands, to Heligoland, a small island nestled in the notch between the north coast of Germany and the west coast of Denmark, then to the coast of Denmark, then back to England to land at Manston, at the eastern tip of England's east coast. If his account is linked to an actual flight, Nemerov did not fly over the assault beaches at Normandy, which were located well south of his route; nevertheless, he flew a hazardous and challenging mission during D-Day, a day when the entire area between England and France was filled with Allied planes and ships. His mission was undoubtedly to report on German ship movements and to attack any targets of opportunity. Any planes flying along the coast of France or the Netherlands on the morning of D-Day would have been subject to gunfire from the ground and attacks by German aircraft. Another squadron pilot confirms that 236 Squadron lost several of its crews to German anti-aircraft fire in the area of the Frisian Islands. The fact that Nemerov was leading the squadron aircraft on this mission suggests his competence as a flier (assuming that the poem reflects the facts of the flight). Yet he describes himself with some humor as

> Pleasant and warm under the perspex canopy
> Of the office fifty feet above a sea
> Hammered and brazen as on the world's first day,
> A peaceable morning. And the sky was blue.

It would be a peaceable flight if they avoided attack, which evidently they did. The skies over France were filled with low clouds, but Nemerov, farther north, apparently enjoyed good flying weather along his route of flight.

> And Daddy sitting there driving along
> Under his silly hat with the stiffener out,
> Wearing the leather gauntlets flared heroic
> Over the white silk elbow-length debutante's gloves
> They used to wear then whatever the weather was,
> And more or less the way you see him now.

Wearing his wheel hat with the "fifty-mission crush," achieved by removing the wire insert around the rim ("the stiffener out"), wearing leather gloves with silk glove liners, he suggests that driving the plane was much like driving the car which he is supposedly doing as he tells the story to his younger listener. In this poem, as in others, Nemerov gives the impression that his role in the war was unimportant, characterizing himself as a "chauffeur," an airplane "driver" wearing a "silly hat."

Refusing to cast himself as a hero, he reserves his strongest statements about the damages of war in poems about others with whom he associated. Instead of writing his war-related volume of poems at the beginning of his writing career, he waited until the end. That volume, *War Stories*, was his last volume of poetry published, five years before he died. It is as if, as he approached the end of his career, he decided to revisit his flying experiences, which he had come to realize had been so significant in his own personal development.

5. Howard Nemerov, U.S. Army Air Forces   97

Correspondence with the American authorities regarding his transfer from the Royal Canadian Air Force to the United States Air Forces in the spring of 1945 suggests that Nemerov was anxious to complete his flying tour and return to the United States. Nemerov's only poetic description of his involvement with the United States Army comes in "A Memory of the War," an earlier poem describing his return to the United States aboard a troop ship, where he was assigned the duty of maintaining discipline in the event of a submarine sighting:

> Most of what I know of war is what I learned
> When mine was over and they shipped me home.
> I'd been a chauffeur with the RAF
> And didn't know the first damn thing about
> The American way of doing anything
> Till they told me I was Officer of the Day
> (at midnight, yet) and gave me a whopping great
> Blue automatic and sat me on D Deck
> At the top of a ladder leading to a hold
> Where a couple hundred enlisted men were sleeping,
> And said I was to sit there till relieved.[34]

When he asks about the need for the gun, he is told "to shoot down the first son- / ofabitch that sticks his head up" in the event the ship might start to sink.

> So that is what I did, and how I learned
> About the War: I sat there till relieved.

The last line ("I sat there till relieved") effectively summarizes Nemerov's reaction not only to the American instance of military discipline, but also to the war itself. He is given a gun and told to point it at a target: German shipping in the RAF, his own fellow soldiers on board the ship going back to the United States. While one target seems intrinsically more appropriate than the other, his role is the same: sit (in the aircraft, on the ship) and be prepared to shoot your weapon when the necessary circumstances arise. That one target was friendly while another was not seems to have made little difference to those issuing the orders. The double meaning of "relieved" to describe the moment when the poet was no longer under obligation to follow orders is clearly evident, the meanings pertaining to emotional as well as military release.

Nemerov was discharged from the army in August of 1945. After his return to the United States, he taught briefly at Hamilton College before joining the faculty of Bennington College, where he taught until 1966. After teaching at Brandeis University, he accepted a position at Washington University in St. Louis, where he remained until his death in 1991.

6

Louis Simpson, U.S. Army

Of the poets discussed here, only Louis Simpson participated in the war as an infantryman carrying a weapon. Simpson was a member of one of the most decorated units—the 101st Airborne Division—which saw some of the most difficult fighting of the war. He was involved in the fighting in the Normandy invasion, fought through the German resistance in western France, rode a glider into a farmer's field in the assault on Arnhem, participated in the American resistance efforts at Bastogne, and served as part of the occupying forces stationed near Berchtesgaden, Hitler's mountain retreat. The harrowing experiences of the men who shared Simpson's time in Europe have recently been represented in the popular televised series *Band of Brothers*. Although that series focused on the men of Easy Company, 506th Regiment, the actions shown in the series were typical of nearly all of the units in the 101st Airborne. Simpson, in G ("George") Company, remained with his unit for several months, serving in France, Holland, Belgium, and Germany. He was wounded in combat, and odds were against his surviving the war.

Originally from Jamaica, Simpson attended Columbia University in New York City briefly in 1942, waiting to be drafted. His instructors at Columbia included Lionel Trilling and Mark Van Doren. He entered the army in January of 1943 and was sent to Texas for basic training. Initially assigned for training with a tank unit in Texas, he frequently wrote to his mother, aunt, and cousin back in New York City, showing flashes of clever humor; describing a recent visit to the local community, he says that he and his fellow trainees

> got as far as Killeen [a town not far from Fort Hood, Texas], which is a thriving community for a couple thousand pale wives from New Jersey, all set to divorce their soldier husbands, about one thousand shoe shine boys, all future Rockefellers, one brindle cow, and a Texan who just sits in the gutter and spits. When we got back this evening our lieutenant was sitting there with a smile and sed: "You men just got back in time to do the day room."[1]

6. Louis Simpson, U.S. Army

After testing to enter the Air Corps, for which he was unsuccessful,[2] and entering a short-lived Army Specialized Testing Program, he was reassigned to the 75th Infantry Division, at Fort Leonard Wood, Missouri. By March of 1944 he was on his way to England, where he joined the 101st Airborne Division, with whom he participated in the invasion of France. Describing his first impressions of his arrival in Europe, he says, "As history grew near and large [D-Day], my mind was censoring the details. The troops were loaded in convoys, went down to the Channel ports, entered ships, and crossed the Channel. Of all this I remember nothing."[3] After the men reached shore, they proceeded past the first signs of fighting:

> Then, against the bank on the left, appears a heap of dusty, gray-green clothing, from which are thrust two boot soles. At the other end, a blond head with open eyes and an open mouth revealing sharp teeth. The complexion is yellow.... Here's another. This one is also on its back, boot soles thrust out. The jacket is tightened with a black belt from which hangs a gray cylinder, the gas mask. Under it and around, a scattering of papers. Another. Half turned on its side, as though sleeping against the bank.[4]

In a letter home, Simpson wrote that the fighting had been "hot and terrible."[5] He was in France from June until the middle of July, when the 101st was returned to England where new men filled the ranks of those who had been killed or wounded in the hard fighting following D-Day. In September the 101st took part in an airborne assault to help capture the bridges over a branch of the Rhine River near Arnhem, Holland. After some difficult fighting, the unit was pulled back to France for rest and relaxation. In the middle of December Simpson and the others in his unit were suddenly loaded on trucks and driven to the Belgian town of Bastogne, where they helped to reinforce other units of the U.S. Army who were being encircled by elements of the German army. After this battle (the "Battle of the Bulge") ended, Simpson was hospitalized briefly for exhaustion and injured feet, then returned to his company in time to participate in the liberation of Brechtesgaden.

During his time "on the line" Simpson witnessed a variety of disturbing wartime experiences, including an ambush on the column of men with whom he was moving, some hazardous fighting at close range, and the nerve-shattering experiences of coming under attack by enemy guns, especially in the defense of Bastogne. Although he appeared to maintain unusual resiliency of spirit at the time, at least as shown in the letters he wrote home while he was in Europe, the emotional weight of those experiences built up within him until he suffered a breakdown soon after he returned from the war. As he says, "I had amnesia; much of the war was blotted out, and parts of my life before the war."⁶ His poetry, he said, helped to restore his balance:

> When I left the hospital I found that I could hardly read or write. In these circumstances I began writing poems. Before the war I had written a few poems and some prose. Now I found that poetry was the only kind of writing in which I could express my thoughts. Through poems I could release the irrational, grotesque images I had accumulated during the war; and imposing order on these images enabled me to recover my identity.⁷

Although it was initially difficult for Simpson to recall his experiences in the war, he eventually did so with impressive results, providing not one but three versions: the first version consisting of shorter, individual war poems (like "Carentan" and "Arm in Arm," among others); the second his long poem, "The Runner"; and the third his prose accounts, especially "On Line." (A slightly different, shorter prose version of his wartime experiences appeared in *Air with Armed Men*, published in England.)

In his shorter poems about the war, Simpson relies on the dream vision to convey his impression of a nightmare world of war, as in "I Dreamed that in a City Dark as Paris": "I stood alone in a deserted square. / The night was trembling with a violet expectancy." In this poem the poet imagines that he is a *poilu*, a soldier in World War I, experiencing the thoughts of a soldier who had died many years before:

>   My confrere
> In whose thick boots I stood, were you amazed
> To wander through my brain four decades later
> As I have wandered in a dream through yours?
>
> The violence of waking life disrupts
> The order of our death. Strange dreams occur,
> For dreams are licensed as they never were.⁸

Unlike Randall Jarrell's dream visions, Simpson's dream vision is a natural result of a mind trying to recapture previous experience, as visions of the past might occur in one's dreams. No poem captures this idea better, perhaps, than Simpson's "Old Soldier." The "Old Soldier" dreams "of battle on a windy night" as "The shadows move once more / With rumors of alarm. He sees the height / And helmet of his terror in the door."⁹ In Simpson's case, however, the dreams are not merely a literary device; they are images of the war that keep replaying in the mind, always with the same meanings but in new and different circumstances.

Simpson wrote his best-known poem, "Carentan O Carentan," in Paris in 1948 after he dreamed that he had been "lying on the bank of a canal, under machine gun and mortar fire." As he drafted the poem he realized it was not a dream but the memory of his first time under fire.[10] "Carentan" is an account of a surprise attack on the men of the 101st Airborne Division as they approached Carentan, a pleasant French village several kilometers inland from the Normandy beaches:

> This was the shining green canal
> Where we came two by two
> Walking at combat-interval.
> Such trees we never knew.

The trees the poet passes by are not the trees where lovers would walk, his first thought. The meaning of these trees cannot be known, for knowledge means death. The camouflaged enemy in the trees is likened to a jungle animal with deadly intent:

> The watchers in their leopard suits
> Waited till it was time,
> And aimed between the belt and boot,
> And let the barrel climb.
>
> There is a whistling in the leaves
> And it is not the wind,
> The twigs are falling from the knives
> That cut men to the ground.

Immobilized by fear and injury, the poet seeks in vain for the guidance that he believes will deliver him from the difficult situation; however, all authority figures are incapacitated and unable to provide help. "Silent" is the master-sergeant who taught him how to shoot; the lieutenant is a "sleeping beauty" who has been "charmed by that strange tune": the captain is "sickly" and is "taking a long nap." The simple ballad style effectively emphasizes the shock and panic over the sudden violence and loss of life.

> Carentan O Carentan
> Before we met with you
> We never yet had lost a man
> Or known what death could do.[11]

Simpson shows that he knows something about how mistakes in war can occur, mistakes that can cost the lives of soldiers. In this case, lack of essential knowledge cost the captain his life: if the captain had been present earlier, "when trenching was begun," he might have noted the presence of the "enemy's masked gun." Either through ignorance or unfortunate circumstance, the captain, whose decisions affected the lives and success of the men in the company, did not sufficiently observe the terrain in which they were fighting and failed to notice tell-tale signs of the probable location of a machine gun. But even the more experienced soldiers (how experienced could they be if they had landed in France only a few days before?) know their lives are subject to the happenstance of war: when they dig foxholes near a church they discover that their holes "were too shallow for our souls / When the ground began to toss." In this graveyard, one soldier takes a "skull to task" for "spying on us," for gaining knowledge that would place the soldiers at a disadvantage.

As Simpson notes in "On Line," when he saw first-hand evidence of the violence of war, what had been theoretical knowledge about the effects of war became visceral knowledge: "If we kill them, they'll kill us back. This is very obvious. But I hadn't really understood it before. I seem to have known many things without understanding them. It is one thing to know, another to exist."[12] This sense of surprise in the face of sudden attack, this short-lived ignorance of the essential destructive facts of war, is found in other poems as well, as in "Arm in Arm":

> Arm in arm in the Dutch dyke
> Were piled both friend and foe
> With rifle, helmet, motor-bike:
> Step over as you go.
>
> They laid the Captain on a bed
> Of gravel and green grass.
> The little Dutch girl held his head
> And motioned us to pass.[13]

The ballad style of "Arm in Arm" (like that of "Carentan") both distances and emphasizes the shock of death, pushing the reader off balance, especially if the reader is expecting, according to previous encounters with the ballad form, a pleasant rhyme with an uncomplicated message. The image of a captain lying on a bed of "gravel and green grass" conflicts with our gradual understanding of what is meant by the word *bed*: gravel is not really what beds are made of, and the sleep of the captain is one from which he will not awake.

"Memories of a Lost War," a poem about the fighting in Normandy, provides a series of episodic scenes, which "jag like a strip of celluloid," illustrating how his memories of the war, lost in his subconscious, reappear randomly but with vivid intensity: how, after the big guns fire,

> In fearful file,
> We go around burst boots and packs and teeth
> That seem to smile....

Or when, after sleeping a disturbed sleep in "June's cool hush,"

> The riflemen will wake and hold their breath.
> Though they may bleed
> They will be proud a while of something death
> Still seems to need.[14]

Eventually, as the army advances further into France, Simpson becomes used to the sight of dead soldiers. Selected by the company commander to become a runner—a task he neither desired nor enjoyed—he has occasion to pass a field "strewn with corpses," German soldiers as well as American paratroopers. He becomes "accustomed to these sights; they were no more to me than shadows and moonlight."[15] This repression of unpleasant sights, a normal reaction to difficult experiences, will eventually grow too great to continue without psychic damage.

The final traumatic experience for Simpson occurs during the Battle of the Bulge, at Bastogne, where the Germans made their final concerted effort to turn back the American and Allied advances. "The Battle" describes conditions at Bastogne, where the men fought in intensely cold and snowy weather against the German forces. Here the language is plain, basic, the language of soldiers, not philosophers. In a simple metrical pattern and rhyme scheme, Simpson includes specific details of the battle:

> Helmet and rifle, pack and overcoat
> Marched through a forest. Somewhere up ahead
> Guns thudded. Like the circle of a throat
> The night on every side was turning red....

As the German artillery barrage continues for several days, the survivors struggle to remain alert in the hopeless cold:

> Most clearly of that battle I remember
> The tiredness in eyes, how hands looked thin
> Around a cigarette, and the bright ember
> Would pulse with all the life there was within.[16]

After advancing through France, and before helping to defend Bastogne, the men of Simpson's unit were moved to an inactive sector near Rheims for rest and re-supply. It was while he was in this location that Simpson had one of the most moving experiences during his time in combat. Coming across the site of a filled-in World War I trench line, he envisions the experiences of the nameless numbers of French forces who fought in that earlier war. He senses the presence of a "company of infantry who had been standing there for generations." Casualties of war, left behind and neglected, they had remained: "Their coats turned to rags, and the flesh withered from their bones, and their skeletons leaned against the parapet."¹⁷ Simpson seems to understand the untold story of these nameless men, and its effect on him is profound:

> The simple and illiterate, those who sustain the labor and pain of existence, those who carry out the orders, are never themselves heard. History neglects to mention them; most art admits little of their existence. Yet on the hill near Rheims, and at other times in my life, I have seen for a moment into the depth of this life, and it has given me an instinctive distrust of expressed ideas. If most of man's life has passed into silence, is not truth itself silent?¹⁸

Simpson's experience at Rheims may have been the defining moment of his poetic impulse, at least as it pertained to his war experiences, for it occupies a significant place in the long poem he wrote about those experiences, "The Runner."

In contrast to the simple, balanced metrical poems of individual battles or experiences which he had written earlier in his career, "The Runner" is unusually long and loosely structured and describes events covering a four-month period, from September to December of 1944. First published in *The Hudson Review* and then in *A Dream of Governors* (1959), "The Runner" is prefaced by a prose description outlining the basic details of the events described: on September 17, 1944, three months after the D-Day assault on the beaches of Normandy, parachute and glider units of the British, American, and Polish forces "descended" in eastern Holland, with the objective of capturing a bridgehead across the lower Rhine River at Arnhem. The assault, though initially carried out with a small number of casualties, was soon impeded by "bitter" fighting, which eventually became a stalemate in the October rains. In mid–November, the American units were "drawn back to Rheims [France], to re-equip and get the drizzle out of their bones." On December 17, however, they were hurriedly carried by truck convoy into the Ardennes forest, where they participated in the defense of Bastogne in freezing winter weather for the next two weeks. The poem concludes as the German assault at Bastogne ends.¹⁹

The poetic form of "The Runner" contrasts markedly with the better-known poems, like "Carentan" or "Arm in Arm." These ballad-like poems have simple rhythms and regular rhyme schemes. "The Runner" is blank verse, unrhymed iambic pentameter, a mode that has been employed in long narrative passages since Shakespeare used it in his plays. "The Runner" should not be thought of as the personal history of Simpson's activities in Europe in poetic form. As he says in the opening section, the poem "is fiction; the episodes and characters are imaginary." The runner is not meant to be interpreted as Simpson, though he tells us in his essays that he was in fact a runner in both the initial action in France and the later defense of Bastogne. A runner is someone who carries messages from the commander to the men. Normally communication would be accomplished via radio; but in certain combat situations, when noise or radio communication was to be kept at a minimum, or when no radio was available, personally delivered messages were preferred. Simpson was likely chosen for this role because of his relatively small size and, one assumes, speed. The name given to the runner in the poem is "Dodd," a name suggesting death, perhaps (the German *todt*), but it also suggests the word *dodge*, to avoid hazard, which the runner must do to stay alive.

There are twelve numbered sections in the poem, each describing a different locale, starting in England and concluding in the Ardennes Forest around Bastogne. Section one describes in detail how the men loaded themselves into the gliders that carried them from England to the fields of Holland: "their box kite," a device that could easily become "a canvas coffin." The emphasis in this section is on the strange way in which they are carried to the war, riding in a craft as "ungainly as a duck," controlled by "slender pilots in their pinks / And sporty caps and glasses." Riding in the glider, Dodd realizes that "his life was in those hands" that held the controls.[20]

The second section describes their surprisingly uneventful and safe landing. It might almost be a practice mission, until Dodd hears "the familiar sound of guns, the battle-roll, continuous," and he realizes that he is back in a hazardous area again. He had been able to put out of his mind the fact that he had previously fought in Normandy and survived. Dodd realizes that he had forgotten "the fear of death," and he thinks that it is "unjust / That he should be required to survive again."[21]

Sections three through seven describe the advance of the unit towards their objective, a bridgehead across the lower Rhine at Arnhem. In the third section, Dodd is called upon to carry a message up to the front of the line of advancing men. After he delivers the message and returns to his original position in the line, the men he passes give him inquisitive looks, as if he will share the important information that he carries. But in fact he knows nothing more than the cryptic information he has passed to the lieutenant at the head of the line.

Suddenly gunfire breaks out behind him, at the head of the line. Dodd immediately hides in the low grass alongside the road. Eventually the firing stops and Dodd hears someone calling for medical assistance.

As the column moves up the road, the men see the body of one man, killed by gunfire, who "lay huddled up / On his left side; his helmet had rolled off; / His head was seeping blood out in the dirt." Later, when the men have an opportunity to rest, he recalls the dead man's words to him when they were in training in England:

> "Hey, runner-boy," he said
> In the familiar and sneering tone
> That Dodd despised. "What're we doin, hey?
> "You've been to college, right?" His little eyes
> Were sharp with mockery—a little man
> Of pocketknives and combs. "You ought to know.
> What's it all about?"[22]

This section indicates the special burden he carries as a runner—that although he is tasked to carry information, he himself has no privileged knowledge. The men who see him carrying messages believe that his special status gives him additional information which will somehow be of personal benefit. But in fact there is no special benefit, only (as Dodd sees it) the additional danger of exposure to the enemy during his message-delivering activities. His burden is increased because the other men know that he has been to college and is therefore in a privileged status—educated, "smart," supposedly knowing the answers to questions about history, politics, war (this is a clear reference to Simpson's background). But Dodd's special educational status has not given him special status or insight. Like all the other soldiers, he faces the same difficulties and hazards of combat as the other men, and his status as a "college boy" makes his situation more difficult, not less.

In the fourth section, Dodd and the other men move ahead slowly, as Air Force aircraft attack the enemy positions ahead of their advance. He sees his first dead German, a soldier "on his back, spread-eagle, / A big, fresh-blooded, blond, jack-booted man / In dusty gray." Dodd looks at the man, then looks away,

> to the front, where other attitudes
> Of death were waiting. He assumed them all,
> One by one, in his imagination,
> In order to prevent them.[23]

In the brief fifth section, Dodd sees more destruction and evidence of war: a crashed Messerschmitt aircraft; a dead German officer, lying on a mattress; a German half-track blown apart, with the crew spilled out, "burned black as rubber."[24]

In the sixth section the unit has stopped for the night, and the men are trying to sleep in the foxholes they have dug. Dodd is awakened to deliver another message, this time back to battalion, not forward up the line. His route takes him through the night-time countryside, made more hazardous by the unknown darkness. Traveling along the road that runs past trees and dikes, he hears gunfire and avoids a flare. When he arrives at battalion headquarters he gives the password ("Kansas") and is told to wait. Then he is given a message to take back to his unit. On his return trip he thinks that it was "weird to be alone in Holland / At midnight on this road," and he reflects on his role as a runner:

> These errands gave him little satisfaction.
> Some might think he led the life of Riley,
> Safe and warm and dry, around Headquarters.
> A man could be a runner all his life
> And never be shot at. That's what they thought.
> . . . .
>
> It wasn't his fault he never had a chance
> To fire back. Now, right here on this road,
> He might be killed by accident. But still,
> That wouldn't be the same as being brave.

Then Dodd expresses the thought that serves as the thematic pivot point of the poem:

> He had no chance to be thought so [brave], no part
> In the society of riflemen.[25]

Dodd sees himself as separate from the "society of riflemen," the heart of the infantry. This thought combined with the belief that the other men think he has been assigned a soft, safe, privileged job in the unit makes him feel uncomfortable. While it is evident that Dodd is not anxious to fire his rifle at the enemy, his actions so far have been those of someone whose only thoughts have been of survival.

In section seven, a brief section but filled with action, the men come under attack by German artillery as "hell broke loose." He hears the "screaming and flat crack" of German artillery units firing air bursts: "The metal slashed / The trees and ricocheted. Bit in the ground." Dodd lies on his belly, "contracting / Under the edge of metal," as leaves in the trees are shredded only a few feet away. He hears cries of someone calling for a medic, but little can be done while the shelling continues.

> His belly and his buttocks clenched each time
> A shell came in. And they kept coming in.

Then he feels a "sting between his shoulder blades" and realizes he is wounded, a thought that brings "a rush of joy," because a wound could result in evacuation from the battlefield. But the wound is slight, and his sergeant instructs him to deliver cases of mortar shells to the mortar team farther along the road. Dodd makes several trips before the attack ends. As he delivers the mortar shells in spite of his wound, he thinks with satisfaction that "he knew that he was brave." One of the mortar men says he is a "good man" for bringing the mortars, and when the attack ends, he is pleased with himself, thinking that he "had done all that could be expected."[26]

However, Dodd's sense of personal satisfaction is short-lived when, in the next section, he brings about his own fall from self-appointed grace, as he embarrasses himself in front of the men in his unit. In this section a temporary stalemate has set in between the Germans and the Allied forces. It is now October and the late fall rains have started, turning the ground to mud. One night Dodd is returning to his own area, and rather than cross a field of dead men, "a place of horrors," where the "dead were mixed as they had fallen," he decides to follow an unfamiliar path. But as he proceeds, a "fearful premonition" stops him, and in "a shadow, cold with dread," he stands listening. When a challenge is made in German, Dodd runs, "blind with panic":

> A storm of shots erupted at his back.
> Brambles tore at his legs. He climbed a bank,
> Clawing, and stumbled down the other side.
> Then, as he ran, he shouted out the password:
> "Ohio!" like a dog drenched with hot water.
> His rifle fell. He left it where it was.[27]

Dodd runs, yelling the password, until he reaches his platoon, but even then in his fright continues to run until he trips and falls, his helmet flying off "with a clang." This flight from terror quickly becomes a standing joke, not only in the platoon, but in the company as well, and the following section, section nine, shows Dodd as the butt of the men's jokes. In this section, it is now November, and the men have been pulled back for rest and relaxation in an area near Rheims, the scene of some intense fighting during World War I. Here Dodd hears the men making fun of his escapade even as they drill:

> The corporal shouted: "When I say Ohio,
> To the rear march and double-time like hell!"[28]

New men reporting to the unit are jokingly told to report to Dodd, now named "Ohio," to pick up their running shoes. Dodd recalls the comments of the disgusted company commander: "'Screaming the password ... throwing away your gun.... Keep out of my sight, Dodd. You make me sick.'"

Dodd's punishment is to dig latrines,

> Pick cigarette butts up, scrub greasy pots—
> Or to do nothing for a live-long day
> But think and try to read, in a cold tent.

Dodd is embarrassed about his regimental ribbons, including a Bronze Star and a "shameful" Purple Heart, shameful because when he received the wound that caused the award, he thought that would mark his "bravery." While the other men go into town to relax, Dodd stays in camp. He falls asleep and dreams a fantastic dream about a stuffed figure of a human standing "with stiff, ballooning arms," dressed in a Prussian uniform, which makes a noise of machine guns when Dodd swings its arms. Then Dodd senses shadows walking with him, talking about immensely high casualties, and he realizes that these are Frenchmen, the dead of World War I. Finally he sees a plain girl dressed in black with large eyes shooting out "tender rays of light." Her name is Mademoiselle de Maintenon, Miss Now. Dodd laughs at the idea of the name, and when he awakes he feels that it was a vision designed to inform and enlighten his spirit. He walks out into the surrounding fields and sees the evidence of the first world war, sensing the presence of the dead soldiers of that war.

> Shadows were standing with him. It was cold.
> They watched, wrapped in old overcoats, forgotten.
> They stamped their feet. The whole world was deserted
> Except for them; there was nobody left.

This vision that Dodd has of standing in the ghostly presence of long-dead soldiers from a previous war curiously helps him to accommodate the pressures of combat. Partly it comforts him as he realizes that he, like these dead others, is one of many who may be sacrificed, accepting the fact that their deaths are the price paid in war. It is not patriotism that justifies their deaths but the sense of fatalistic acceptance of the duty required of them. This experience on the fields near Rheims was clearly significant for Simpson personally as well as aesthetically (as the turning point for Dodd in "The Runner"). When Dodd returns to camp, he learns that they have received sudden orders to move out, and the men are loaded into trucks and taken to Bastogne.

The next section, section ten, describes the long, uncomfortable truck ride to Bastogne and the subsequent march to their position on the edge of town, in the Ardennes Forest. When they start to dig in, snow starts to fall. Dodd is assigned the task of standing guard, and while he surveys the precariousness of their position, a runner approaches him, giving him the message that

> "We're up a creek, that's what!
> They're coming—panzers from the Russian front,
> Under Von Runstedt. Panzers and SS.
> . . . .
> Everyone else is pulling out but us."[29]

Section eleven contains the description of the German attack, with tanks, on the American positions. Before the attack comes, Dodd decides to make himself a cup of coffee to warm himself, lighting a small fire in a ration box to heat the melted snow. Then Dodd hears voices and the sounds of tanks, and at the foot of the slope below their position, he sees a cannon barrel sticking through the trees, sliding out "like a snake's head, slowly swinging":

> It paused. A flash of light came from its head;
> A thunderclap exploded to Dodd's left;
> Metal whanged on the slope, a spume of black
> Hung in the air.[30]

Following the tank comes "a swarm of walking men," dressed in gray and white, with capes and hoods, the German soldiers. Dodd takes up his gun and attempts to fire. But his first attempt is unsuccessful, because he has failed to release his safety catch. As a bullet "cracked by his head," he takes aim and fires. Although Simpson does not bring attention to the fact, this is the one time in the poem when Dodd fires his rifle. By doing so, he has finally become a member of the "society of riflemen." Simpson provides more details about this moment in "On Line": "I aim at one, at the belt line, and squeeze the trigger. The M-1 goes off, kicking into my shoulder, and the cartridge case flies into the snow. I aim at another. He flops down out of sight."[31] The language here ("flops down") ambiguously offers the possibility that the German fell of his own accord rather than as a result of being hit by the bullet Simpson fired.

Just as it seems that the German tank is about to overrun their position, it is hit by fire from an American tank:

> The tank shuddered. It slewed broadside around.
> Inside the plates, as on an anvil, hammers
> Were laboring. It trembled with explosions,
> And smoke poured out of it.

With the German tank destroyed, the fighting subsides. Dodd looks back in his foxhole and sees his coffee mug, still warm. The fight had begun and ended in a manner of minutes.

Vernon Scannell observes that this section of "The Runner" is especially effective in the way that it captures the essence of hard fighting: "Simpson's description of combat here must rival any other account of battle in either the verse or prose of the Second World War." Scannell says that Simpson uses "a language that is absolutely direct, unadorned, as steely and functional as the armaments he is observing in action," "manipulating the pentameter so that the violent, spasmodic and unpredictable nature of what is happening is reflected in the movement of the verse."[32]

In his narrative essay published later, Simpson recalled the moment when he saw the American tank commander after a fight with German tanks: "the hatch was open, and the tank commander was in the turret, looking down the road. A German tank was burning. I can see him still, like a man at ease in the saddle, as I go on my way, looking back."[33] Simpson does not identify the man in the tank, but it could have been Creighton Abrams, then a lieutenant colonel, later army chief of staff.

In the short final twelfth section, the defense of Bastogne continues. Like the other men in the unit, Dodd is struggling to keep warm and to stay healthy and to hold up under the steady assault of the German artillery barrages. The first sergeant calls for Dodd and tells him he must take a message back to battalion in the dark. Before Dodd leaves, the first sergeant warns him of possible German patrols and wishes him "Good luck!"

> Dodd waved his hand, although it was too dark
> For the other to see him. And set off
> In what seemed to be the right direction.[34]

At this point the poem ends, seemingly with an anti-climactic ending to a long and involved story. Yet a resolution has been achieved: by firing his weapon in the fighting at Bastogne, he has become a rifleman, even if the results of his actions are unknown. He has regained the confidence of those above him, as they have relied on his expertise as a runner, entrusting him with a message to higher command. And, most importantly, he has survived.

In fact, it was at this point that Simpson was temporarily removed from the front lines as a result of deteriorating health. As he says in "On Line," "At this point memory becomes dim. I recall walking into the command post to take another message. The first sergeant looked me up and down from face to feet," and told him to join a small group of men who were soon evacuated and taken out of the front lines by an ambulance: "I found myself being helped up by careful hands.... I climbed onto a stretcher that was suspended against the wall. The ambulance started, and I fell into darkness."[35]

Simpson said that when he wrote "The Runner," he wanted to describe "the dogface soldier's war."

> I wanted to represent the drudgery of that life, the numbing of intellect and emotion, and the endurance of the American infantry soldier. I wanted to write a poem that would be abrasive, like a pebble in a shoe. Some readers thought this flat poem a mistake, but other readers, who were infantrymen, appreciated the details. To a footsoldier, war is almost entirely physical.[36]

This long narrative poem accomplishes a number of tasks. First, it gives a realistic description of the sequence of events that worked upon one man in a series of combat situations (and, by extension, all the men who shared those experiences). It describes, as clearly as if it were a written history, the hazards and challenges of an infantry soldier surviving some of the toughest fighting in Europe. It also describes the evolution of Dodd, the runner, who moves from nervous apprentice to more seasoned veteran, someone who has learned to control his fears and do his job under fire to the best of his ability. The final line, "set off / In what seemed to be the right direction," suggests that while Dodd can never be certain of his path in a wartime environment, he has increased confidence to deal with unexpected situations to the best of his ability, without panicking as he had before.

It also completes the allegory of the "runner," a soldier whose additional task (besides fighting and surviving) is to carry messages from the advanced positions to the rear and back again. Although this job should give him special status and knowledge, it in fact adds additional burdens to his other duties. Although he carries important messages, he cannot benefit from them; he has no special, privileged information that will help him to survive the war. If anything, his job requires him to be exposed to enemy fire more than the normal infantry soldier. He has survived, not because of the information he carries, but because he has learned through painful personal experience, running through the war, fearful for his safety and survival. One of the main thematic ideas of "The Runner" is the notion that the individual soldier never has enough information, never has the essential information that can lead to his survival. This lack of knowledge is especially frustrating as well as ironic for someone like the Runner (Dodd/Simpson), who has some college education and should be a privileged participant in the conflict.

The metrical pattern of "The Runner," iambic pentameter, contrasts noticeably with the short rhymed lines of the ballad-like poems depicting the intense combat episodes of the more familiar shorter poems, but it is appropriate for a long narrative verse. Iambic pentameter approximates normal spoken prose; its metrical structure provides the poet with opportunities for poetic expression suitable for the scene or moment described. It is also appropriate for the topic, an account of the achievements of the "forgotten men" of the war (like those World War I soldiers whose presence Simpson felt in Rheims), who did their duties with little or no notice, unlike the commanders who made the decisions that put the lives of the men in danger.

After being evacuated from Bastogne, Simpson recovered in a hospital well behind the lines. During his time in recuperation, he visited Paris, enjoying the pleasures of the city after six months in or near the front. He eventually rejoined his regiment near the German border. They crossed the Rhine and then began "a race to the interior," moving rapidly through Bavaria to Berchtesgaden, the mountain hide-away of the senior German staff, where they heard "without emotion" the news that the war in Europe had ended. At the war's end, Simpson, like many of the men in his unit, was in a run-down and weary condition: "We had been exhausted, degraded, and reduced. War made you rub shoulders with many kinds of people, forced you to live intimately with them, with the stink of their bodies and the dullness of their minds."

> The difference between one mind and another and the mysterious difference between man and woman had ceased to be of interest. What were ideas, after all? They seemed unreal. What remained? One's boots stepping over the pavements of foreign cities; one's profile, with the cap tilted at the right angle, glimpsed covertly in the glass of a window; one's skin, shaved parade-smooth; one's own mind, drab and savage as a rat in a corner.[37]

Simpson provides one final, ironic vision of the treatment accorded the men who survived the war in "The Heroes"; its bouncing meter mocks the image of returning soldiers, immobilized by their war experiences, and subjected to the misguided efforts of society to rehabilitate them:

> I saw them in long ranks ascending their gang-planks;
> The girls with the doughnuts were cheerful and gay;
> They minded their manners and muttered their thanks;
> The Chaplain advised them to watch and to pray.
>
> They shipped these rapscallions, these sea-sick battalions
> To a patriotic and picturesque spot;
> They gave them new bibles and marksmen's medallions,
> Compasses, maps, and committed the lot.
>
> A fine dust has settled on all that scrap metal.
> The heroes were packaged and sent home in parts.
> To pluck at a poppy and sew on a petal
> And count the long night by the stroke of their hearts.[38]

After the war Simpson completed his undergraduate education at Columbia University. He worked for a while as an editor in New York City and concluded his academic career at the State University of New York at Stony Brook, where he worked from 1967 until his retirement in 1993.

In his war poetry Simpson provided masterpieces of both the short, well-crafted ballad and the long, factual account of blank verse. Both in form and content, his poems are among the finest of those produced by the war poets.

7

James Dickey, U.S. Army Air Forces

Reviewing *Helmets*, Dickey's third book of poetry, William Meredith said that Dickey's poems "arise from experience that requires poetry to comprehend it." Dickey, he adds, "sees things his own way, almost willfully, and his strategy is to bear down until the reader receives the same intensity of vision."[1] This insight into the unique nature of Dickey's poems could come only from someone who had been in a similar situation during the war; like Dickey, Meredith needed poetry to comprehend his wartime visions. For James Dickey, the war experience molded his poetic outlook; the war was a transforming experience. It transformed the lives of those who participated in it, even when it cost them their lives. Late in his life, Dickey "continued to believe that the war had been the major experience in his life; indeed, he considered it a metaphor for life itself."[2] Never one to settle for the plain experiences of life, in his poetry Dickey regularly manipulated facts and events to provide their best creative advantage.

James Dickey was born and raised in Atlanta, Georgia. He left Clemson University after one semester and reported to an air force basic training camp near Miami Beach, Florida, in December of 1942. He attended aviation cadet training at High Point, North Carolina, from April to June, confident of his ability to become a pilot: "I know I'll be commissioned as a pilot," he confidently wrote his mother in May.[3]

After completing his initial cadet training successfully, he traveled to Nashville, Tennessee, for two months, to undergo a series of tests to determine whether he was best suited to be a pilot, navigator, or bombardier. Approved as a pilot candidate, he traveled to Maxwell Field, Montgomery, Alabama, for preflight training, a ten-week course he attended in August and September. He then reported to primary flight training school at Camden, South Carolina. This was also a ten-week course of instruction in which he would have received approximately seventy hours of flying time. After this course concluded, the next step in his training would have been basic flight training at another field, where he would have received an additional seventy hours of flight instruction. He would then have proceeded to advanced flight training, where he would have received from 70 to 100 hours of training in the type of aircraft he would have been assigned to fly operationally.[4] However, Dickey did not complete his training at Camden successfully.

Dickey attended flight school at Camden from October through December of 1943. At Camden he would have learned about basic aircraft operation and controls and would have had to demonstrate mastery of fundamental flight maneuvers. In this first phase of flight training, failure could result from an inability to safely control the airplane (as in the case of Randall Jarrell), or it could result from a serious infraction of the standard flight rules or procedures. It is not clear exactly what caused Dickey's removal from the flight training program. Although he later intimated that his removal had been due to a shortage of people in other career fields, it is more likely that he was transferred as a result of failing to demonstrate satisfactory airmanship.[5] In a letter to his brother Tom, written early in October, he reported that when his instructor had finally cleared him to fly solo, he had made a bad landing, and his aircraft had made a "ground loop"—in which the aircraft swings around rapidly, typically scraping a wingtip:

> I cut the motor and came in. I made the prettiest landing I ever made—the plane only bounced 30 ft. in the air four times. By the time I had it on the ground and was congratulating myself I noticed a very peculiar thing—one of the wings was dragging in the dirt. The plane went 'round and 'round and finally stopped, but not before I banged my thumb up against the instrument panel.[6]

In the same letter to his brother he reports that he has a total of five minutes of solo flying time and is "quite a bit behind."

Although Van Ness suggests that the worst part of the landing was bouncing the plane "30 ft. in the air four times," ending the landing in a ground loop would have been much worse. Accumulating only five minutes of solo time (flying by oneself, without an instructor present in the airplane) suggests that his instructors were reluctant to send him up alone (the five minutes of flying time probably came on his first solo, which ended with the bad landing). It is likely that he was eliminated from the program as a result of a deficiency in flying skills. In January 1944, he wrote his parents from his next station, Buckingham Field, near Fort Myers,

Florida, where he was attending "aerial gunnery school"; after two months at this school he was transferred to radar school at Boca Raton, Florida, where he completed training as a radar observer in a three-month program. He then was assigned to Hammer Field, Fresno, California, in the aircrew training program for night intercept fighters.

The air force's widely-printed account of its training programs, *AAF: The Official Guide to the Army Air Forces*, issued in 1944, describes the training program Dickey must have experienced: "Aviation cadets with special qualifications who are eliminated from flight training for reasons which do not disqualify them from further aircrew duties are eligible to train as radar observer, night fighter. Because their work requires a thorough knowledge of flying technique, they must have had at least 50 hours' flying time." If Dickey had completed at least 50 hours of flying time at Camden, he would have completed more than half of the primary training flying schedule. According to the *AAF Guide*, students in the radar observer course "first take a six weeks' gunnery course, followed by nine weeks' radar operations [training]. Training is designed to enable them to fly with a pilot in a 2-seated night fighter and direct the pilot to enemy aircraft by means of radar." Night fighter replacement training units (RTUs) conducted training for aircrews for a period of five months. This sequence of training periods matches almost exactly the time Dickey was involved in his training programs at Fort Myers, Boca Raton, and Fresno.[7]

At Hammer Field he trained in the AT-23, B-26, P-70 and the P-61, the aircraft he flew in the Pacific theater. With the advanced electronics equipment it carried on board, the P-61 was capable of identifying enemy aircraft in flight, tracking them, intercepting them, and destroying them. After he completed his training at Fresno, he was placed on orders, dated 21 December 1944, assigning him and fifteen other officers (including 2nd Lieutenant Donald Armstrong and Flight Officer James Lally, who figure in his later poems) to overseas duty in the Pacific. Dickey and the other replacements traveled by boat to Hollandia, Dutch New Guinea, arriving at the end of January 1945. By February he had joined the 418th Night Fighter Squadron at San Jose, Mindoro, in the Philippine Islands. The pilot he was teamed with, Earl Bradley, agreed to Dickey's request to name their aircraft the "Flaming Terrapin," after a line in one of Roy Campbell's poems. By March Dickey had flown over Manila, which was in flames as a result of Allied bombing efforts to drive the Japanese out of the city.

In May he was involved in an aircraft accident when the C-47 in which he was riding crashed on takeoff near Manila, and he suffered a cut hand.[8] This incident provided the basis for his later poem, "The War Wound." In June his unit moved to Okinawa, where the aircrews were involved in bombing raids on Formosa (Taiwan). In late July, the 418th began to practice flying fire-bombing raids into the islands of southern Japan. During his combat missions he apparently never fired his guns at an enemy aircraft, but he did complete at least one aerial intercept of an enemy aircraft, although the results of that intercept were inconclusive. He and his pilot also intercepted a lost air force bomber and led it to a safe landing, an incident that confirms Dickey's capability to perform radar intercepts successfully. In October he was in Atsugi, Japan, with the occupation forces. By November he was on his way home, suffering from "combat fatigue."[9]

Dickey had participated in the aerial combat aspect of war, an experience for which his stateside training had not prepared him. He encountered a variety of stressful situations, including flying over the vastness of the Pacific, flying at night, flying bombing runs, flying intercept missions, surviving enemy attacks, and surviving the accidents that are always associated with an active flying unit. By the time he returned to the United States, he had flown 38 combat missions and had been awarded the Air Medal. Initially assigned the rank of flying officer, he ended the war as a second lieutenant. Although he later claimed to have been a pilot in the war, he was not. Possibly, eager reviewers made that claim for him; if so, he never corrected statements to that effect that others had made.[10]

Dickey's job as radar observer was to steer the pilot towards the position indicated on his radar screen so that the pilot would be in an appropriate position to open fire. During the one time that Dickey and his pilot, Bradley, were able to close in on a hostile aircraft at night using this method, they were unable to complete the intercept successfully; apparently the aircraft they were intercepting was a slow-moving training biplane.[11] Because Japanese night aerial attacks were relatively infrequent and ineffective as the months passed in 1945, the P-61s were used less in the night intercept mode and were increasingly used as attack bombers and patrol aircraft protecting Allied naval shipping.

The P-61 was a modern, high performance aircraft containing the latest electronic instrumentation, and Dickey's job was to operate those instruments; he was less a flyer than he was a "systems operator," to use modern terminology. The P-61 featured a large single wing holding two engines, one on either side of the fuselage. Twin booms extended behind the engines for several feet where they were connected by a long horizontal stabilizer. The radar observer's position, at the rear of the cockpit, was thus surrounded by aircraft structural components. The closed in-flight environment in which Dickey operated figures significantly in a number of the war poems he wrote later.

There were three crew positions on the P-61: the aircraft operating manual describes them as pilot, gunner, and radio operator. The pilot's position was in the top of the fuselage just behind the nose of the aircraft; the gunner's position was located behind and slightly above the pilot's position. The radio operator's position was located at the rear of the center fuselage section, well to the rear of the pilot's and gunner's positions. The aircraft operating handbook listed the position as radio operator instead of radar operator for security reasons: illustrations in the operating manual showing the equipment located at the position of the "radio operator" included many blanked out areas. The radar operator operated some radios, but his primary task was to operate the on-board radar equipment. Much of this equipment was located in the lower fuselage area between the pilot and radar operator positions. For a variety of reasons, the guns in the top turret were removed in some models or fixed in a forward-firing position under the control of the pilot. In the Pacific theater, at least, the position of the gunner was seldom filled. Especially on the long-range missions which the P-61s flew in the Pacific, extra fuel was more valuable than an unneeded man sitting in the gunner's position. Thus in most combat sorties in the 418th, there was a two-man crew, the pilot in the front of the aircraft and the radar observer at the rear.

When the aircraft was in flight, the pilot had the usual full range of vision forward, but the radar operator's forward view was completely blocked by the radar equipment and other aircraft components. Visibility for the radar operator was restricted to side windows and a large rear window. The side windows offered a limited view of the ground beneath the aircraft; the primary objects to be seen from these windows were the aft fairings of the twin engines, one on each side, extending back from the large single wing of the aircraft. A large curved plexiglass panel behind the radar operator's position allowed the radar operator to see the twin booms extending from the engine mountings. The plexiglass panels also provided an excellent view of the sky above. The radar operator had a good view of the territory behind, but not of the territory ahead.

In addition, he was separated from the pilot by several cubic feet of radar, radio, and navigation equipment; he could not see the pilot directly, and their primary means of communication was via intercom. The radar operator's radar set depicted islands, large ships, and other large aircraft as yellow or green images on a darkened radar screen. Although the relatively clear view to the rear might have been enjoyable at times, it must have been a disconcerting experience to be flying blind, lacking any possibility of direct forward vision, especially when the aircraft was diving toward the earth on a bomb run, or flying through turbulent air caused by bad weather or the thermal effects of bombing.

Dickey's unique situation in the aircraft is indicated most completely in "The Jewel." This poem, which initially seems intended to recapture the experience of preparing to fly a night mission, concludes with considerations of the meaning of the past war experience from the perspective of the present, postwar, day. The poem begins with a series of images of the poet/crew member studying his reflection in his coffee cup as he and the other crew members prepare themselves mentally for the tasks ahead:

> Forgetting I am alive, the tent comes over me
> Like grass, and dangling its light on a thread,
> Turning the coffee-urn green
> Where the boys upon camp-stools are sitting.
>   Alone, in late night.[12]

As he drinks his coffee before the mission, he masks his fear by smiling: "I smile back a smile I was issued." Then, referring to himself as a "man doubled strangely in time," he sees himself walking to the aircraft, flashlight in hand, the flashlight beam serving as a "third, weak, drifting leg." Once in the aircraft, he

> packs himself into a cockpit
> Suspended on clod-hopping wheels,
> With the moon held still in the tail-booms....

"Clod-hopping wheels" is an apt description of the large, oversize tires on which the P-61 moved while on the ground. The image of the moon in the tail booms refers to the unique structural features of the P-61, the twin booms extended behind the wing and connected in the rear by a horizontal stabilizer. From Dickey's radar observer position in the rear section of the aircraft cockpit, he would have had a clear view of the full moon to the rear of the aircraft as it flew west. In this location in the cockpit, isolated from the pilot who sat in the front part of the cockpit by the wing and the full load of electronic equipment necessary to operate the radar, Dickey could easily imagine himself as having "taken his own vow of silence," although the phrase refers primarily to the practice of observing "radio silence" as they flew their night missions to avoid indicating their position or intentions to enemy listening stations.

Once in place in the aircraft, Dickey would be able to catch occasional glimpses, through the maze of electronic gear between them, of the pilot positioning himself in the front "cabin," or cockpit:

> Across from him, someone snaps on
> The faceted lights of a cabin.
> There like the meaning of war, he sees
> A strong, poor diamond of light,
>   Alone, in late night.

> And inside it, a man leaning forward
> In a helmet, a mask of rubber,
> In the balance of a great, stressed jewel
> Going through his amazing procedure,
>   Alone, in late night.

The poet equates the pilot's preparation in the front cockpit with the "meaning of war," because the switches and controls that the pilot manipulates will not only cause the aircraft to move through the night skies, they will also allow the pilot to fire the guns or drop external ordnance hung on the massive wings of the aircraft. The distancing of the poet from the pilot reinforces the idea of the isolation of the main figure, who is "alone, in late night" even though teamed with a fellow crew member in the aircraft. The "jewel" refers to the facets of light that shine through to the rear position on the aircraft, but the terminology also suggests that the cockpit itself is a jewel, a shining focus of "amazing procedures" involved in the operation of the aircraft.

Thus far, the poem seems to be an unexceptional, impressionistic account of what it might be like to prepare for a night mission. But the final stanza of the poem brings a complex close:

> Truly, do I live? Or shall I die, at last,
> Of waiting? Why should the fear grow loud
> With the years, of being the first to give in
> To the matched, priceless glow of the engines,
>   *Alone, in late night?*

The question, "do I live?" refers both to the remembered moment and the present time of remembering. In the remembered moment, the poet wondered if he would survive the mission, hoping he and the pilot would be able to avoid unpleasant experiences. In the present-day moment, as the poet recalls the meaning of such scenes from his participation in a war that occurred years before, he struggles to understand completely the still-developing impact of that experience. The fear that occupies his mind is both the fear of the dangers of the mission to be flown and, in the present moment, the attraction of the memory of being in the war, when he "gave in" to the excitement of participating in the war, represented here by the "priceless glow" of the engines, their red-hot exhaust, which he could clearly see from his location in the airplane.

This poem describes the key perspective that characterizes Dickey's best war poems, that of the excitement of remembering his participation in the war and the occasionally disturbing thoughts of the challenges of those missions and of the physical and emotional damage that those wartime missions caused. As someone who shared the hazards of aerial combat with others in his squadron, James Dickey never was able to say that his involvement in the war had been wrong or immoral, although poetic art and tradition—as well as contemporary poets—occasionally seemed to demand such denial of him. Because he wrote few poems about his wartime experiences until he returned from overseas, his later, more mature war poems are about remembered events or experiences seen from a then/now split perspective.

"The Enclosure," like "The Jewel," appears to describe routine operational procedures but at the end describes a new and strange kind of transformational experience. The "enclosure" of the title is initially the American nurses' compound, where the nurses are housed in a protective environment:

> Down the track of a Philippine island
> We rode to the aircraft in trucks,
> Going past an enclosure of women,
> Those nurses from sick-tents,
> With a fume of sand-dust at our backs.[13]

The men on the truck "leapt to the tail-gate" of the truck to see the women, then "drew back" from the "guards of the trembling compound," where the women "like prisoners paced." Without transition, the poem abruptly shifts to an enclosure of another kind, the cockpit of the aircraft: "In the dog-panting night-fighter climbing, / Held up between the engines like a child," the poet rests his head on his hands and imagines what he might see in the nurses' compound, through the "dark and heart-pulsing wire" that surrounds them:

> Their dungarees float to the floor,
> And their light-worthy hair shake down
> In curls and remarkable shapes
> That the heads of men cannot grow,
> And women stand deep in a ring
> Of light, and whisper in panic unto us
> To deliver them out
> Of the circle of impotence....

In a Chagall-like vision of suspended animation, the poet sees himself as a man "suspended above them, / Outcrying the engines with lust." But the man is "carried away" from the women "without damage," who wake to the noise of the "engines' matched thunder." The noise of the aircraft's engines gradually fades until the women can hear only the "whine of the mosquitoes" and avoid touching the netting beneath which they remain, "Not touching it, sleeping or waking, / With a thing, not even their hair."

The man, conveyed into the night by his aircraft, sits in his cockpit,

> In a braced, iron, kingly chair,
> As the engines labored
> And carried him off like a child
> . . . .
> To the west, and the thunderstruck mainland.

The first of the poem's two visions, which concludes here, is of the poet denied sexual satisfaction with the women whose job is to tend to the health and welfare of the men. The second is depicted much more quickly, signaled by a transition into a more recent time:

> It may have been the notion of a circle
> Of light, or the sigh of the never-thumbed wire,
> Or a cry with the shape of propellers,
> Or the untouched and breath-trembling nets,
> That led me later, at peace,
> To shuck off my clothes
> In a sickness of moonlight and patience.
> . . . .
> And a white gaze shimmered upon me
> Like an earthless moon, as from women
> Sleeping kept from themselves, and beyond me,
> To sweat as I did, from the north:
> To pray to a skylight of paper, and fall
> On the enemy's women
> With intact and incredible love.

The war over, the poet on duty in Japan is able to achieve in a Japanese bathhouse what was denied him by the system under which he fought while at war. The ironies of sexual satisfaction being provided him by the women of his "enemy" are shown in the image of reversed worlds, in which the light of the night inside the bathhouse is like an "earthless moon," the moonlight he has associated with sexual frustration when he flew his missions from his wartime base. The setting changes from friendly to enemy territory, from the well-disciplined American soldier denied the one thing he believes he needs the most, to a traitorously behaving man who has finally been able to achieve sexual release with Japanese women, a form of satisfaction obviously of some personal as well as thematic significance to Dickey. While most readers might not completely share his sense of sexual frustration and satisfaction, we cannot doubt the validity of Dickey's representation of those feelings. The second image is not a particularly idyllic vision, with the threat of violence explicit in the phrase "fall / On the enemy's women" suggestive of the kind of war the poet had waged before the peace, dropping his ordnance on their homeland. There are several "enclosures" in the poem: the compound of the American nurses, the poet's position in the aircraft, the aircraft itself, and the bathhouse where the poet's final consummation takes place. The image of an enclosing space is also indicated in circles created by the moon and the circular arcs of the aircraft propellers.

As these poems illustrate, one of the most obvious and important aspects of Dickey's poetry is his use of strikingly different realistic elements, or elements drawn from disparate areas of experience. "The Performance," for instance, combines two disparate aspects of a single individual, who is described as a pilot and an amateur acrobat. One of Dickey's best and most frequently anthologized poems, it supposedly describes the death of one of the squadron pilots, Donald Armstrong, who was killed when his P-61 crashed during a low pass across a Japanese-held island. Armstrong was killed instantly, but his observer, Flight Officer James Lally, was injured and survived the crash only to be beheaded by Japanese soldiers.[14]

In Dickey's poetic version of events, Armstrong is the single participant in the action and survives the crash (Lally is not mentioned). The poem focuses on Armstrong's efforts to perform an acrobatic feat—the handstand—before he is beheaded by his Japanese captors. Dickey describes two separate events: the first is Armstrong's "real" performance, when he attempts to stand on his hands in the American camp before the mission, which Armstrong performs with minimal success, his feet "looming and waving" in the light of the sunset. The second performance is mythic, perceived in the mind of the poet, as he imagines the final minutes of Armstrong's life in the hands of his captors. In these final moments, the poet imagines Armstrong performing not only the handstand, but also the back flip, the kip-up, and other gymnastic feats perfectly, amazing and astonishing his captors so completely that they become temporarily disoriented and momentarily fail to carry out his execution.

In the poem there are two complementary scenes: the first, Armstrong's imperfect efforts in the camp of the American fliers, is balanced by the second, Armstrong's impossibly perfect final performance. In both scenes, there are similar elements: the impressed observers, tools of war, and the play of light. The poem opens with the poet remembering "the last time" he saw Armstrong, who was

> staggering oddly off into the sun,
> Going down, of the Philippine Islands.[15]

This initial image foreshadows the disappearance of Armstrong into the Japanese empire, signified by the setting (rising) sun. In the first moments of the poem, the attention is on the narrator rather than Armstrong:

> I let my shovel fall, and put that hand
> Above my eyes, and moved some way to one side
> That his body might pass through the sun,
> And I saw how well he was not
> Standing there on his hands,
> On his spindle-shanked forearms balanced,
> Unbalanced....

Our attention turns from the narrator to Armstrong, back to the narrator, and finally back to Armstrong as he struggles to maintain his balance, breathing hard from the physical exertion so that the dust flies up, his blood rushing to his head ("blood turned his face inside out").

The link between Armstrong as performer and the narrator as observer is mirrored in the vision that follows immediately, when

> Next day, he toppled his head off
> On an island beach to the south,
>
> And the enemy's two-handed sword
> Did not fall from anyone's hands
> At that miraculous sight,
> As the head rolled over upon
> Its wide-eyed face....

The narrator, holding a shovel, is analogically linked with the Japanese executioners, holding the execution sword. The narrator in a way shares in the responsibility for the death of Armstrong, which he describes in the poem, but the narrator also is credited with raising Armstrong to a higher level of existence by indicating the extraordinary abilities Armstrong demonstrates in the moments before his death:

> Doing all his lean tricks to amaze them—
> The back somersault, the kip-up—
> And at last, the stand on his hands,
> Perfect, with his feet together,
> His head down, evenly breathing....

Like Armstrong, the narrator has been working the ground with an implement, so that when Armstrong kneels, at the closure of the poem, "beside his hacked, glittering grave," the poet, with shovel in hand, becomes part of the burial detail for Armstrong as well. There is also the suggestion that death may await the narrator, the shovel of the narrator and the sword of the executioners' tools signifying death.

Armstrong never, in fact, gave the kind of performance Dickey describes in the poem: Armstrong was apparently killed in the crash, and Lally was captured and beheaded. Dickey engages in a poetic act of profound transformation when he describes Armstrong completing his performance "having done / All things in this life that he could." As a pilot, as a soldier, as a person, Armstrong ends his life with an act of physical perfection, an achievement always important to Dickey the man and poet. Even the act of his beheading appears to be controlled by Armstrong, who "toppled his [own] head off." As "The Performance" shows, Dickey's approach is to identify the basic elements of wartime experience and reassemble them in a modified pattern, a mosaic in which the essential elements are present but modified in a unique blend of original and imagined moments. Dickey transforms the basic fact of Armstrong's nearly unsuccessful attempts to perform a handstand into a statement of extraordinary, if unusual, human achievement in strange and hazardous circumstances.

Dickey's poetry is immersed in the idea of metaphor—not simple metaphor, however, but a more complex notion of metaphor, in which the elements of the described experience are compared to another kind of experience, one in which the elements of the basic experience are isolated, mixed, and recombined in a new and unusual result. In an address that he gave while serving as poetry consultant to the Library of Congress, he said that

> The deliberate conjunction of disparate items which we call metaphor is not so much a way of understanding the world but a perpetually exciting way of recreating it from its own parts.... It is a way of causing the items of the real world to act upon each other, to recombine, to suffer and learn from the mysterious value systems, or value-making systems, of the individual, both in his socially conditioned and in his inmost, wild, and untutored mind. It is a way of putting the world together according to rules which one never fully understands, but which are as powerfully compelling as anything in the whole human makeup.[16]

In the metaphor-making process he describes, Dickey juxtaposes aspects of the Freudian ego and id, setting the "socially conditioned" mind against the "inmost, wild, and untutored" mind. The juxtaposition of polite, cultured perception and undisciplined, primitive urges is evident in nearly every work Dickey has written. It is the one quality that makes Dickey's poetry and prose special and successful; it is also the one quality that often disturbs readers who are made uncomfortable by what they perceive as Dickey's manipulation of the elements of reality into an unabashed, unrealistically exaggerated masculine vision.

To Dickey, metaphor is the most dynamic agent of the imagination at work, and many of his poems are examples of how strange and unusual "items of the real world" can be linked or arranged, not just for startling effect, but for thematic impact. While Dickey may have developed this Freudian approach to his poetry-making after World War II ended, the experiences of war were crucial in forcing the awareness of the juxtaposition of the formal, "polite," approach to life with the violence of wartime experience. There can be no more startling contrast than that between military preparation for combat, in which the goal is a highly structured, machine-like approach to efficiency in combat, and the violence and incoherence of combat itself. The many valid reasons for using such an approach cannot hide the disparity that any new member of the military feels when confronted with a system that insists on strict regimentation of behavior for the sole purpose of the destruction of human life or supporting resources.

Another of Dickey's poems about the war, "The War Wound," illustrates how he combines a "socially conditioned" response with a "wild, inmost" impulse. In the poem, the poet reflects on a cut that he received on the palm of his hand during the war when he braced himself during an aircraft accident. A piece of shattered glass cut his hand, leaving a scar in the shape of a half-moon. After the war, the wound reminds the poet of the "fury" of war of which the wound itself, though small, is a constant remembrance. He asks his half-moon wound to "shine" as a reminder, to "burn like a poison" to warn him when his two children are involved in dangerous activities, to serve as a constant reminder of the "world-fury" that caused it and which it constantly represents.[17] Its moon shape is linked to the cycles of the moon, the passing of time, and is a personal reminder of the night missions the poet has flown. The poet invites the extreme conditions of violence represented by the wound to return to disturb his more polite, socially conditioned postwar world when a violent act is about to occur.

Other evidence of Dickey's fascination with the magical powers of metaphor as a world-changing tool is shown in "Confrontation of the Hero," an early poem written about an experience that occurred in 1945 but not published until 1992. In this poem the narrator, a World War II veteran, places his foot on an island in the Pacific

> forward
> Sleeping in its flesh, road by road
> Into the island, and the coral shudders,
> Gives way, turns easily, a zodiacal wheel,
> And the beasts step up from their stars over you
> And disappear in the sea and earth of noon.[18]

The "zodiacal wheel" is the unique alignment of the twelve constellations that constitute the zodiac, the term given to those artificial groupings of stars assumed to outline the shapes of animals or people through which the sun and planets appear to travel on their annual journeys through the daytime and nighttime skies. Because the planets, moon, and sun are limited in their apparent travel through this relatively narrow band of the heavens, supernatural forces and influences became associated with the alignments of the heavenly bodies and the constellations dating to earliest recorded history, a belief evident in the modern attraction for reading daily horoscopes.

In "Reincarnation (II)," a poem not specifically based on wartime events but linked to them in theme and location, a man is transformed into a large white sea-bird, an albatross, and undertakes a migratory flight across the Pacific. The narrator/bird finds himself

>   Aloft   a night five thousand feet up
>   Where he soars among the as-yet-unnamed
>   The billion unmentionable stars
>   Each in its right relation
>   To his course   he shivers   changes his heading
>   Slightly   feels the heavenly bodies
>   Shake   alter   line up in the right conjunction[19]

After he reaches the island he has been seeking, he mates with another bird and then heads north again, relying on an innate sense of direction provided by the starry environment of the night sky:

>   In midair   beasts
>   Balanced on starpoints
>   Latitude and longitude correct
>   Oriented by instinct   by stars
>   By the sun in one eye the moon
>   In the other....

Dickey's explanation clarifies the concept he was attempting to communicate:

> I tried to show two things in the poem: first, the recognition of this being that he's now a bird and no longer a man, and his realization that he can navigate by means of the stars; second, the gradual fading of his identity as a human being through this long voyage. On the long nuptial down from the polar regions toward the Galapagos Islands, where he will mate with another bird to produce offspring, he loses the last memories of his human life. When he mates and perpetuates his kind, he becomes completely what he is in this phase of his existence. In one phase he was a man; in this phase he is a bird.

He also has a notion of another instinctual thing, death. Most of the poem has to do with instinctual navigation, and at the end of the poem I try to introduce the supposition that death, for a bird that navigates by instinct, also navigates by instinct, and will coincide with him at some distinct point of latitude and longitude. And when they meet, he will be changed into something else. Yes.[20]

As Robert Kirschten observes, of all of Dickey's animal poems, this poem "is the most mystical, or cosmic, because of its celestial scenery and because the bird's unearthly motion so closely resembles the 'spiritual walking' of the poet's constantly reindividuated Absolute of Motion."[21] Kirschten's "Absolute of Motion" concept includes aspects of Dickey's astronomical-astrological vision, which is neoplatonic in nature:

> Explicitly analogized to the Neoplatonic commonplace of the harmony of the spheres, Dickey's poetic motion is not only a cosmic principle but also a mediating magical link between man and nature. The poet thus acquires the restorative powers of the gods, because the objects in his universe are attuned to each other in an empathic harmony animated by an emanating movement shared by men and stars.... Dickey can harmonize natural opposites—life, death, and rebirth—through an emotional proportion we no longer believe to be scientific fact.[22]

Though he was not given much formal training as a navigator, Dickey would certainly have been instructed in dead reckoning procedures for estimating the aircraft's position based on aircraft heading, airspeed, and winds aloft. One of the key tools in estimating aircraft position is celestial navigation, which relies on knowledge of the positions of the sun and stars to determine the location of the aircraft according to celestial latitude and longitude coordinates. As a radar observer, Dickey would have had the primary responsibility for tracking the position of the aircraft, and must have been cognizant of the rudimentary techniques of celestial navigation, especially considering the significant amount of over-water flying he and his pilot experienced over the western section of the Pacific Ocean.

Although Henry Hart suggests that Dickey learned the fine points of navigational techniques later in life,[23] he must certainly have learned the basics during his months in the Pacific and, during the Korean War, with the Air Force, when he taught radar observation and navigation courses at air force bases in Mississippi and Texas. That he renewed his interest in basic navigational techniques and methods later in life is evident in the pages of his 1987 novel *Alnilam*. Although the book is primarily concerned with the activities of a group of young aviation cadets who form a secret society based on the teachings of Joel Cahill, a cadet who dies mysteriously while circling a forest fire, the book includes several references to activities of veterans who participated in the war before arriving as instructors at the South Carolina training base.

In one episode, Whitehall, who had been a navigator on B-17s in the South Pacific, describes how, with the aid of his navigational tools and techniques, he was able to guide an aircraft surrounded by bad weather and over open ocean back to its home base. In a novel which frequently presents critical and occasionally cynical depictions of the men associated with the military services, this episode stands out as an example of skilled work performed well and a description of a significant, even heroic, achievement. Whitehall describes his sextant as "a beautiful thing; all that precise engineering, all those angles and mirrors, those numbers that match up on the sun and the planets and the stars, and on the moon, and give you your lines of position."[24] Whitehall explains to his listeners in the novel that "all celestial navigation is spherical-trig problems, figuring out the sides of particular triangles. But the tables do all that for you; all you have to do is a specialized form of addition and subtraction. The logarithms are all built into the tables."[25]

Using his sextant Whitehall obtains fixes on three stars, Deneb, Altair, and Vega. A break in the clouds occurs just as he needs a fix on Vega, and he plots his new heading confidently. Everything falls into place for him, because, as he says, "the stars and the books had got together; the stars had gone back into the tables. They were something you could understand, at least in some way; the only way that mattered."[26] Whitehall's navigational ability not only leads to his success in returning the mission safely to the home base, for which he receives a medal, but more importantly from a personal perspective, it gives Whitehall a special feeling of confidence that can hardly be matched or understood by those unfamiliar with the demands of his profession. Once he realizes his crew will return safely, Whitehall notices that "some kind of change had come over everything: everything that I could see from where I was sitting; everything I could reach":

> Here I was, sitting there with my implements, with the big area map in front of me and the little map of big New Guinea to one side of me, with the Weems plotter across the map, with the E6B, the compass, the dividers, the driftmeter, everything giving a kind of glad light, giving it back off me, as though I were shining, and they were reflecting.[27]

Dickey's experience as a radar operator and navigator taught him that knowledge of star positions and apparent star movement—due to the earth's rotation—could provide the means for accurately locating oneself at any location on the face of the earth, if one had the appropriate star almanacs at hand, of course. But those almanacs could become, in Dickey's vision, magical hermetical documents that could provide the key to life when used by someone with the ability to read the sky as well as the tables of star locations and times. In this episode from *Alnilam*, that knowledge leads to demonstrated skills that result in the transformation of the navigator into something like an angel—a shining image of the voice that leads the men to home and safety.

The transforming experience of long-distance flight is evident as well in Dickey's best-known war poem, "The Firebombing." This poem gives an account, not of a B-29 incendiary raid, as Joyce Carol Oates assumed in an early review, but—if it is based on any actual mission at all—of one of the few practice firebombing raids the crews of the 418th flew.[28] The narrator of the poem mentally reconstructs the mission in an effort to comprehend the damage his raid might have caused to the people who suffered the effects of the bombing. As in almost all of Dickey's war poems, there is a two-part time sequence, the "now" of the present day serving as a doorway into the "then" of the war. Dickey the poet-narrator, living some years after the war in his home within the comfortable suburban Atlanta environment, recalls his wartime tasks as a flier engaged in the task of firebombing Japanese territory. He tries to imagine what it must have been like on the ground when the fires he imagines he helped to start consumed the property and lives of hundreds and perhaps thousands of Japanese citizens. But as he says repeatedly throughout the poem, he is unable imagine those scenes, at least not with accuracy or empathy.

Although he has spent twenty years living in the suburbs, putting on weight and growing older, he is able to recall with amazing vividness the details of the mission: flashlights, cowl flaps, the tilt of the propellers. Even as he recalls the first of the images of the flight line, he also recalls the images of the "enemy filling up the hills / With ceremonial graves." He believes that his conscience should be bothered about the results of his fire-bombing missions, but any sense of remorse is offset when he first provides an image of the enemy as agent of death for American soldiers, "ceremonial graves" referring to the ceremony involved with cutting off the heads of captured soldiers and airmen. Such an image works directly against the capacity to develop sympathy for those upon whom he will eventually drop a load of fire:

> Some technical-minded stranger with my hands
> Is sitting in a glass treasure-hole of blue light,
> Having potential fire under the undeodorized arms
> Of his wings, on thin bomb-shackles,
> The "tear-drop-shaped" 300-gallon drop-tanks
> Filled with napalm and gasoline.[29]

The speaker meditates that "others try to feel for them [the victims]. Some can, it is often said."

As he relives the firebombing mission, he recalls vividly the details of the flight through the night, the ocean over which he flew, the city which he bombed, and the return to his home base. But he is unable to visualize, to realize the nature of the damage he had caused: "Twenty years in the suburbs have not shown me / Which ones were hit and which not." "My hat," the narrator says, "should crawl on my head / In streetcars, thinking of it, / The fat on my body should pale." "Death," he thinks, "will not be what it should; / Will not, even now...." At the end of the poem, having recovered the details of the flight, he thinks: "All this and I am still ... unable to get down there or see what really happened." His unique position in the aircraft is only one of several reasons why the Dickey narrator cannot "see" what happened.

"The Firebombing" suggests a contrast between duty and the results of duty's tasks: cities are consumed with flame as a result of the flier's "detachment, the honored aesthetic evil." The narrator of the poem recalls his skillful flying, as he "sail[s] artistically over" the heads of his victims.

The most striking, memorable images in the poem are those associated with the progress of the flight through the night. As his aircraft departs his home base on Okinawa, for instance, he sees

> The moon-metal-shine of the propellers; the quarter-moonstone, aimed at the
>   waves,
> Stopped on the cumulus....

As he flies over portions of the Japanese mainland, he describes

>   Enemy rivers and trees
> Sliding off me like snakeskin,
> Strips of vapor spooled from the wingtips

As he prepares to drop his load of napalm, jellied gasoline, his hand

>   turns whiter
> Than ever, clutching the toggle—
> The ship shakes   bucks
> Fire hangs   not yet fire
> In the air above Beppu

His northerly heading over the resulting firestorm is fixed by the position of the moon behind him:

> The moment when the moon sails in between
> The tail-booms   the rudders nod   I swing

> Over   directly over the heart
> The *heart* of the fire.

His return to Okinawa follows "The huge, moon-washed steppingstones / Of the Ryukyus south, / The nightgrass of mountains billowing softly / In my rising heat."

Although the narrator reminds us that he is trying to imagine the awfulness of the destruction he has helped to create, the poem is as much about the challenge of the mission and the hazards faced by the fliers as it is about the destruction they bring to the enemy population:

> One is cool and enthralled in the cockpit
> Turned blue by the power of beauty,
> In a pale treasure-hole of soft light
> Deep in aesthetic contemplation,
> Seeing the ponds catch fire....

The cockpit is a "treasure-hole" of light, reminding us of the "jewel-like" aspect of the pilot's or aircrew member's domain.

Dickey writes the poem as if the Dickey-narrator is the only person in the aircraft, the pilot. No other aircrew member is mentioned. By posing as the pilot, Dickey suggests he is single-handedly responsible for the success of the mission and the destruction that it caused. If Dickey had placed himself in his true historical position, as one member of a two-man crew, the sense of personal responsibility would have been diminished. But even with Dickey posing as primary agent, the impact of the poem is one of moral ambiguity, a quality on which many readers have commented. Some aspect of this ambiguity may result from the fact that Dickey and the members of the 418th probably never participated in firebombing missions designed to weaken Japanese resistance. They did, however, fly a few practice missions. According to Dickey's pilot, Earl Bradley, the 418th used fire bombs twice: "These flights were mainly for us to learn some of the techniques involved so we could pass the information along. The war ended before we ever got into full swing."[30] It is not clear that Dickey flew on any of those practice missions.

The poem has been the target of criticism since it was first published in *Buckdancer's Choice* in 1965. After the poem appeared, the poet Robert Bly attacked "The Firebombing" and other poems in *Buckdancer's Choice* for not demonstrating an openly critical attitude towards the Vietnam war.[31] Bly's attack came at a time when many of the country's writers and artists were protesting American involvement in Vietnam. It is not clear that Bly understood "The Firebombing" to be about World War II and not Vietnam, but Bly apparently believed that there was a thematic association (because of the poem's focus on aerial attacks on an Oriental population) and that any poem about war appearing at that time should be implicitly if not explicitly critical of the American war efforts in Vietnam.

Dickey himself said that no poet could write about guilt effectively unless the poet had "earned" that guilt. Dickey may never have believed that he had truly "earned" that guilt, though he participated as a military serviceman. As he has said about the poem, it expresses his guilt about the fact that he is unable to feel guilt for what he did in the war.[32] One possible reason for his inability to feel guilt might be that he could never forget his original reaction to Japanese atrocities in the Philippines, including the beheading of James Lally. In a letter to his parents dated May 1945, he wrote, "Everything you hear about the Nips is true. They are really brutal. I wish we could kill them all."[33]

What might appear to be an inhumane attitude towards the Japanese soldiers and their actions was in fact an attitude shared by almost all American military personnel who served in the Pacific. For most American soldiers who fought in World War II, their hatred of the Japanese was much stronger than it was for those Americans who were fighting the Germans, partly because of the greater cultural differences, but mostly, perhaps, because of the shock, violence, and destruction of the Japanese attack on Pearl Harbor. Few knowledgeable individuals were surprised when the Germans invaded Poland, whereas most Americans were profoundly shocked by the attack on Pearl Harbor. For Dickey to fail to demonstrate any feelings of guilt is consistent with his wartime attitude (shared by millions of combatants and non-combatants at the time), and to later pretend that he did feel guilt would have been dishonest. And though there were numerous instances in which Dickey didn't mind lying in the cause of art, this was not one of them.

A second reason for his inability to feel guilt could be his sense of identification with his unit, the 418th NFS. As is evident in his letters home and his poems, he saw himself (or wanted to see himself) as an integral part of the squadron. He volunteered to write a portion of the squadron history, which was published after the war.

Perhaps the most cogent reason he was unable to feel guilt was that he remembered the terrific sense of power that flying a heavily armed combat aircraft could bring. As Van Ness reports, although worried about his chances for survival, Dickey believed that participating in the war was important: "You can never do anything in your life that will give you such a feeling of consequence and of performing a dangerous and essential part in a great cause as fighting in a world war."[34] To employ the language of the poem itself, the narrator feels "the greatest sense of power in one's life."

If he had chosen to, in "The Firebombing" Dickey might have described the magnitude of that power and the fascination he must have felt for it. It has been documented repeatedly that the one impulse that keeps the combatant going when the threat of death is imminent is the sense of power to be derived from the implements of war and the adrenalin surge that accompanies a life-threatening situation. Why Dickey did not let himself indulge in his "inmost, wild" perceptions of such power is not clear; certainly he felt little restraint when he did so in connection with other aspects of the id, especially sexual desires and activities. Perhaps his mind had been too "socially conditioned" to approve of the violence of war as a fit subject for poetry. Perhaps too, his role as radar operator instead of pilot served to remove him from the full impact of the destruction brought about by his night bombing experiences. While he was responsible for steering the aircraft toward the target, he was not responsible for controlling the aircraft when it dove towards the earth and released its bombs; he could see only what the results of the mission had been.

Finally, "The Firebombing" earns our attention more by the nature of its subject than by its poetic merits; it is the only poem in the inventory of war poems written by a respected poet who actually participated in a firebombing raid (or a close approximation). We, like Bly, may be disappointed that no larger thematic issue seems to come out of it than the recognition that the firebombing possibly constituted a terrible act, but the poem's uncertain tone can be attributed to the tension between Dickey's strong feeling about the rightness of his involvement in wartime flying activities and his lack of guilt about the damage he and other aircrews had caused. (It is possible that the images of the burning Japanese city in his final novel, *To the White Sea*, were created in an effort to accomplish what "The Firebombing" failed to do.)

"The Driver" is Dickey's poetic summary of his Pacific war experiences. In the poem he describes himself sitting in the driver's seat of a sunken half-track off the shore of a Pacific island: "At the end of the war," the poet says, he arose from his bed in a tent and walked

> Where the island fell through white stones
> Until it became the green sea.
> Into light that dazzled my brain
> Like the new thought of peace, I walked
> Until I was swimming and singing.[35]

As he swims, his "long legs of shadow" point to the surface of the ocean beneath where his soul "could take root and spring as it must." He sees a "rusted halftrack" that

> Moved in the depths with the movement
> One sees a thing take through tears
> Of joy, or terrible sorrow....

Sitting in the driver's seat, "driving through the country of the drowned," he sits "still, / Getting used to the burning stare / Of the wide-eyed dead after battle." Looking up, he sees the water's surface, the "uneasy, lyrical skin that lies / Between death and life, trembling always." From his point "at the wheel of a craft in a wave / Of attack that broke upon coral," beneath the surface of the water, he sees an airplane fly over. Able to see the end of the war as one who is simultaneously alive and one who might be dead, he tries to express the idea that he can "'become pure spirit'" in a "bright smoke of bubbles." But his attempt to communicate in a world of the dead fails, and he realizes he is about to lose "the power of speech in the presence / Of the dead," and that he must "leap at last for the sky / Very nearly too late,"

> Where another
> Leapt and could not break into
> His breath, where it lay, in battle
> As in peace, available, secret,
> Dazzling and huge, filled with sunlight,
> For thousands of miles on the water.

Life in combat has been an unreal, restricting experience, like living beneath the water. Once peace occurs, however, there is a possibility of life without such restriction. As a member of the armed forces who could have joined the "country of the drowned," Dickey makes a leap for life, experiencing a symbolic rebirth out of the sea.

After the war, Dickey attended Vanderbilt University, where he received A.B. and M.A. degrees in English. He taught at several colleges and universities and worked in advertising before achieving literary success with his novel *Deliverance* and *Buckdancer's Choice* and other poetry collections. He joined the English department at the University of South Carolina in 1969 and remained there until his death in 1997.

8

Richard Hugo, U.S. Army Air Forces

Like Louis Simpson, Richard Hugo established his reputation as a poet after the war ended; like Simpson, Meredith, and Dickey, Hugo used his war poems to process his wartime experiences. Initially Hugo wrote few war poems, preferring instead to write about his life in the environments of Seattle and other areas in the Pacific Northwest.

Born Richard Hogan in 1923 in a suburb of Seattle, Hugo was raised by his maternal grandparents after his father left his mother. When his mother remarried, Hugo took his stepfather's last name for his own in November 1942, just before he enlisted in the army air forces. Following a period of initial testing, he qualified as a cadet in the training program for bombardiers. He began a ten-week pre-flight training program around the first of July 1943, and entered a six-week gunnery course in the middle of September. By the first of November, he was in bombardier school at Deming Army Air Field, New Mexico. At Deming he trained in twin-engine AT-11 aircraft, in which he practiced his bombing techniques. While he was in training at Deming, he gave some indication of his future literary interests by serving as the editor of his bombardier training class yearbook, in which he stated his appreciation for the efforts of the men who had helped him put the yearbook together: "In all sincerity and unashamed, I stand and decree myself to feel humble, and at the same time proud to be connected with such men." Of his motivation for joining the air corps, he said later that he volunteered "for the cheapest kind of romantic personal reasons." He said that he felt "weak and inadequate, and foolishly thought facing and surviving danger would give me the spiritual depth and a courageous dimension that I lacked and desperately wanted."[1]

Hugo graduated from bombardier class 44-5 on April 1, 1944, and proceeded to combat crew training in the B-24 bomber, where, for a period of three months, he and the other members of his crew practiced formation flying in the large, four-engine aircraft. After their crew training was complete, they departed the United States for Italy, where they joined the 825th Bomb Squadron, one of the units of the 484th Bomb Group, located at an airfield at Torretta, near Cerignola, in southern Italy, about thirty miles east of Foggia. His other crew members were Howard Steinberg, pilot; Robert Swanson, co-pilot; Ryan O'Brien, navigator; Ed Self, engineer; Stewart, radio operator and gunner; Anthony Cartwright, an "English immigrant," tail gunner; and Knapp, the ball turret gunner. In addition to these seven there were two side gunners. The members of the crew all flew together for the full time of their stay in Italy.

Their airfield was located in the relatively flat farming terrain near the southeast coast of southern Italy, below the spur on the Italian boot. This location placed them in relatively close proximity to their most important targets: Odertal, Vienna, Linz, and Munich, to the north, and Ploesti, a key oil production area in Romania, well to the east, just north of Budapest. The bombing missions to these targets were not easy, even when German resistance was light, as they required long distance flights, often through bad weather. The flight to Ploesti was particularly hazardous, as the crews had to fly over extensive stretches of rough, mountainous terrain, where there were few safe landing fields in the event an emergency landing was necessary. German defensive firepower was especially intense, in the air and on the ground; the anti-aircraft fire was notoriously thick near Ploesti and Vienna (also an oil production and manufacturing area). German fighter aircraft were especially tenacious in their defense of these cities.

Hugo and his crew flew a total of 35 missions, from August of 1944 until March of 1945. The missions were spread out over a period of eight months due to bad weather and the need to fly other training and resupply missions. When the squadron did fly, it could suffer appalling losses. The one mission that brought the 484th Bomb Group the greatest number of losses occurred on 17 December 1944, a mission to Odertal, Germany, when the unit suffered 30 percent losses, nearly one plane out of every three failing to return safely. On this particular mission, the weather was especially bad, with snow and heavy cloud formations reducing visibility, causing the bombers to break up their normal formations en route to the target. To reduce the possibility of the bombers' running into each other in the clouds, they proceeded individually, hoping to rejoin near the IP (initial point), the point at which the bomb run to Odertal would begin. Unfortunately, the German air force had been alerted to the attack, and German fighter aircraft were circling in the tops of the clouds, waiting for the bombers to appear. A large number of German aircraft had been hurriedly assembled to support an attack on the American infantry at Bastogne, in what would become known as the Battle of the Bulge. The bad weather in Europe was preventing the German aircraft from attacking at Bastogne, but it did not prevent their rising to intercept the force of B-24 aircraft. (About half of the American bomber force that had departed Italy arrived near the southern border of Germany, the others having turned back due to bad weather or aircraft malfunctions.)

The first few B-24s that broke through the clouds were immediately set upon by, according to various estimates, between 50 and 80 Me-109s and FW-190s, some firing rockets as well as machine guns. The B-24s, strung out haphazardly, were just starting to lower their ball turrets into firing position. Unfortunately, the ball turrets were not lowered in time to fire upon the German aircraft, which attacked the bombers at will from underneath. One of the B-24 pilots on the mission, whose plane was shot down during the attack, recalled the details vividly:

> All hell broke loose! The whole damn Luftwaffe had appeared out of nowhere and had singled out our flight for the first attack! I could feel our plane vibrate as all the firepower I had [front turret, tail gunner, side gunners] went to work! Tracers were flying everywhere and enemy rockets exploding all around us! Flying bits of glass and smoke filled the flight deck as bullets ricocheted off our seats! I glanced past Frisco [the co-pilot] out the right window and saw a Fock-Wulfe 190 break into smoke off my wingtip and go down in flames. Simultaneously, his buddies shot out my two left engines and then a third. I broke the formation in a steep glide to the left in an effort to tack onto the lower lead flight of the group. In the same second Art [the navigator] grabbed my arm and yelled that the bomb bay was on fire! I took a quick glance and saw a seething inferno of flame. I gave the order to abandon ship.[2]

The pilot bailed out of the aircraft and subsequently became a prisoner of war.

Fortunately for Hugo and his crew, they were not part of the first group that the Germans attacked; their aircraft followed behind the lead formation. A friend of Hugo's, a fellow bombardier, was in one of the stricken B-24s, which Hugo saw spin to its destruction in the clouds below: "He died at Odertal near the Polish border, nailed by centrifugal force to the interior of a B-24 that would never pull out of the tight spin down five miles of sky. I remember the Messerschmidts shooting into the bomber even after it was hopelessly locked in the spin. I remember my terror that day, the unbelievable number of German fighters that struck."[3] The news of the terrible B-24 losses on the mission was lost in the news about the Battle of the Bulge, which started on that date.

The impact of this and similar missions was sudden and overpowering; as he says, "I woke up one day, around my fifteenth mission, and realized I could be killed." After that point, "things were never the same."[4] As a result, "the sky became more and more frightening as I neared my thirty-fifth bombing mission."[5] Hugo was probably sharing the fear, common among aircrew members, that the odds against survival appeared to increase the closer they came to their final mission. He acknowledges that he was losing his desire to fly: "I flew because others were flying and I couldn't have faced their scorn" if he had quit.[6] It didn't help that Hugo and his crew could have been killed—but weren't—when their heavily loaded bomber crashed on takeoff, in mid-December, on the mission prior to the Odertal mission. For some amazing reason, the bombs and fuel failed to ignite during the crash, although the aircraft was totally destroyed.

Hugo's position inside the B-24 undoubtedly helped to reinforce his feeling of helplessness. Like Joseph Heller's Yossarian, the bombardier in *Catch-22*, who felt vulnerable riding in the glass nose of the medium bomber B-25 (the aircraft Heller was flying in combat in Italy at about the same time Hugo was flying in B-24s), Hugo must have felt similarly entrapped in his bombardier's position in the nose of the B-24. While early models of the B-24 featured large glass nose compartments (much larger than that of a B-25), the models in which Hugo flew had been equipped with a gun turret which fired twin .50 caliber machine guns. The base of this turret was located just above the bombardier's compartment; beneath the turret was a wide, thin glass window in the bottom front portion of the aircraft which slanted to the rear, allowing the bombardier to have a clear, if limited, view of the terrain over which the aircraft was flying. This was a desirable feature in that it allowed the bombardier to adjust the route of flight of the aircraft so that its bombs would fall on the target. The bombardier utilized a highly technical device, the Norden bomb sight, through which he could view the track of the aircraft over the earth passing below and make the necessary adjustments to ensure an accurate bomb run, using the controls of an autopilot steering mechanism located near by.

The main disadvantage of the bombardier's position was that, like the glass nose of the B-25, it was fairly vulnerable to ground or aircraft fire coming from beneath. In case of the need for an emergency exit, there would have been a struggle to move back to an escape hatch, which was the crew entrance door (or the bomb bay in flight). One of the major fears of all crew members on heavy bombers like the B-24 and B-17 was the difficulty of escape from the aircraft once it was disabled in flight; if it entered a descending spin, centrifugal forces made it nearly impossible to escape the aircraft unless the crew member was located near one of the escape exits. The fear of entrapment was felt even at the beginning of the mission, during takeoff, when the heavily loaded bombers were most vulnerable to disaster if the aircraft suffered a loss of power on takeoff. This in fact happened to Hugo and his crew, and they were fortunate to escape with minimal injuries. Although Hugo mentions this event briefly in his memoir of his wartime activities, "Ci Vediamo," his emotional reaction is impressively documented in his poem, "Where We Crashed."[7] This 115 line poem is actually short, because only thirty-five lines include more than one word. The effect is a torrent of words as the eye races down the page in a furtive attempt to establish meaningful syntax and logic. Syntax and logic are completed only at the end of the poem, when the reader discovers that no one was killed (though some were injured) as a result of the crash, as the crew members stand in a group anxiously out of breath after running from the damaged aircraft.

The poem begins in a relatively matter-of-fact manner, as Hugo (there is no doubt that he is the main character in the poem) is announcing the airspeed readings over the interphone as the aircraft gains speed on takeoff. This would have been one of the duties of the bombardier, to inform the pilots that the aircraft had attained calculated flying speed without their having to look at the airspeed indicator, their attention being occupied with maintaining visual perspective by looking out the front of the aircraft. He calls an airspeed of one hundred and thirty five knots, a rather high speed for takeoff but necessary for a heavily loaded aircraft. Something happens (we are not told what, whether an engine fails or a landing gear collapses), and the aircraft slams onto the runway. The glass windows of his bombardier's position break immediately, as the weight of the aircraft comes down on its nose. The glass breaks slowly, as if the action is occurring in a dream. As the aircraft slides along the runway, the poet thinks of its load of gas and bombs and realizes he could die in a sudden explosion.

As the aircraft continues its slide, the poet imagines the explosions (from the fire that could set off the load of bombs they carry) that will soon occur. Then he realizes that the aircraft is starting to swing as a tire comes loose and a landing gear strut drags in the ground. The aircraft turns as it slides down the runway, grinding and tearing parts of the fuselage. Then a hole opens in the side of the fuselage and the crew members force their way out of the aircraft and run into a nearby field, swearing in frustration at their slow running pace as they worry about the imminent explosions. After running a safe distance from the aircraft, the poet looks around and sees other crew members standing nearby: Stewart, the radio operator, from Klamath Falls, Oregon; O'Brien, the navigator, from Los

Angeles, with a broken foot; Knapp, the ball turret gunner; and Steinberg, the pilot, looking dazedly around him with a gray face. They are standing in the grass, in the rain, holding back the Italian farmer who ran to help them, yelling, joking, all safe. For some miraculous reason, there was no fire, no explosion, and the poet realizes that he survived without being killed. A picture of their aircraft, the "What's Up Doc," as they had named it, shows a twisted, broken, malformed wreck.

Hugo's exciting adventures in the air continued, as his crew was selected to fly a special diversionary mission to Innsbruck, while the main body of bombers was attacking Vienna. In addition to the task of steering the aircraft over the target during the final minute of the bomb run and managing the mechanisms to release the bombs, the bombardier also had the task of removing the safety pins from the miniature propeller mechanisms on each of the bombs prior to starting the run into the target. These miniature propellers would start to spin once the bombs were dropped, arming them in the air as they fell. If the pins were not removed, the bombs would not explode when they struck the earth. On this mission, when it was time to drop the bombs, the bombs did not release from the aircraft. As Hugo says, "the [bomb] racks were frozen and the bombs were stuck."[8] The aircraft was flying in clouds at an altitude of 25,000 feet with the bomb bay doors open; the moisture from the clouds had probably coated the surfaces of bombs and bomb bay with ice. In addition, Hugo's throat microphone had malfunctioned, and he had no way of telling anyone about the problem. The crew probably realized the bombs had not dropped, as the aircraft always gave a leap up when it lost the weight of the bombs.

After making his way to the pilot's compartment, he related the problem to Steinberg, the pilot, who told him to take a screwdriver and pry the bombs loose from their release shackles. This was no easy task, as it required Hugo to position himself on the bomb bay structure and reach down with one hand while the cold wind whipped into the aircraft through the open bomb bay doors:

> I wedged myself between the racks, wrapped a mugger's grip around the left rack with my left arm, and signalled the engineer to open the doors. As the doors rolled open, the blast of air into the bomb bay shocked my eyes. I'd had to leave my parachute behind because the space between the racks was too narrow, and I was standing in that roaring rush of air, one arm tight around the shackle, on about ten inches width of catwalk [the support structure over the center of the bomb bay], five miles above the earth.[9]

Just as he reached to pry the first bomb loose, they all fell from the aircraft; the navigator, O'Brien, had managed to successfully pull the emergency bomb release. Because they had been orbiting in the clouds as they attempted to work the bombs loose, they had no exact idea of their location. Hugo believes that they might even have dropped their bombs on Switzerland, a neutral country, because Innsbruck, their intended target, was only 50 miles from the Swiss border. Even though they were unsure of their bombing success, or even of their target, the officers received the Distinguished Flying Cross (DFC) for the mission (enlisted members were seldom awarded medals). Although Hugo thought that the mission did not merit the awards they received because they were unable to bomb with accuracy, he was happy to receive the medal, because "those medals and citations meant discharge points," which enabled them to leave the service sooner when the war was over.[10]

The only poem Hugo wrote in which he directly described his experiences as a bombardier on a mission was the early "Mission to Linz," which describes the events and sensations of a typical bombing mission.[11] The mission profile provides the framework, within which is included the emotional reaction to its departure and return segments. This four-part poem describes the progress of a bombing mission to Linz, Austria, a long, hazardous flight to hostile territory to the north followed by a relaxing flight south to the crew's home field. In the first part of the poem, prior to departure, the speaker imagines the flight north into enemy territory, and the long distance to be flown. His bombardier's tasks require him to become part of the mechanisms of war, like the bombs, marked with yellow bands around their green casings, and the engine components, the Pratt and Whitney engines, the Hamilton Standard propellers, and the Norden bomb sights.

The poem is about the process of remembering the mission as well as recounting its details, and its lines describe the strange impulse to recall the events of unpleasant and hazardous actions. They become a kind of refrain, marking the sequence of events in the mission. First the poet thinks of visual details, a pleasant vision of the Swiss Alps in summer, but he rejects that vision as part of the details of the poem because he thinks of it in part as a "beautiful" moment; the poem is not intended to be about pleasant moments, but about *terrible, awful* moments. Next he thinks of the sounds of the mission, the rotation of the gun turret in the nose of the aircraft, the sound of flak bursting nearby. But even these specific details are insufficient to convey the complete, nerve-wrenching personal reaction to the mission, and the poet is tasked with the challenge of representing in something like poetic form an experience that was so powerful and energy-draining that it is nearly impossible to characterize poetically.

In part two of the poem the bomber has departed and the voices of the crew members are heard as they respond to the pilot's request to provide necessary details about their oxygen supply and general condition. The aircraft form into six "boxes," or units, of six aircraft each. At their increasing altitude the sun pales in the thin air high above the Adriatic Sea. The fifty-caliber guns are test fired, as the engines generate a noise that is like a silence, a reference to the fact that the constant engine noise becomes an accepted part of their operating environment, unheard but always there.

At high altitude, it is difficult to discern movement north, although their instruments tell them that they are moving north into central Europe at a steady airspeed of 154 knots. As the aircraft passes over the high mountains of the Alps, the target area grows closer, and the poet calculates the odds of survival, estimating that they could lose three aircraft out of thirty-six. Three out of thirty-six aircraft lost would not appear to be a high loss rate, a little over 8 percent. But if every mission resulted in an 8 percent loss rate, no crew would (statistically) survive longer than twelve missions, and all would perish three times before reaching the end-of-tour goal of 35 missions. Many crew members dreaded the final missions as they neared the required number, because they believed the odds of their survival were staked impossibly high against them; the more missions they survived, the greater were the odds against their continuing survival.

Part three of the poem describes the bomb run over the city, beginning with the turn to the initial point of the run, at which point the aircraft must hold heading and altitude steady if the bombs are to be dropped accurately on the target. The aircraft must fly at a steady rate and altitude towards the target, Linz, if they hope to deliver their bombs accurately. Then the anti-aircraft fire begins; the flak explodes and the poet begins to pray as the flak bursts cause his greatest fear. He knows that a plane disappears so quickly that its disappearance might have been an illusion, except that the sudden disappearance of a bomber meant that ten men and their aircraft had been instantaneously blown into fragments.

On the eight-minute run-in to the target the crew members can tell how close the flak bursts are by the sound and feel of the bursts. Then the poet sees one of the aircraft broken in fire, an image that will remain in his memory forever, as the stricken aircraft tilts and a wing comes loose, fluttering down like a severed arm twenty-five thousand feet until it strikes the earth. The image of a bomber's metal wing, heavy with two engines, breaking off and fluttering towards the ground like a piece of paper is one that the mind cannot immediately comprehend (if it can ever be completely comprehended); nor is it possible to know the chaotic conditions inside the stricken aircraft, the struggles of the crew members inside trying to escape before the fuselage strikes the earth.

Then they are over the target and the bombs are released, falling and converging beneath them. When the bombs hit the ground below, the vision is of a puff of smoke like a small coin dropped in dry dirt, the damage done to the people on the ground as remote and as unknown as that experienced by the destroyed aircrew. Bombs gone, the aircraft dives away from the target as it races away from the target area. After the aircraft turns to the south, the poet touches himself, knowing that doing so is evidence that he is still alive.

The brief fourth and final part of the poem describes the return to the home field, to the warmer temperatures, to a friendlier earth, where, if a crew member dies, his body can be buried with appropriate if ineffectual ceremony instead of disappearing in an instant in the skies over a hostile country. On the return trip the engines have a different sound: as the aircraft descends for landing, the reduced power settings of the engines signify a safe landing at the end of the mission.

The poem effectively conveys the feeling of dread that settles over the crew members as they prepare for departure, a feeling that intensifies as the aircraft climbs for altitude to enter a hostile land bordered by mountains and clouds, natural threats against the survival of any aircraft. Then comes the bomb run to the target where the aircraft, held immobile on its predetermined track, is unable to maneuver to avoid the flak bursts. (Apparently on this mission there were no intercepting German aircraft.) Then the turn to the warmer, friendlier skies of the south, where the body begins to relax and the feeling of dread dissipates as the threats to their survival disappear behind them. The route on the map becomes symbolic, especially when it is repeated habitually: north, to a cold, hellish environment of clouds and hostile fire, then south, to a land of warming, comforting sun and the safety of solid earth.

A friend of Hugo criticized the poem because, according to Hugo, "he said I showed no awareness I was bombing people, and in a rare burst of intellectual superiority I said that's exactly the point. We were not bombing people. Towns looked as real as maps."[12] Hugo's friend had reacted to the poem much as Robert Bly reacted to James Dickey's "The Firebombing," complaining that the poet seemed to have no sense of the terrible destruction his bombs were causing. But this should not be thought of as a personal, aesthetic, or philosophical failure on the part of the poets; to have attempted to describe it from the perspective of people on the ground would have been false to the fliers' experience. Dickey and Hugo would hardly have been in a position to appreciate the damage on the ground, confined as they were in a vulnerable aircraft and susceptible to enemy attack. In such a position, under those circumstances, it would have been indeed remarkable for any crew member to dwell on thoughts other than immediate survival. If any crew member were so sensible and empathetic as to be capable of fully imagining the threats to life on the ground as well as in the air, that crew member would probably not be emotionally capable of fulfilling his crew duties for any length of time. The response to the poem that Hugo relates shows the difficulty of later, post-wartime readers trying to understand the perspective of poems written by men who experienced the war in the air, especially readers who know only of life on the ground (and perhaps who know little of combat). These readers, especially if they are poets concerned to write about the injustices of the human condition, might wish the poet had written a different poem, about the suffering on the ground, a poem they might have written, but which would have been foreign to the experiences of the men who flew in combat.

After the war ended, Hugo returned to the United States and entered the University of Washington. He received his undergraduate degree in 1948, and began course work for a master's degree. In the graduate English program at the University of Washington, he was a student in courses taught by the poet Theodore Roethke, who had a strong influence on Hugo's eventual decision to become a poet. After completing graduate work for the master's degree, he began working for the Boeing Company as a technical writer, a job he held for over ten years. In 1961 A Run of Jacks, his first volume of poetry, was published, and the success of this volume convinced him to become a poet. In 1963 he left the Boeing Company to spend a year in Italy with his wife; upon his return, he accepted a position in the Department of English in the University of Montana at Missoula, an institution with which he remained affiliated until his death from leukemia in 1983. In 1967 he visited Italy again, alone this time, "revisiting a land he had known first in its grim sadness" where he discovered "something about the value of emotional openness and the strength that it represents" for a poet.[13] The result of his visit to Italy was his third book of poetry, *Good Luck in Cracked Italian* (1969), which contains the best and most enduring poetry about his wartime experiences.

"Docking at Palermo," the first poem in the book's opening section, "Where All the Doors Open In," describes his arrival in Palermo, Sicily, and establishes the elegiac, emotional mood for most of the poems that will follow.[14] Although Hugo was never in Palermo during the war, he knew of its military significance. As he enters an area of significant military activity on his way to Italy, he concludes with the thought that now that he is returning as a non-combatant, he will be able to experience the country with a more personal perspective, one reflecting a profound sadness as he thinks of the men who died and the conditions under which they flew and lived.

When he arrives in Naples ("Napoli Again") he recalls his time there during the war when he departed Italy for his return to the United States. He visits the Galleria, where he sees that the shattered glass of his wartime visit has been replaced, and he pays inflated prices for his cappuccino.[15] When he sat in the Galleria twenty years earlier, he was wearing his uniform with his silver bombardier's wings, characterized by a bomb poised over a target framed by wings.

Not every poem in *Cracked Italian* involves reflections about the war. But whether he is in Venice ("The Bridge of Sighs"), Padua ("Galileo's Chair," "Morning in Padova"), or Rome ("Castel Sant' Angelo"), he is constantly evaluating the achievements of the past through the perspective of the present, a pattern of looking with a historical framework that he carries into his war-related poems.

The twelve poems of the second section of the book, "Side Trips Back," are directly about Hugo's wartime experiences in Italy. In the first poem in this section, "G.I. Graves in Tuscany," Hugo considers the loss of lives the war caused, remembering long lines of American bombers on their way to attack and return from enemy targets.[16] But images of the war from an airborne perspective are not what he wants to think about; he wishes instead to think of Italy itself, the land from which he departed and to which he returned when he flew his missions.

As he travels through Italy, Hugo detects some animosity against Germans, and he worries that his name will create a hostile reaction. (His family had come from Germany two generations earlier.) When he shows his American passport, however, the reaction is positive, and the Italians seem happy to see him. When he witnesses an ill-planned ceremony for the war dead ("Viva La Resistenza"), he is soured by the false sense of patriotism it is designed to inspire. When he visits Cerignola ("April in Cerignola"), the town he and other flyers often visited for relaxation during the war, he notes that neither the iron grillwork nor the spring season he now sees was here during the war. Visions of the past and present mix: he sees the towns and villages as they were when he was there, not as they are now. There were no men then, and the women hid behind walls with bullet holes in them. The poem suggests T. S. Eliot's famous line, "April is the cruelest month," in its opening and closing lines.[17] Hugo never knew Italy in the spring, his tour of duty having run from August until March; his return to the location of his wartime flying location combines reflections on the deaths of his fellow flyers with the greening of the earth.

In "Tretitoli, Where the Bomb Group Was," Hugo's double vision of the past laid over the present is the main theme of the poem: he views the modern scene with eyes conditioned to remember what it looked like during the war. The nuns are teaching school in a building which the flying crews used as a mess hall, forcing down powdered eggs and Spam as they worried about the hazards of their next target. He thinks of the fliers who perished, especially on the terrifying mission to Odertal, and of their various good-luck routines before the flight.[18] The poet recalls singing dirty songs in the building which the nuns now use for their school, where twenty years earlier he was receiving an education of another sort. He sees farmlands now where there were none before, and thinks of the three women who gave most of the members of the squadron venereal disease, and especially of his strong desire then to walk away from the war across the plains of Italy. It is impossible for him to see the land as it currently exists without superimposing on it his remembered visions of the past: the squadron huts and tents, the location of the parking area for trucks, the bomb dump; even the runway he knew so well is gone, and he has to guess at its location.[19] "Where We Crashed," previously discussed, appears next in the sequence of poems in this section. It serves to mark the poet's complete return to the past, as it tells the story of the nearly catastrophic event ever-present in the poet's mind, framed by opening and closing statements in the past tense, first calling the airspeed for takeoff, and then, brief moments later, standing outside the wrecked aircraft, still in shock, beginning to realize that he was still alive when he could just as easily have been killed in the accident.

"*Spinazzola*: Quella Cantina La" is the central poem of this section. In this poem Hugo describes an incident that happened to him during the war when, by following directions confusedly after visiting a friend at a distant airfield, he found himself in a field of grass outside a town called Spinazzola, far from his intended destination and far from his flying field.[20] While resting in this field he experienced a sense of release from the war that somehow allowed him to deal temporarily with the stresses of flying. In the field, he watched the grain ripple in the wind like waves in a sea. During the war he had been strongly affected as a result of watching the play of the wind on the grain and had momentarily lost his desire to return to his base. He wrote two poems about this experience; the first was "Centuries Near Spinnazola," published in *A Run of Jacks*. He later thought that this poem failed "miserably."[21] "Centuries" is more concerned with fitting Hugo's moment in the field of grass into the general course of war beginning with the time of the Greeks (Sardis and Xerxes). It describes the misguided impulse of war as perceived in the public mind, from which the poet wishes to distance himself. The event in the field serves as little more than an entry into the larger topic of public perception of war.

"*Spinazzola*: Quella Cantina La," the later poem about this experience, is about the event itself and what it meant to Hugo, about how it served to focus on the emotional impact of the war on the poet. The tone of the poem is established in the opening lines, describing how the flow of the wind seemed to carry him away from the pressures of flying in combat; it seems deliberately to contrast itself to the earlier poem. He thinks now of how the wind blowing across the grain suggests to him the forces of war affecting the lives of the men who must fight it; they are moved by a force much greater than their individual wills to resist it or to do anything but move as the forces drive them. He is at a loss to explain how that image is so powerfully suggestive of the situation in which he found himself at the time. The poet is unable to explain how these various elements—the wind, the wine, the drone of bombers, the sun—created such an unusually strong impression on his mind, then as now. The poem explains what the poet cannot explain, about how the pressures of flying in combat in a hazardous environment cause emotional distress. The images in the poem are mixed; he can't explain what their meaning is, but he does know that all are important and interconnected. His memory, he says, has been weakened, made more fragile, by the recollection of his wartime experiences.[22]

Although aircraft engines should make the same sound at any part of the flight (so the poet thinks), the engines seem to create a much louder noise when they fly towards the target than they do afterwards, as the plane returns to the home airfield. The descriptive terms in the poem convey the emotional impact of each aspect of flight. As the poet sits in the cantina in Spinazzola drinking wine, remembering the experience, all scenes and locations merge: the cantina, the field, the airfield, the aircraft, one vision shifting over another, mixing together, like ripples across the field of grain. He imagines the waiter serving him wine until the last bombers, lost twenty years earlier, return home.[23]

The lost bomber fleet represents the past experiences of Hugo the former flier as well as the planes and fliers lost during the war. Hugo's image of lost bombers returning to their home base is similar to John Ciardi's image, in "V-J Day," of all the bombers that ever departed the island of Saipan returning, landing gear jammed, unable to land. This poem serves as the emotional pivot of the book, as it effectively combines the present peaceful environment with past images and sensations of war seen through the perspective of a man who is able to see the present only through the eyes of the past.

Seemingly, every place in Italy carries memories of the war for Hugo; when he visits the island of Capri, he recalls sharing a meal with a friend, Richard Ryan, a week before Ryan ditched in the Adriatic Sea, in "Note from Capri to Richard Ryan on the Adriatic Floor." Angry at the foolish loss (as Hugo sees it) of a friend when he tried to land the aircraft in the waters of the Adriatic instead of trying to land on the mainland, Hugo tries to imagine what his friend now looks like now, bones resting on the ocean floor, among the barnacles and eels. The poem concludes as the poet sits on the rocks, looking angrily at the sea.[24]

The final three poems in this section ("The Yards of Sarajevo," "Paestum," and "Galleria Umberto I") mark the poet's movement out of his consideration of his wartime experiences. Sarajevo is one of the targets Hugo and his crew bombed during the war; it is also the city which could be said to have started World War I, where the assassination of Archduke Ferdinand occurred. Most historians agree that World War II was the continuation of issues World War I did not settle. "Paestum" describes an ancient Greek site, south of Salerno, where in 1943 a Red Cross station was established to treat the wounded; when Hugo visits the site it has become commercialized. In "Galleria Umberto I" Hugo returns to Naples, the Italian city where he began his wartime revisitation travels; there he pays another visit to the Galleria, now fully repaired after the war. Acknowledging the fine literary effort to describe the symbolism of the Galleria in John Horne Burns' novel *The Galleria*, Hugo sums up the participants' attitude towards war. Don't blame us, the participants, for our actions, he says; we were just doing what we were told, trying to survive.[25]

The final two sections of *Cracked Italian*, "Maratea" and "Remote or Stone," describe other aspects of Italian life that Hugo noted during his stay. Although these poems are not about the war, echoes of the war are heard in their characters (the man at Maratea, who lost an arm at Tobruk), settings ("Montesano Unvisited"), or theme ("Pizzeria S. Biagio"). We also learn the significance of saying good-bye in cracked Italian: as Hugo takes leave of the Vitolo family, his hosts in Italy, we understand that his "cracked Italian" is both ineptitude with the local language and his deep-seated sadness as he says goodbye.[26]

It is worth noting that Hugo's second trip to Italy and the publication of *Cracked Italian* occurred during the tumultuous years of changing American attitudes towards the war in Vietnam (1967–1969). It may well be that popular demonstrations of American angst over an unpopular war and awareness of the imperfect adjustments of returning soldiers might have helped to push Hugo towards his determination to revisit his own war experiences and work towards some resolution of their impact on him.

Although *Good-Bye in Cracked Italian* can be considered primarily about Hugo's war experiences and his efforts to interpret them, the effects of the war continued to find their way into his poems from the beginning until the end of his poetic career. Wartime contexts or references to flying appear early in his poetry, in "Memoirs," in *A Run of Jacks*, and in "Antiques in Ellettsville" and "Fort Casey, without Guns" in *Death of the Kapowsin Tavern*. In addition, in both of these books bird flight is an important symbolic aspect in many of the poems.

In "Flying, Reflying, Farming" (in *What Thou Lovest Well Remains American*, 1975), the poet is traveling across the countryside in a commercial airliner, flying high over the ground. When the airplane groans and bounces, he is reminded of his experience during the war when he saw an aircraft flip on its side as a wing broke loose, and he recalls his profoundly disturbing sense of fear and distress at seeing that sight.[27] After the airplane descends and lands, the poet recalls how, thirty years earlier, he and his crew members had laughed and congratulated themselves after surviving another tough mission.

His 1977 *31 Letters and 13 Dreams* was published after he suffered a nervous breakdown while he was a visiting professor at the University of Iowa.[28] While the *Letters* poems show a man communicating earnestly with his friends about the inspiration and achievements of poetry, the *Dreams* poems show a kaleidoscope of seemingly disconnected images that his subconscious is attempting to organize. When wartime images reappear, they are typically associated with anxiety and fear. "In Your War Dream" opens as he dreams he has to fly his wartime bombing missions again. He dreams that he is back at his Italian airfield, eating bad food and worrying about whether or not he will survive the mission.[29]

In another dream poem, "In Your Big Dream," he imagines he is climbing above the clouds, higher than the birds, to a place where he feels at home. And in "Here, but Unable to Answer," one of Hugo's last poems, written to his stepfather, Herbert Hugo, he compares his stepfather's desire to serve in World War I to his own service, concluding with a restatement of what has by now become a familiar theme, the profound disruption of his mental equilibrium caused by his wartime experiences: the memories of hazardous flying, bad nerves, his hands "still trembling with sky, that deafening dream exploding me awake."[30]

Clearly, Hugo's wartime experiences disturbed him well past the time his service ended. The eight-month period from August 1944 until March 1945 stamped his psyche as no other during his lifetime. It is as if, having seen too much in that short time, his unconscious and subconscious unpacked those impressions over the remaining thirty-seven years of his life.

9
Lincoln Kirstein, U.S. Army

Lincoln Kirstein is both an anomaly and a touchstone in this collection of assessments: the least poet of the eight poets considered here, he produced the most important single book of poetry about the war, *Rhymes of a Pfc*. Thirty-five years in the making, *Rhymes of a Pfc* constitutes the most comprehensive verse history of the World War II army experience. While no one poem in the collection stands out with the distinctiveness of a poem like Jarrell's "Death of the Ball Turret Gunner" or Dickey's "Performance" or Meredith's "Love Letter from an Impossible Land," the total effect of the 95 poems in *Rhymes of a Pfc* is truly impressive. Indeed, one reason why few poems stand out in the collection is that all the poems demonstrate an exceptionally high level of poetic achievement.

Kirstein is best known for his publications about ballet, especially for his work with the New York City Ballet. But throughout his varied and energetic career in the arts, he was consistently occupied with artistic expression in the written word as well. Although Kirstein's first book of poetry, *Low Ceiling*, appeared in 1935, several years before the first books of Jarrell, Ciardi, or Shapiro, in later years Kirstein seems to have completely disregarded the book, failing to include any of the poems (or even mention the title) in his *Collected Poems*. But his *Collected Poems* includes all of the poems in *Rhymes of a Pfc*.

The poems of *Rhymes of a Pfc* are frequently comic, even incongruous, in their effect, because they exactly catch the rugged, earthy flavor of the wartime experience from the viewpoint of the soldier. Their rich mixture of narrative personas and metrical schemes effectively captures the humor and experience of World War II army life, at least as it was lived behind the lines. The intellectual content of the poems is enhanced by the personalities of the personas of the poems as well as their form and content, for many of the individual poems are told from the perspective of a variety of participants in the war, told in a personal and engaging manner.

The primary voice is, of course, that of the poet himself. But there are other personas as well, voices of soldiers and civilians, enlisted men and officers. The cumulative effect of the voices is to lend a credibility and emotional impact to a series of poetic accounts that in the hands of another poet might have added up to a dry, abstract assessment of the events encountered along the way to war and back.

In its final version, *Rhymes of a Pfc* is a collection of 95 poems describing the poet's progress through the phases of preparation for and participation in various aspects of the ground war in Europe. Although few describe combat directly—Kirstein was not an infantryman—the poems provide an accurate and unified vision of the war. No two poems are exactly the same: each employs a different meter, rhyme scheme, or verse development; each describes events from a new perspective, often in the words or thoughts of new and unique characters. They are similar to a collection of snapshots in a photograph album, some taken in training, some en route, some on the European battleground, some after the war, all contributing to a complete visual catalog of the war. *Rhymes of a Pfc* creates a series of striking visual portraits, of the poet, of individuals, of groups of men and women caught up in the war, in scenes set from Virginia to England to France to Germany. It is a verbal photograph album of a GI's war, and Kirstein is the photographer. This effect is not accidental, as we can see as we discover the details of Kirstein's background.

Named after Abraham Lincoln, Kirstein was raised in Boston in a culturally important and affluent family. His father was president of the Boston Public Library as well as an important corporate officer in Filene's department store. Kirstein graduated from Harvard University in 1930, where he made the acquaintance of fellow students James Agee and Walker Evans, and studied under such distinguished teachers as Alfred North Whitehead and John Livingston Lowes. At Harvard he was one of the founders of the *Hound & Horn*, a well-received literary quarterly. He published a novel, *Flesh Is Heir*, in 1930, and a history of classical dancing (*Dance: A Short History of Classic Theatrical Dancing*) in 1935. *Dance* was reprinted frequently and remains the definitive work on the subject. At Harvard he developed an interest in art and photography (he had written on El Greco). He had, he says, "a small talent for drawing" and at one time thought he "might as well become a portrait painter."[1]

In recounting the genesis of *Flesh Is Heir*, he says:

> I wanted my novel to be illustrated by actual photographs, of scenes and persons I'd known, transposed for the sake of decency into a typological gallery. These would not have been literal portraits but symbolic snapshots suggesting an immediacy of time, place, and person with a fresh candor. I strove for a

"photographic" atmosphere, which would be at once hard focus but stereoscopic.[2]

Referring to *Flesh Is Heir* and *Rhymes of a Pfc*, he added, "both might have been illustrated by photographs."[3] His association with James Agee, with whom he perused photographs in magazines in Harvard's Widener Library, and his walks with Walker Evans, who photographed many of the older homes of Boston in Kirstein's company, added to his appreciation of the fundamentals of grouping, setting, and detail, so important to the poems of *Rhymes*. As he studied the art of photography, so too did he study the art of poetry.

Kirstein tells us that the poems in *Rhymes* were not produced intact during the wartime period: "the one writing here is not he who jotted jingles in Normandy, Lorraine or Bavaria. The residue is a product of thirty-five years, dating from 1943, into the present decade."[4] The poems are based on the practices and achievements of important poets in the American and English poetic tradition. Kirstein acknowledges sources whose poetry or poetic theory directly influenced him: Henry James, Gerard Manley Hopkins, T. S. Eliot, Walt Whitman, Marianne Moore, W. H. Auden, and especially Rudyard Kipling. As Kirstein says, "for me, Kipling was a far more masterful model than Clough, Tennyson, or Browning. For metrical music, ... [Kipling] stands with Hopkins and Auden as a lord of the English language."[5] Inspired by Kipling's model, Kirstein "aimed to compose a sequence of narrative verse, hopefully, neither careless nor monotonous, borrowing from common parlance its coarse-grained savor."[6] To Kirstein the poetic mode of Kipling, whose poetry helped to establish the pattern for much of the popular poetry of World War I, was appropriate as a model for the poetry of World War II as well; Kirstein's challenge was to modify the models of Kipling to meet the conditions of an army made up of members of a later generation.

His solution was to adapt the varied metrical patterns and rhyme schemes of Kipling according to models demonstrated by Auden and Hopkins, also masters of meter and rhyme. From Kipling he learned also to adapt the everyday language of the worker to poetic form. From Hopkins he learned to match metrical form to religious thought and enjambment, and from Auden he borrowed tone of voice and intellectual action as a substitute for the physical action of Kipling. Of course he borrowed or incorporated the ideas of other poets as well, especially Eliot and Moore. The result of these modifications is a body of poetry that combines meter and rhyme with processes of meditation and introspection. These poetic models are ingredients in Kirstein's poetic plan, which includes assessment of the historical events in the war, like the Normandy invasion, the attack on Saint-Lô, the Battle of the Bulge, or the capture of Hermann Göring.

In the years before the war, Kirstein traveled to South America, officially as the coordinator and manager of a touring American ballet troupe, and unofficially as someone taking the political pulse of the countries through which the troupe moved, reporting his observations to his Harvard friend, Nelson Rockefeller. Rockefeller was concerned that the American attitude towards war events in Europe was not being shared or supported by many Latin American countries. Kirstein's reports gave Rockefeller honest personal assessments of a kind not to be obtained through official diplomatic channels. As a result of these activities, Kirstein was able to delay his entry into the armed forces, though he was not in any way reluctant to enter military service.

Kirstein was eventually inducted into the army in February of 1943. Although he had hoped to work in the area of intelligence and counterespionage, he trained with the Army Corps of Engineers at Fort Belvoir, Virginia.[7] While he was in training, he wrote to a friend in New York City:

> I find the army a mystical experience. You advance through purgatory with your eyes open and it's no dream.... I got here on a fluke. I am about as equipped to build bridges, roads etc as to train lions. It's awful to think that the boys here are so kind and generous in barracks and so uninterested in their largely irrelevant fates. Anyway I meditate constantly and I am in good muscular condition physically and morally. I find I'm being propelled into being an officer or at least going to officer's school. I have no desire to command or fight or interest in engineering. But I find that unfortunately you can do almost anything and that your interest is a luxury which is strictly rationed....[8]
>
> I am now stationed at Fort Belvoir for two months. I have been training with a regular combat battalion. Now we are on advanced maneuvers—bridges, demolitions and night problems. I won't pretend I'm a good soldier nor would I have ever volunteered or accepted a commission. But being an anonymous recruit has certain compensations. I can shoot a rifle and do many physical things that I never thought possible.[9]

As his training draws to an end, he writes, "My future is obscure. I'm too old for specialist training, not effective as officer material—so I don't know what will become of me. I find little waste in the army so I'm not over worried."[10]

According to David Leddick, Kirstein was denied the possibility of a commission in the armed services as a result of the unofficial surveillance of U.S. diplomatic activities he had undertaken during his 1942 South American visit on behalf of Nelson Rockefeller.[11] Kirstein eventually found a home in the army as a member of the U.S. Arts and Monuments Commission, a group whose primary task was to track and recover important works of art that had been removed and placed in hiding by a number of high-ranking German officers, chief among whom was Hermann Göring. Although Kirstein's low military rank initially created a problem, his influential political friends were able to convince the approving authorities that Kirstein's knowledge of and involvement in the arts qualified him for the job, and early in June 1944 Kirstein left for England, the first stop in his work on the Arts and Monuments Commission.[12]

Kirstein's role in the war was atypical; college educated but in the enlisted ranks, he was able to obtain some maneuverability in an army that was unsure of what to do with him:

> To me, already thirty-six, war was largely didactic. I'd had Harvard, spoke French, some German, and held no rank. Since I never sewed my single stripe on a sleeve, since duties were those of courier, driver or interpreter, external signs of authority were not obligatory. A sly fellow with determination could easily pass where disoriented superior officers might be hindered. In volatile areas there was often no occasion to brandish credentials, so one moved freely in restricted zones.[13]

The combination of age, education, experience, language skills, and (ironically) low rank enabled Kirstein to move about behind the front lines in Europe with relative ease, encountering individuals and witnessing events that eventually formed the core episodes described in *Rhymes of a Pfc*. He seems not to have been unduly disappointed by his low status in the army; certainly that status did not lessen his ability to travel and to meet and interact with important figures like Generals George Patton and Lucius Clay. Although it was reasonably simple for men with homosexual urges to avoid military service, as Leddick observes,[14] Kirstein did not do so. It was important to him to participate as a member of the armed forces. Certainly his education and his age gave him the perspective and the self-awareness necessary for detached observation of the events of the war.

The poems in *Rhymes* reflect Kirstein's physical mobility during the war as well as his poetic license: they are varied, energetic, unpredictable, kaleidoscopic, full of army slang, describing a wide range of scenes and events. They are as technically amazing as they are intellectually engaging. Vernon Scannell was one of the first to appreciate Kirstein's poetic mastery, calling *Rhymes of a Pfc* "the most original volume to be inspired by the Second World War."[15] Scannell especially admired "the speech rhythms, the witty and vigorous employment of invective and profanity, [and] the muscularity and sheer energy of the writing."[16]

Rhymes of a Pfc was first published by New Directions in 1964 as a collection of 65 poems; a second edition, containing 85 poems, appeared two years later. The final edition, with ten new poems, was published by David Godine in 1981. Twenty of the thirty poems added between 1964 and 1981 describe events and scenes in France and Germany (11 and 9 new poems each). The poems added later are specifically about two topics: impact of the war on fine arts (a logical result of his war efforts to recover stolen art) and the effort to capture lived experience in poetic form.

That Kirstein felt moved to add these poems demonstrates his concern that *Rhymes* be as complete a poetic statement as he could make about his participation in the war. At some point Kirstein must have decided that these poems would constitute a record of what was to him an important phase in his life, his life in the army, and that they would stand as a complete artistic document, different in form, but similar in spirit, to other documents that described important periods in his life, like *Mosaics*, *Quarry*, and *Flesh Is Heir*. The later poems contain elements of greater philosophic complexity and depth than many of the poems in the early edition. Kirstein also provided in his third and final version a set of notes designed to explain some of the technical terms and army jargon found in the poems and to give the historical context of some of the events. These notes are helpful as well in giving a clearer understanding of Kirstein's purpose in creating his comprehensive poetic survey of the war in Europe.

Kirstein's poems are typically told from one of three viewpoints: that of the poet himself, that of other individuals who describe experiences similar to those the poet might have known, and that of an independent, detached observer. This is not to suggest that Kirstein developed *Rhymes* according to a formula, but rather that he was concerned about balancing three visions: one of himself as poet, one of others in the military or combat environment, and one encompassing other general impressions. Generally, there is an equal division among those poems in which Kirstein appears as persona (an undisguised "I" as speaker) and those poems in which other characters either narrate or occupy the focal point of the action of the poem. The focus on individuals who were a part of the war effort is a logical outgrowth of Kirstein's interest in the individual rather than the group or philosophical conflicts illustrated by the war.

The initial poems describe Kirstein's experiences as a recruit and novice in the army; once his initiation is complete, however, the poems include an increasing number of new narrative personas from whose point of view events along the path to combat are presented. Kirstein broadens the scope of experience as seen through the perceptions of others, and the impressions become those of the full range of individuals caught up in the war; as a result, the vision of the war takes on a universal perspective as opposed to the unique perspective of the poet. Of course the poems are entirely the result of Kirstein's mind, but the truths of the various viewpoints are validated by their variety, by their details, and by the fundamental human sensations they depict. Their believability is necessary if one is to trust them as representative pictures of the wartime experience, an effect Kirstein clearly desires. But just as he is interested in establishing their validity as true visions of the wartime experience, he is also concerned with establishing another kind of truth: the centrality of poetry as a means of capturing and representing these experiences.

Kirstein's emphasis on the special importance of poetic expression as a means of conveying essential insights about wartime experience is developed through the gradual inclusion of poems which feature poetry in their subject matter as well as style. While any poem inherently displays a theory of poetry, three poems in *Rhymes* are specifically about poetry as a form for interpreting wartime experience: "Tudoresque," "Inter-Service," and "Siegfriedslage." Those poems appear in the later sections of the book, after the personal viewpoints have been established. Kirstein's purpose in addressing the nature of poetry is twofold: to reaffirm its value as a mode of wartime experience, and to establish the volume's continuity with and development from earlier representations of war poetry, especially that poetry produced by the British war poets of World War I, whose work he knew well.

Kirstein begins his sequence with a brief introductory section (*World War I*) in which he establishes his personal perspective and identifies the events in his youth which predisposed him to accept army service in World War II. He is the narrator and chief figure in each of the three poems in this section. These first poems tell us much about Kirstein's personal history, about his literal baptism into manhood, when his uncle introduces him into the world of men, swimming nude in the Boston YMCA (in "Fall In"); as he follows a shell-shocked veteran of World War I around at night ("ABC"); and as he is initiated into homosexual experience as a child while older Americans are participating in the war in Europe ("World War I"). These three poems establish the patterns of the awareness of war and the homoerotic impulse which frequently appear later in poems directly about Kirstein's experiences.

A kind of thesis statement for Kirstein's personal perspective on the individual's ability to respond to the pressures of war is presented in the initial poem, "Fall In"; after nearly drowning in the YMCA pool into which his uncle urged him, he recognizes that although he failed to swim successfully, his uncle is equally, if not more, at fault for forcing Kirstein into the pool: "He knew I knew who'd flunked his foolish test." The episode gives Kirstein one of the key premises on which his war poems are based:

> The rage of armies is the shame of boys;
> A hero's panic or a coward's whim
> Is triggered by nerve or nervousness.
> We wish to sink. We do not choose to swim.[17]

The first four poems in the next section, *Stateside*, describe Kirstein's experiences in the initial phases of military indoctrination; their titles are essentially self-descriptive: "Basic Training," "Barracks," "Map & Compass," "Cadets." Then come four poems which feature distinct, unique character voices. "Top Kick" describes a First Sergeant who worries about his physical frailty. In "4F," an individual working for the Luce publications (*Time* and *Life*) attempts to rationalize his non-participation as a soldier. "Gloria" is a comic epic of a female impersonator who convinces the navy authorities that a navy friend is not a homosexual. "Syko" is a showpiece of poetic technique in which a distraught soldier describes his Section 8 discharge (for psychiatric causes), managing to express his story in meter and rhyme even as his power of coherent expression erodes.

In addition to depicting a variety of types caught up in the movement towards war, Kirstein shows that all share the common disadvantage of a lack of ability to deal adequately with the war. This trait is evident in nearly every poem in every section, from training to combat. Central to this second section are descriptions of homoerotic experiences, an essential part of Kirstein's preliminary military environment. The importance of these episodes for Kirstein is established by the introduction of homosexual behavior in the opening section. The effect of Kirstein's emphasis on homoerotic behavior suggests that it was an important aspect of military life for a significant number of recruits as well. This aspect of Kirstein's poems was noted by Vernon Scannell, who commented, "Nowhere else in poetry have I read such frank and penetrating examinations of that special sexuality fostered by the conditions of military life, the licence extended by the imminence of violent death, and the disturbing relationship between intense physical fear and erotic desire."[18] The most important perspective established in this section is that the pressures of the inevitable transfer to a combat environment create complex stresses which are depicted in the personalities and actions of the people described in the poems.

The poems in the third section, *U.K.*, continue the motif of mental preparation for the war combined with a considered examination of the effects of the war on the English people. Appropriately, the eleven poems in this section are more or less evenly divided between those reflecting Kirstein's experiences ("Convoy," "Troop Train," "Pub," "Evensong," and "Riverscape"), and those demonstrating the perspectives of other individuals ("Tea," "Engineer," "Boy Scout," "Bobby," and "Junior"). As his military experience increases, his cast of character-participants increases also.

If the previous section heavily emphasized the sexuality of men preparing for war, sexual attraction is almost entirely missing here. Instead, this section is devoted largely to matters of the intellect, represented primarily through the long central poem, "Tudoresque." This poem describes Kirstein's reaction to this wartime visit to England, a country envisioned in his youth through the imaginative readings of Shakespeare that he shared with fellow Harvard undergraduate James Agee and through their viewing of the pictures of World War I in the *Illustrated London News* which they saw in Harvard's Widener Library. Though end rhymed and meter measured, this poem is in a way one of the least poetic in the book. It is also one of the most directly personal. In it Kirstein describes the visions of an heroic England that he and Agee shared through their readings of Shakespeare's history plays and their fascination with the characters of Bolingbroke, Prince Hal, and Hotspur.[19]

At Harvard, Kirstein developed an appreciation for combat experiences as expressed in poetic form, especially through the concept of the ideal soldier-king as represented in Shakespeare's *Henry IV* (parts 1 and 2) and *Henry V*. Kirstein now sees an England in which war is real, in which the ideas presented in Shakespeare's plays can be compared with the actions and demeanor of the English people. He concludes the poem with an account of a visit to a London theater to see John Gielgud's *Hamlet*, in which Peggy Ashcroft played Ophelia with a hand wounded by debris from a flying bomb. Kirstein's Harvard impressions have been significantly altered, and he sees, like Hamlet, the characters of Rosencrantz and Guildenstern as symbols of a youthful life that cannot be regained.[20]

This long, loose poem establishes an important theme: the poet's attempt to synthesize the events and impressions of the war in terms of both personal experience and the poetic tradition. In this poem, Kirstein explores the ability of poetic tradition to adequately convey the truths of war. His immediate problem is to adjust his perspective of the truths with which war poetry engages. The special historical framework of Shakespeare's history plays, while instructive, does not really offer helpful answers to the problems of war. *Hamlet*'s message is, as Hamlet, says, "ripeness is all." Simultaneously with offering his personal vision, as expressed in the Kirstein persona and the personas of other characters, he attempts to establish a poetic interpretation of the war, especially the effort and challenge associated with capturing the poetic essence of a topic basically at odds with poetic expression. He begins to see that although there may be little coherence or continuity in art's efforts during wartime, artists have no choice but to make the effort.

By January of 1945, Kirstein was in France, assigned as an assistant to the monuments officer of fellow Bostonian George Patton's 3rd Army.[21] The *France* section of *Rhymes* is the first of the three combat-related sections; the poems in this section provide character sketches of a variety of men, officers as well as enlisted, and of their experiences of the war. One of the individuals described is a major from Mississippi who discovers to his surprise that the brick he uses in the construction of his personal fireplace is abandoned German dynamite ("Chimbly"). Others include a captain who finds it more difficult to communicate with a French woman than to parachute into German-held land ("Chateau"); a colonel who is caught up in an American brawl over scarce gasoline supplies ("Hijack"); black soldiers in a white man's war ("Black Joe"); and Red Cross workers providing an impersonal but touching glimpse of a far-away America ("Red Cross"):

> Standing in line, three hundred joes grin boylike and self-consciously,
> Nudging the quicker ones ahead step up for doughnut and coffee.
>   Doughnuts are tender cakes with holes which Yankee maids of standards pure
>   Substitute symbolically for many acts they mayn't endure.[22]

In this section too is Kirstein's sympathetic poetic portrait of General Patton ("Patton"), whom Kirstein encountered while driving a chaplain to the Third Army Headquarters for a conference. After the conference ends, Patton invites Kirstein to share some hot tea with whisky, which "Nurse" will provide.

> "Chaplain says you come from Boston. Then you know it is my home;
> Now both of us are many miles from Bulfinch's golden dome.
> By springtime it is where I hope the both of us may come
> Provided we ain't dead."

When Patton's vehicle overturned a year later, killing him, Kirstein says that he thinks of him "as a saint."[23] This poem illustrates Kirstein's gift for capturing the vernacular of his speakers, famous or less well known, and placing their language within a regularized poetic framework.

The *France* section is unusual too in that poems representing the perspectives of other characters outnumber those told from Kirstein's persona. It is as if the story of the war in France has priority over Kirstein's individual description. The events and experiences are too varied and too unusual to be compassed within the purview of one individual. Here Kirstein witnesses the effects of the war: air strikes, dead animals, burned-out tanks, displaced persons. Kirstein most clearly depicts the action of the war that is surrounding him, and of which he is most often an interested but essentially powerless observer. The best example of such a poem is "Air Strike," an effective combination of image and assessment:

> Abruptly from out our west, heralded by a droning hive,
> Swept over level throbbing air, the stinging squadrons, death alive.
> Hand upon hip in proud amaze, soldiers dropped hatchet, nail, and saw:
> Four thousand planes roared overhead. We all were speechless in our awe
> Of Yaveh, Thunderer, Battle God, who in His just, avenging wrath
> Hath lent us much materiel bigger and better than Jerry hath.[24]

The poet ponders the meaning of the vision of a sky full of bombers: the support personnel required, the cost of such a fleet, the morality of bombing, the politics of war. But the final meaning of the vision is most directly expressed in subsequent events:

> But at the morrow's trumpet-sun, the big guns sounded strong and slow.
> We'd cracked their salient, and we were some kilometers past St. Lo.

The one poem in this section in which poetry is the main topic is more about a specific volume of poetry rather than the art of poetry, but the importance of that volume and its appearance in the narrative at this point underscore the enduring value of poetry. The poem, "Inter-Service," begins as a complaint about the unhappy side effects of Eisenhower's directive to integrate soldiers of the British and American armies. Kirstein, as narrator of the poem, complains of the ways in which an upper-class British officer (actually a Scot) unfairly usurps the American enlisted men's water and bivouac area. This intruding British officer represents practically every injustice visited on the American enlisted men, and they are prepared to hate him wholeheartedly until they discover the book the British officer reads for relaxation: the *Oxford Book of English Verse*.[25]

To Kirstein the *Oxford Book of English Verse* represents the poems and achievements of those English poets who have most affected his poetic outlook, and it makes little difference to him which poems the Scots officer is reading. More importantly, however, a link to the poets of World War I is established. The book represents some of the key British poets who wrote of World War I: Wilfred Owen, David Jones, Siegfried Sassoon. These poets were able to "purge the curse of class," and "honored their General Staffs in style" by penning indictments of the system that bought about the deaths of so many men in the trenches in World War I. Kirstein is aware of the physical and mental damage that war brought to these poets (Owen was killed; Sassoon suffered a mental breakdown; Jones was wounded; other important British soldier poets suffered similar fates).

The poems in this section begin to develop a sense of the strangeness of war, as Kirstein describes towns, buildings, and estates, which serve as settings against which the tales of the war are told. Increasingly in this section the poet assesses the effects of the war on the French people and on the structures which represent not just the French culture but the larger European culture: architecture, art, music. The effects of the war are described indirectly, as increasingly the poems of this section deal with native inhabitants and locales, as in "Lucky Pierre," "Chateau," "School," "Interpreter," "Snatch," "Zone," "Trinity." Of 41 poems in this section, the longest in the book, twelve address, directly or indirectly, these issues.

Two of the central poems in this section, "Comité des Forges" and "Reveillon," directly address the ambiguous nature of the effects of war. In "Comité," army artillery strangely avoids the direct destruction of an ironworks center controlled by an international cartel, and the poem juxtaposes the intentional avoidance of a facility normally targeted for destruction with images of townspeople threatened by small arms fire. In "Reveillon," the poet shares a New Year's Eve with a widowed upper-class mother whose son has inexplicably leapt to his death. The sexuality of the earlier poems expands in this section to describe heterosexual as well as homosexual love. The cast of characters involved in war activities includes civilians as well as soldiers, women as well as men. The war is near, and its effects are often threatening, as when the poet describes a night attack by German aircraft ("Bedcheck"), the harassing fire of a distant German gun that is linked to homosexual urges ("Load"), or his visit to a burned-out German tank ("Guts").

In the *Germany* section of *Rhymes of a Pfc*, the war is close and the effects of the war more disturbing and complex. The action of the war itself is shown vividly and dramatically in "4th Armored," which was, as he relates in his notes, told to him by an infantryman, an Iowa farmer, who witnessed the events the poem describes. It is the central poem of the section, located in the center of the section, and the intensity and coarseness of its language matches the events it describes:

> Them Hitler-youth kids. Was they fierce!
> We see one stand up with his girl, her about twelve, maybe thirteen,
> Both of them with their type bazooka.
> Charlie have his Heinie P-38. Wasn used to it then neither.
> One hunerd yards, a long shot fera pistol. Hell, long fera carbeen.
> Hot damn. That kid drop like a hammer hit him.[26]

This poem represents the harshness and brutality of war, not especially the kind of war fought by the soldiers of the 4th Armored, but by any men in combat in Europe in the Bastogne area, where the Battle of the Bulge was fought. Appropriately, it is the only unrhymed poem in the book. As Kirstein says, the impact of the story "knocked rhyme out of me."[27] This is Kirstein's acknowledgement that some incidents in war do not easily lend themselves to the creative manipulation of language for artistic or esthetic effect.

Kirstein provides an apt and appropriate poetic summing-up of his feelings and experiences in the war in "Armistice," as he and some fellow soldiers stand around a fire in the rain after learning that the war in Europe has ended.[28] The poem demonstrates those characteristics that make *Rhymes of a Pfc* so wonderfully representative of the World War II GI experience. There are the humor (the play on words in "to pool our luck"), the GI slang ("sweat it out"), the playful misuse of grammar to fit a rhyme ("I deemed you and you deemed I"), the hint of sexuality ("love each other, sure"), the details of GI life ("we shudder in each leaky coat"), the vague guilt of non-combatants depending on the combat successes of the front-line troops ("Battles of braver joes than us"), and the ability to describe the lasting importance of a common incident (the symbolic significance of "Copper embers in the rain"—as the fire of the European war dies, the rain replenishes the summer earth). More important than all of these is the visual impact of the poem—the image of a moment at the end of the war in Europe captured in a Bill Mauldin kind of verbal snapshot of men immobile in the rain realizing that they might live to return home after all.

If "4th Armored" addresses the unavoidable brutality of war, "Siegfriedslage" addresses the subject of its poetic interpretation. It is one of the central thematic poems in this section, and the crucial poem in the volume addressing the issue of poetry as a vehicle for the description of war. The poem, one of the last written, well after the end of the war, combines ideas connected with Kirstein's work for the Arts and Monuments Commission with a fortuitous meeting with the poet W.H. Auden. From February until September of 1945, Kirstein was in Germany, where the work of the Arts and Monuments task force began in earnest. One of the more significant finds he and his group made was the recovery of the Ghent altarpiece, the *Adoration of the Lamb*, by Hubert and Jan van Eyck, in a salt mine near Salzburg.[29] His involvement with the recovery of important works of art must have resulted in complex reflections on the effect of war on art, ideas that find expression in "Siegfriedslage." The poem describes the unusual meeting of Kirstein with Auden, who was working on behalf of the American forces in the preparation of the U.S. Strategic Bombing Survey, organized to study the "effects of bombing on Germany, in preparation for final attack on Japan, and to determine postwar defense."[30] Kirstein was able to accompany Auden to Tergensee, where Auden was to interview

Martin Niemoller, World War I submarine captain hero and staunch opponent of Hitler, whom Hitler had interned during the war. Kirstein compares the forest setting to Siegfriedslage, the forest camp of Siegfried, hero of Wagner's *Ring of the Nibelungs*. In this location, discussion turns to the nature of war and war poets.

Auden (called "Morden" in the poem) delivers the opinion that "poetry's not in the pity" (an allusion to Wilfred Owen) but "in the words. What words are wide enough?" Auden (according to Kirstein) appears to be wondering how words can begin to describe the effects and the experiences of a wartime environment. In answer to this question, the poem provides a list of characteristics and opportunities that demonstrate the materials of war poetry, and—for purposes of illustrating the achievement of *Rhymes*—catalogues the moments of inspiration for the poems in the volume:

> Yet if one's greedy in our craft or art,
> Shrewd, apt, ambitious—here's a recipe
> To fix some blood-types for a wounded heart,
> Resecting style, or better, grafting tones
> Eavesdropped in anguish o'er field-telephones,
> Wise walky-talking through our murky mess,
> Rococo bingo, gangbang or deathdance,
> A microscopic keyhole on distress—
> Merciless, willful, exquisite, grim, frank....[31]

The list Kirstein provides is essentially complete; we may not care for each item, but we cannot dispute their aptness or necessity. A war poet—and poems about war—must be shrewd, apt, ambitious, merciless, willful, exquisite, grim, and frank. These are characteristics of any poet who would write poetry of lasting appeal and value, but their possession is especially essential in wartime. The artist's task is to capture the moment as faithfully as possible, using the tools and materials at hand. Description of events while they are happening is as important as interpretation, if not more so. Assessment of events will follow in time; but later assessment will necessarily be based on those accounts, prose or poetic, that are written in the moment. The poet's purpose in time of war is to make the verbal picture as he or she sees it. Another eye will evaluate the value it possesses.

In the poem Kirstein answers the other question about war poetry, which is, Why write it at all? As he returns to his unit, Kirstein reflects, "How one believes, nay, must believe in ART." Kirstein believes that he knows the essential meaning of their investigations: "OUR PRESENT VICTORY'S BUT OUR FUTURE ROUT."[32] If it is in the nature of war to destroy the peoples and the cultures of the time, then, according to Kirstein, art becomes more, not less, important, for it is only through art and poetry that the full meaning of the effects of war can be interpreted and understood, even if (as Kirstein seems to suggest in this and later poems) one of the meanings discovered is that wars and wartime destruction will continue.

That Kirstein intended this to be the key poem in the thematic exploration of the link of poetry and combat experience is suggested in the fact that it was one of the last poems to be added to the volume, and was in fact included only after the death of Auden in 1973. Auden was, to Kirstein, the most important living poet writing in English, so their meeting shortly before the end of the war was as thematically appropriate as it was totally unpredictable.

The figure of Morden/Auden represents poetic tradition, poetic assessment, and poetic authority. If Auden was less than an authority on war, he certainly was one of the masters of poetry and poetic theory, and the poet against whom all poets writing before and after World War II measured themselves. His appearance lends resonance to Kirstein's effort to link poetry and wartime experience. His characterization in the poem as a comic figure of disorder and misrule lends validity to the issue of the purpose of poetry, validity that could not be derived from ideas expressed by the type of soldier or civilian who appears elsewhere in the volume. In this section, even more than in the *France* section, the emphasis on the cultural impact of the war deepens. Of eleven poems in this section, eight relate to the fine arts or native artifacts, as Kirstein directly places the effects of the war against the setting of the communities through which he and his fellow Arts and Monuments members are traveling. As someone who prided himself on his knowledge of the fine arts, Kirstein was both delighted and appalled by the treatment of important works of art which he came to know in his role in the recovery of stolen art works, and the art-linked poems in this section reflect that response. The war ends not in triumph but in weariness, as the poet continues his attempt to understand the larger meanings of the war.

The next section, *Peace*, is essentially a continuation of the search for meaning described in the previous two sections. In the original edition, this section was not separately identified, and its poems were included in the *Germany* section. Of the eight poems in *Peace*, six have to do with the impact and aftermath of the war, addressing the issues that characterized the German war effort, and questioning the subsequent effects of the war. In "Truce," Kirstein suggests that there is never a satisfactory answer to the problem of war; peace is usually only an interval before the next conflict.

Only four poems are found in the final section of the book, *Postscript*, poems which summarize and synthesize the messages of the earlier sections. They include, in "GI Bill," a moving and meaningful summary of the futility of the war effort and a profound questioning of the effectiveness of the lessons learned in the war, as a history professor ("an idiot AWOL from their war") attempts to teach them "lessons" that can scarcely match those they learned out of school.

The poems of *Rhymes of a Pfc* effectively summarize some of the more important lessons of the war, presented in a form designed to stimulate and challenge those who would study them. In its total effect, Kirstein's *Rhymes* describes some of the personalities, major and minor, involved in the conduct of the war; it describes the equipment, events, and moods of war; and it combines both personal and poetic perspectives to give a sense of the chaos and drive that characterize the conduct of war in any era.

But its most enduring legacy is the collection of images of the many characters who populate his road to war, from the banks of the Potomac to the banks of the Rhine. Most of these individuals are, like Kirstein the narrator, singularly ill-equipped to react to the war or to accommodate its pressures and meanings. They are all a little comic, a little foolish, a little selfish, a little nervous—a lot like most of us, acting the way we would act had we been there. They remain fixed in our memory frozen in a pose that catches their spirit exactly: Red Cross girls serving doughnuts, GIs watching bombers passing overhead, Patton offering tea, a foot soldier excited and appalled by the act of shooting children, Auden discussing poetry in the German forest. All are snapshots in the book of war.

10

Conclusion

The poets and the poems examined here bear witness to the truth of Harvey Shapiro's assessment that the American poets of World War II "viewed themselves as individuals caught in a giant machine that was so complex and far-flung the mind could not encompass it. They were astonished at the way their lives had been altered."[1] The poems of these nine poets show the large patterns of movements the typical soldier (or airman, or sailor) experienced: the route to the war, through indoctrination and training; the war itself, reflecting on those with whom they fought, those whom they fought, and those whom they had left at home; and finally, the return home and the adjustments that followed.

The most impressive poems about the combat experience come, not surprisingly, from those poets who saw combat. These include almost all of the poems of Louis Simpson, which document the appalling destructiveness of the life of the infantryman, fighting the war at close range. Next are the poems of John Ciardi, who participated in a different kind of combat, in the skies over Japan; his poems effectively capture the stress and uncertainty of the life of an aerial gunner in a high-altitude bomber. Howard Nemerov's poems are similar to Ciardi's, in their attention to incidents and details that characterize aerial warfare, especially as they are determined by the particular type of aircraft involved in combat. James Dickey's poetry demonstrates this aspect as well, as his environment in the rear position of a P-61 night fighter informs nearly every one of his poems about the war. Richard Hugo's poems are almost exclusively about his B-24 combat missions and his short- and long-term emotional response to them.

Every poet considered here expresses ideas about the deaths of fellow soldiers, whether they occurred as a result of combat or other activity. Simpson describes the deaths of many combatants, German as well as American, and Kirstein reports on deaths in similar fashion. Ciardi wrote several elegies before he wrote his own ("Elegy Just in Case"); Nemerov and Meredith documented the flying failures of the men in their units in an almost off-hand fashion. Dickey transformed the death of one man in his squadron into an event of near-mythic proportions in "The Performance." For Hugo, the deaths of the men in his unit who were lost in combat saddened him profoundly. Shapiro used the occasion of the deaths or wounds of the men near him as an opportunity for poetic experimentation as much as for subjects of sympathetic response, while Jarrell placed the deaths of men he never knew in a broadly framed triptych under the themes of waste, despair, and guilt.

Once the war ends, most of these poets generally turn their attention to new ideas and new issues. Jarrell, for instance, never writes about the war after it ends, nor does Shapiro. Similarly, Meredith rarely looks back to his war experiences, even though he was also involved in the Korean War. Those who became poets after the war ended—Dickey, Hugo, and Simpson—wrote their war poems in the subsequent two decades. Two of the poets—Nemerov and Ciardi—continued to make the war the subject of numerous poems written well after the war ended. John Ciardi, especially, was extensively occupied with the most important issues of the war— the human cost of waging war, especially as it was calculated by those who sent other men off to fight. Finally, of all the poets, Kirstein determined to create a complete poetic narrative of the route to war and back; most of the poems in his *Rhymes of a Pfc* were completed years after the war ended.

Although all of the poets entered the war in different places and at different times, it is instructive to realize that all of these men were engaged in their military disciplines at one specific, crucial period in the war, during one eventful week in the middle of December, from the 15th to the 21st of December, 1944. Placing them in their geographical and professional environments helps to create a truly global vision of the range of human and military experience the writings of these men provide. During this period Louis Simpson is huddled in a cold, shallow foxhole in the Ardennes forest during the Battle of the Bulge, trying to stay warm and alive while German forces shell his position and make at least one unsuccessful assault. On the 16th of December John Ciardi is flying his second mission as a B-29 gunner over Nagoya, Japan, and the hazards of this line of work are beginning to be made clear to him. On the 17th of December Richard Hugo sees at least one of his unit's B-24 aircraft fall towards the earth in a spin while flying towards the German refineries at Odertal, killing a good friend and the other members of the crew. The German aircraft attacking his bomber formation are able to do so because bad weather is preventing them from attacking American soldiers in the Bastogne area, where Louis Simpson is trying to survive.

Lincoln Kirstein is probably driving an unarmed Jeep on the back roads of France, carrying a variety of passengers to a variety of locations. During this period Karl Shapiro is working as a hospital clerk on the island of Biak in the South Pacific, and William Meredith is flying anti-submarine patrols in his Curtiss Helldiver aircraft over the waters surrounding the Hawaiian Islands. Howard Nemerov is flying anti-shipping patrols over the North Sea and along the coasts of England. James Dickey is completing his training as a radar observer in P-61s in the United States, and in two weeks' time he and other members of his unit will ship out for the South Pacific. Finally, Randall Jarrell is helping to develop the celestial navigation skills of bomber crews at Davis-Monthan Field in Arizona. Each man, in his own way and in his own locale, is a part of the American machinery of war (in Nemerov's case, on loan to the Royal Air Force thanks to the Royal Canadian Air Force; in another month he will become officially a member of the United States Army Air Forces, though he will continue to fly with the RAF until just before his return to the United States). The military machinery of which they are a part is large and shapeless, like a huge, imperfectly made elephant, but each man is in the process of processing the experiences that will eventually lead to a unique poetic picture of that part of the elephantine machinery with which he is most familiar.

The poems of these nine men give us a reasonably complete picture of the various theaters of war and aspects of the military experience during World War II; the only major arena of military activity that is not represented is life on one of the great naval ships (if Richard Eberhart had found his way onto an operational naval vessel in the Pacific, this lack might have been remedied). In spite of the great variety of experiences these men describe, there are some commonalities and differences in their works. Many, for instance, found training experiences tedious and frustrating; all recognized that they were parts of the great impersonal mechanism of war, and were accordingly more or less willing to become a part of that mechanism. All created striking visual images of their part of the war effort. All spoke of the deaths that resulted from war, whether in training or in combat, directly or indirectly witnessed. All were concerned about how they, as poets, could create meaningful expressions of lived experience without being absorbed or deformed by that experience. All demonstrated exceptional energy and determination in their efforts to survive the war and to continue to be (or become) poets. And all adapted the terminologies of the military services to convey the unique insights they had gained in the course of their movements through the war.

Shapiro, for instance, is especially fond of using the words of the soldier in an experimental way, as if to see what spirit would rise when these words were uttered. In "Troop Train," he describes the tools of the soldier that, as they are in transit, are little more than specialized baggage to be carried with them, yet in the way they are described (their packs as "murdered bodies," their helmets loose, like empty buckets holding nothing of the man who would wear them), they evoke the progress towards the war, progress that constricts them as they move closer to the war. Shapiro seems to have delighted in writing poems that challenged conventional thinking about military goals, actions, and processes. As the reviewer for *Poetry* said in the June 1945 issue, Shapiro's "brisk individual accent" created poetry of a unique and often puzzling aspect, a product of a "nimble imagination integrated with, and controlled by, a skeptical and sophisticated intelligence."[2]

Determined to avoid being called a "war poet" but increasingly identified as one as the war progressed, Shapiro wrote war poems that demonstrated ambiguous vacillation between sentiment and irony, in "Elegy for Dead Soldier," the non-ironical and sentimental language of "V-Letter," the hell-bent for catastrophe pace of "Scyros," and the extended hyperbole of "The Fly." Shapiro's "The Leg," an imaginative investigation of a soldier's loss of a limb, is more accurate and empathetic (and therefore more disturbing) than Jarrell's unemotional, abstract account of a loss of a limb in "Siegfried," for instance. But even in this poem we sense Shapiro's attempt to detach himself emotionally from the human cost of the war, as the amputated leg becomes a symbol of an abstract philosophical idea. Not himself a combatant, but close enough to serious fighting to know something of it, Shapiro was able to write about the war with some insight and accuracy. The poetry that results combines the language of wartime experience with the detached perspective of a sensitive observer who recognizes the line dividing sentiment from irony, even if he is unsure himself how to walk that line.

In contrast to the occasionally inconsistent ironies of Shapiro are the heavier philosophic statements of Randall Jarrell. Insulated from the harsher realities of the war by a stateside assignment and a regular work routine, his secure position in the training establishment of the U.S. Army Air Forces afforded Jarrell the luxury of undertaking serious commentary on the bureaucratic processes of the military machine at minimum personal risk. Distanced from the war, Jarrell imagined the worst that could happen (possibly assisted by newsreels and photographs from popular magazines), relentlessly depicting the inhuman mechanisms of the forces involved. As a result, his word pictures of doomed combatants (the gunner, the ball-turret gunner, the pilot from the carrier, the Eighth Air Force crew members), as well as other victims of the war, are less concerned with obtaining the reader's empathy for the real participants in war than with cataloguing repeated examples of human folly, loss, and waste. Instead of seeing the cost of the war in human terms, Jarrell opted for philosophic complexity and intellectual abstraction. In his poems with a strongly religious context, like "Burning the Letters," "Eighth Air Force," and "The Angels at Hamburg," the presence of the religious element is as much a contributory cause of distress and despair as it is philosophical context against which the meanings of the activities are to be evaluated. In these poems, Jarrell paints a Brueghel-like canvas of human suffering against a background of fiery, war-torn landscapes, the purpose of which is as religiously pedagogic as medieval iconography.

To reinforce the impersonal actions of the State, he invokes a language of trade, economics, and bureaucracy. The most common language of the Jarrell poems relates to the bureaucratic actions of the State, especially how soldiers are treated by the State: placed in long lines for food and supplies, in hospital beds, in graves. The shorter Jarrell poems are more generally effective than the longer poems, primarily because Jarrell does not load these poems with the religious and philosophical baggage that can place a greater stress on the poem than it is capable of bearing. Personally absent from almost every war poem he wrote, Jarrell was more interested in writing poems with intellectual import, as he states in his letters to Lowell, and this emphasis resulted in poems that can become more intellectual exercises than statements of and about the human condition. His reputation as the war ended was based on the poems of *Little Friend* and *Losses*, poems that were widely respected, and perhaps more respected than liked. This emphasis on intellectual significance continued into his postwar poems, and he may have found some difficulty in writing about postwar topics that were less easily amenable to philosophical contextualizing than wartime actions.

Whereas Jarrell imagined the unhappy life of a gunner, his central symbol of the victims of war, John Ciardi *was* a gunner. Like Jarrell, Ciardi was fully capable of providing complex philosophical contexts against which to display the details of a particular character or event (as in "Reflections While Oiling a Machine Gun" or "V-J Day"). Unlike Jarrell, however, Ciardi is often located at or near the center of the poem. While Jarrell portrayed the gunner as an unfortunate, doomed other, Ciardi knew that *he* was the gunner. If something bad happened to the gunner, it happened to *him*. By placing himself at the center of the poem, Ciardi made the events of the war intensely personal, and the philosophical lessons those poems convey result from his sense of self as a part of an immense conduit channeling destructive power to an enemy homeland in the Pacific. The lessons he was in a unique position to learn came at a high personal price. Ciardi knew that he could pay that price at any time; after he had written elegies for a number of the men whom he had known, he wrote his own "Elegy Just in Case," giving it a grimly ironic tone, one that would amuse others if he lived but still carry a heavier meaning if he did not.

Like Jarrell, Ciardi believed that poetry was more important than war, and he was clearly relieved when his writing skills brought about his transfer to a staff position. His poetry literally saved his life, bringing about his reassignment to a desk job days before his crew was lost on a bombing mission. Like Jarrell, Ciardi developed a sense of anger over the events of the war. But whereas Jarrell's sense of anger was largely intellectual, Ciardi's was personal, and therefore more deeply felt and more meaningful when encountered in his poetry. Ciardi's language emphasized the complex meanings of operational language: squadrons turning; firing pins, probabilities, reports and rosters, interphones, parachutes and guns. Every term referring to equipment used carries complex meanings of struggle and survival.

Like every other poet considered in this study, Ciardi did not describe himself as an especially important member of the war effort; in looking later at a photograph of himself in his flying gear during the war, he sees only deception and pretense in his pose and equipment. Yet he does not deny the fact of the photograph or its significance at the time it was taken. Like Shapiro, Ciardi was suspicious of the motives and practices of the military organization of which he was a part. Unlike Shapiro, however, Ciardi was forced to depend on that organization to ensure his survival (to the degree it could be ensured due to the hazards of combat). For Ciardi, poetry was a means of processing the effects of combat that he experienced and of coping with its personal and philosophical adjustments.

William Meredith gained a new perspective of his surroundings when he became a naval flier assigned to fly first in the Aleutian Islands and then in the Hawaiian Islands area. Distanced from heavier combat, Meredith found that the main challenge was survival in a hostile environment. Flying initially in a geologically young area, Meredith relied on words evocative of unusual sights to convey the meanings of the visions of the indescribable combination of ocean and islands over which he flew. The poet describes the effects of attempting to fly in a standardized military manner in a natural environment that shows evidence of continuing to evolve geophysically. The vision of navy pilots flying, often with tragic results, in an environment naturally harsh and unforgiving, is the dominant image in his wartime poetry. Unlike Jarrell, Meredith does not blame the military bureaucracy or any other component of the State for this situation. Possibly because he was in a privileged status, as an officer and a pilot, he felt little of the sense of injustice that an enlisted man, working at less stimulating tasks in larger, more impersonal military organizations, might feel. Meredith never complains that the inhuman workings of an abstract system are responsible for the predicaments he and others are facing. Instead, his concern is for describing the unusual nature of the environment and context of the flying activities in which he is involved, as in "June: Dutch Harbor" or "Homeric Simile." Throughout his war poems Meredith struggles consistently to frame his exceptional flying experiences in an appropriately traditional poetic perspective. Beyond relying on standard poetic forms such as the sonnet and ballad, he frequently relies on literary references (to Milton, Wordsworth, and Spender, for example), as well as literary devices, like the simile, to add resonance to his works. This strange combination of unfamiliar natural settings with seemingly affected literariness produces results that emphasize the strangenesses of an unusual war fought in a harsh environment.

Like Meredith, Howard Nemerov shared the privileged status of pilot and officer; unlike Meredith, he was flying in a land where history and tradition spoke to him from every checkpoint along his route of flight, even if he fully appreciated that fact only later in his poetic career. Nemerov's early war poetry addresses the ironies of war, juxtaposing the conflicting aims and results of organized military campaigns. Gradually, however, his war poetry grew increasingly personal, and his later poems, especially those written shortly before he died, describe less the waste of war in general and more his personal involvement as an aircrew member. While he could share the frustrations of Jarrell and Shapiro over the ill treatment received in training, his unhappiness focused on specific individuals with whom he came in contact, not the larger workings of an impersonal system. His best poetry depicts the chances of war as they affected his combat arena of coastal patrol duties. Self-deprecating about his own role as a pilot, he nevertheless was able to impart a sense of the complexities and difficulties of the flying missions in which he was involved. He shared with Ciardi an interest in the language of operational equipment: striking arms, guide bracket posts, engine fairings, barrage balloons, takeoffs, gunsights.

His poems contrast the confident language of military and technological techniques with more hesitant personal uncertainties about the practical effects of that language: in "Models," for instance, the pilots are told, after firing their guns, to turn to a heading of north and fire one more burst. The purpose of such an activity seems logical: "to set the shaken compass true again: / It straightened the molecules." But then comes the realistic response of the skeptical aviator: "or so they said."[3] Nemerov's reading of the landscape over which he flies is different from Meredith's: where Meredith sees a strange new natural world, in his poems written long after the war, Nemerov thinks of literary or historical significance. Meredith's landscape has only a remote connection with established literary tradition, which he attempts to bridge with literary references. Like Meredith, however, Nemerov shares a nervous disdain of those whose flying skills are not sufficient to assure their survival.

Nemerov's war poetry contrasts the directives and expectations of the authority figures of the wartime system with the reactions of those imperfect individuals who are called upon to fulfill those directives and meet those expectations. Unlike Randall Jarrell, in whose war poetry the State systematically victimizes its participants, Nemerov does not complain about the impersonal workings of the system that directs the actions of its wartime workers; he accepts as a fact of the war that the system must exist. Instead of complaining about the awfulness of its monolithic force, he describes instances of conflict or stress that occur when flawed human beings are tasked to fulfill directives that assume success and do not appear to consider the possibility of failure.

Unlike Nemerov, whose presentation of himself as pilot was self-deprecating, James Dickey was not hesitant to centralize his experiences as a flier in his poetry; his flying experience provides the creative locus of the action of his war poems. Not happy about flying as a radar observer in the P-61—he would much rather have been a pilot—he apparently established or helped to support a postwar myth that he was one. In his poems involving flying, he appears to be the solitary individual in the aircraft, thus suggesting that he is the pilot, holding the responsibility for the progress and resulting actions of the aircraft. In "The Enclosure" and "The Firebombing," the Dickey persona appears as the sole occupant of the aircraft, operating in a condition of tension resulting from a feeling of entrapment and personal frustrations (sexual desire, inability to act independently, guilt over lack of guilt). In "The Jewel," the other crew member, the actual pilot, is an accessory to the drama of the poet's experience, which is central. Like the other poets who were involved in flying duties, Dickey does not complain specifically about the hierarchy's indifference to personal desires, perhaps because he, as they, believed he had a useful, if small, role in the conduct of the war. He, like they, believed he was capable of exerting at least a nominal amount of autonomous behavior, a belief that could be sustained when operating in an impressive machine of war instead of viewing oneself as one small part of a body of men.

10. Conclusion

The essential characteristic of Dickey's poetry is its emphasis on the surrealistic aspects of war experience, represented most familiarly in "The Performance," "The Enclosure," or "The Driver." Words like *amaze*, *miraculous*, *glittering*, *dazzled*, or expressions like "moon-metal-shine," "treasure-hole of soft light," "country of the drowned" convey transformational meanings, elevating the common experience into magical, aesthetically unique visions. In the war poems, these episodes typically occur in flight-related moments. Rarely does Dickey invoke the technical language of flying, in contrast to the other flyers—Ciardi, Meredith, Nemerov, Hugo. An operational phrase or an image instead immediately calls forth an exceptional vision, a transforming moment.

In contrast to the relatively insulated worlds of the aviators, Louis Simpson lived the exposed, vulnerable life of the infantryman. Simpson speaks the common language of the soldier: we not only know very well we are in the army, we know the ranks of those involved (captain, lieutenant, master-sergeant, chaplain) and the equipment they carry (rifle, helmet, binoculars, trenching tool, boots, cigarettes, compasses, maps). His vocabulary of soldier experience helps to put us there, to share with him the terrifying awfulness of war. No philosophical detachment for him; philosophy was the occupation of a mind at leisure. Simpson's concern was survival. Simpson never complains about the system that brought him, by a haphazard and circuitous route, to a position in the 101st Airborne Division. If Randall Jarrell had met him in 1943 or 1944, Jarrell might well have considered Simpson the perfect example of the innocent victim, a perfect prototype of the "Gunner," one who would soon have his medals sent home to his cat. Simpson's education (he had completed some courses in his undergraduate study) was more a burden to him than a blessing, as his fellow soldiers often harassed him for being a "college boy," and he was too busy with technical and physical training to think much about moral nuances of armed conflict.

Simpson's war poetry describes violent and disturbing episodes during the seven-month period (June to December of 1944) when he saw intense combat in Europe; he published no poems about his training experiences. His earliest poetry helped him to recover from the trauma of combat, helped him recreate images of the war that his mind, as a defense against the violence he had witnessed, had blanked out. The title of his long poem, "The Runner," symbolizes his main concern, to keep moving. By moving he could confirm that he was still alive. His best poetry about the war reflects a postwar awareness of the significance of the geographical and cultural environment through which he had moved as a frightened foot soldier.

Like Simpson, Richard Hugo relied on his war poetry, written after the war, to make sense of the emotional pressures he faced as a crew member on B-24 aircraft involved in bombing well-defended targets in central Europe. The cumulative impact of his experiences flying 35 missions into the cloud-filled and uncertain skies of Europe gave him a burden of unhappiness that was scarcely lightened by his subsequent representation of those experiences in poetic form. The poems of *Good-bye in Cracked Italian* enabled him to process his wartime experience, especially as they were generated by return visits to Italy after the war ended. In these poems Hugo imagines his earlier self in key moments of distress and temporary relief and in describing those moments is able to acknowledge the deep personal grief he felt as the result of the incidents he witnessed. While his poems can include the vocabularies of technical terms ("Mission to Linz" is the best example), the language of his most impressive war poems is almost exclusively pictorial, providing images that simultaneously provide a framework of understanding and relief to the poet and insight for the reader.

In contrast to Simpson, Lincoln Kirstein wrote no poems in which he witnessed combat directly, because he was never in combat; his *Rhymes of a Pfc* is an effort to give a true picture of the war as he saw it as a soldier in a support role. It would have been inappropriate, even unethical, to include a poem in which he might imagine a combat scenario involving himself. One poem in *Rhymes* describes combat; but as he explained in his notes, it was related to him by someone who was in combat. Kirstein's focus at all times is on the people with whom he traveled, whether literally or figuratively. He describes a wide variety of senior and junior officers and enlisted men, from generals to privates, usually showing how they attempted to manipulate their circumstances for their personal (often sexual) or professional benefit. But mixed in with these personal vignettes are occasional philosophic insights about the motives and results of the applications of force in war, as in "Air Strike" and "Comité des Forges." Like Simpson, he provides a catalogue of army terms and tools: hatchets, saws, K-rations, bazookas, pistols, field telephones. If Simpson wanted to give a complete sense of what the combat environment was like, Kirstein's goal was to give a complete picture of army support operations in the areas behind the front lines.

Kirstein is not especially bothered by the petty injustices of the military system, whether in training or in the operational arena. As a result of his thorough familiarity with the men with whom he works, and of his support duties and maturity (he was 38 years old when the war in Europe ended), he could understand the perspectives of both officers and enlisted men. He does not see the military system as an impersonal force; it is instead a collection of individuals with varied idiosyncrasies and motivations, whose behavior he delights in describing. If to Kirstein the war was an inconvenience, an interruption in the more useful artistic life (as it appeared to be for Shapiro), it was also a necessary process to be seen through to its conclusion. Kirstein is less concerned with the underlying moral complexities of the military than he is with its impact on art: on his art (as represented in his poetry), certainly, but even more on the arts in a larger sense, the sculpture, architecture, and fine arts of western Europe. *Rhymes* contains, especially in its *Germany* section, many poems about the effort to appreciate or protect the cultural artifacts that the war had damaged or destroyed, the natural result of his involvement in the Arts and Monuments Commission. Kirstein describes the loss of much of this art with the knowledge that the war could have destroyed more than it did, and that the human travail depicted in that art included the kind of turmoil the war represented. If Jarrell obtained his poetic inspiration from photographs in news magazines, Kirstein desired that his poems become word-based visual images, photographs, of the men and events he had seen personally.

The nine poets considered in this study bring a variety of perspectives to their versions of the wars they saw. If we can imagine a scale of involvement in the war with detachment at one end and personal involvement at the other, it is easy to see that one's location and duties in the war largely govern the kind of poetry that results. The farther from the war the poet is situated, the larger are the issues that the poet describes; the closer the poet is to the war, the more immediate is the focus. Jarrell, far from the battlefield, produces a poetry of detachment that criticizes the State and views the common soldier, the gunner, as a tool of the system. Drawing upon the tenets of religious belief and philosophy, his poetry occasionally takes on the tone of the biblical prophets, presenting images of despair and waste. Although his poems describe individuals supposedly involved in the actions of war, they are more often stereotypes than representatives of the human condition. At the other end of the spectrum, Louis Simpson depicts the immediacy of the war, whether stylized in ballad form or presented realistically in blank verse. The figures in his poems are both individual and symbolic, and the actions described are smaller in scope but more intense, more realistic, than those of Jarrell. We are very much aware of the local terrain in Simpson's poems: roads, trees, ditches, bushes. There are few landscapes in Jarrell's poetry; instead, we have a series of symbolic backgrounds, arranged like a series of stage sets through which Jarrell's unfortunate victims pass.

The poetry of these two poets establishes the range within which the remaining poets can be located: Hugo stands next to Simpson, describing the conditions of aerial combat as well as the emotional cost in intensely personal terms. Kirstein follows next, as he creates a series of characters engaged in the real activities of supporting the war effort. Shapiro is located at a near distance to Jarrell, as he consistently places his subjects in some kind of poetic framework, and the frame often competes with the subject for the attention of the reader. Meredith stands well down the scale from Jarrell, with his emphasis on a natural setting serving as his philosophical base, against which he draws portraits of himself and his fellow aviators distanced from the earth and sea over which they fly. Approaching the center from opposite sides are Dickey, slightly on the abstract side as a result of his poems' surrealistic quality, and Nemerov, on the realistic side for the increased appearance of himself as a participant in his later poems. In the center is Ciardi, with his balanced mixture of personal involvement and philosophic perspective.

Positioned on this spectrum, the most philosophical poems are in danger of losing their appeal due to the heavy thematic baggage they carry. Similarly, those poems that are the most realistic run the risk of sacrificing their poetic qualities (while retaining their value as documents of lived experience). Those poems that base their philosophic impact on real experiences, included within the information in the poem, become enduring testaments of poetic expression, combining intellectual insight with visions of the experience itself. The best poems of these nine poets achieve this goal, and, taken in sum, present a truly remarkable panorama of the American military experience in World War II.

Chapter Notes

Introduction

1. Karl Shapiro, "The Death of Randall Jarrell," in Robert Lowell, Peter Taylor, and Robert Penn Warren, eds., *Randall Jarrell 1914–1965* (New York: Farrar, Straus and Giroux, 1967), 203.

2. Vernon Scannell, *Not Without Glory: Poets of the Second World War* (London: Woburn, 1976), 14.

3. Harvey Shapiro, ed., *Poets of World War II* (New York: Library of America, 2003), xx.

4. Ibid., xxii.

5. Karl Shapiro, "The Death of Randall Jarrell," 292. While Shapiro's comments about "waiting out the war in uniform" might apply to himself and Randall Jarrell, they do not necessarily apply to the other poets considered in this study.

6. M. L. Rosenthal, *Randall Jarrell* (Minneapolis: University of Minnesota Press, 1972), 15.

7. W. H. Auden, "Private Poet," in Lincoln Kirstein, *The Poems of Lincoln Kirstein* (New York: Atheneum, 1987), 317.

8. "Correspondence," *Poetry: A Magazine of Verse*, February 1943 (61:5), 639.

9. "Our War Correspondents," *Poetry: A Magazine of Verse*, April 1943 (62:1), 57–8.

10. "News Notes," *Poetry: A Magazine of Verse*, February 1945 (65:5), 286–7.

11. Henry Treece, "The War and My Poetry," in Oscar Williams, ed., *The War Poets: An Anthology of the War Poetry of the Twentieth Century* (New York: John Day, 1945), 20.

12. Hayden Carruth, *Reluctantly* (Port Townsend WA: Copper Canyon, 1998), 143–5.

13. Joel Roache, *Richard Eberhart: The Progress of an American Poet* (New York: Oxford University Press, 1971), 137–44.

14. Oscar Williams, ed., *The War Poets*, 8.

Chapter 1

1. Karl Shapiro, "American Poet?" in Karl Shapiro, *Creative Glut: Selected Essays of Karl Shapiro*, ed. Robert Phillips (Chicago: Ivan R. Dee, 2004), 239.

2. Karl Shapiro, *The Younger Son* (Chapel Hill: Algonquin, 1988), 118.

3. Karl Shapiro, *Poems 1940–1953* (New York: Random House, 1953), 57–8.

4. Karl Shapiro, *The Younger Son*, 120.

5. Karl Shapiro, *Poems 1940–1953*, 30–1.

6. Karl Shapiro, *The Younger Son*, 159.

7. Karl Shapiro, *Poems 1940–1953*, 56–7.

8. Karl Shapiro, *The Younger Son*, 168.

9. John Updike, "Introduction," in

Karl Shapiro, *Karl Shapiro: Selected Poems*, ed. John Updike (New York: Library of America, 2003), xxv.
10. Karl Shapiro, *The Younger Son*, 167.
11. Ibid., 166.
12. Ibid., 167.
13. Karl Shapiro, *V-Letter and Other Verses* (New York: Reynal & Hitchcock, 1944), vi.
14. Karl Shapiro, *The Younger Son*, 167–8.
15. Ibid., 104.
16. Ibid., 168.
17. Karl Shapiro, "American Poet?," 239.
18. Karl Shapiro, *Poems 1940–1953*, 105.
19. Ibid., 91.
20. Ibid., 149.
21. Karl Shapiro, *The Younger Son*, 240.
22. Ibid., 241.
23. Karl Shapiro, *Poems 1940–1953*, 90.
24. Ibid., 61.
25. Karl Shapiro, *The Younger Son*, 237.
26. Ibid.
27. Karl Shapiro, *Poems 1940–1953*, 42.
28. Karl Shapiro, *The Younger Son*, 237.
29. Vernon Scannell thought that the "Elegy for a Dead Soldier" demonstrated a "curious lack of the poet's real involvement with his subject matter, a lack which is emphasized rather than diminished by the frequent extravagance and sensuousness of language and imagery" (Vernon Scannell, *Not Without Glory: Poets of the Second World War* (London: Woburn, 1976), 206.
30. Karl Shapiro, *The Younger Son*, 164–5.
31. Karl Shapiro, *Poems 1940–1953*, 154–5.
32. Susan Schweik, *A Gulf So Deeply Cut: American Women Poets and the Second World War* (Madison: University of Wisconsin Press, 1991), 90.
33. Karl Shapiro, *The Younger Son*, 255.
34. Ibid., 136.
35. Ibid., 137.
36. Karl Shapiro, *Poems 1940–1953*, 74–5.
37. Karl Shapiro, *Reports of My Death* (Chapel Hill: Algonquin, 1990), 10.
38. Karl Shapiro, *Trial of a Poet* (New York: Reynal & Hitchcock, 1947), 10. The version of "Recapitulations" in *Poems 1940–1953* is much changed in tone and content from the earlier version in *Trial of a Poet*.

Chapter 2

1. Vernon Scannell, *Not Without Glory: Poets of the Second World War* (London: Woburn, 1976), 190.
2. Lorrie Goldensohn, *Dismantling Glory: Twentieth Century Soldier Poetry* (New York: Columbia University Press, 2003), 174.
3. Vernon Scannell, *Not Without Glory*, 190.
4. Lorrie Goldensohn, *Dismantling Glory*, 178.
5. Randall Jarrell, *Randall Jarrell's Letters*, ed. Mary Jarrell (Boston: Houghton Mifflin, 1985), 60.
6. Ibid., 66.
7. Ibid., 67.
8. Ibid.
9. Ibid., 68, 69.
10. Oscar Williams, ed., *The War Poets: An Anthology of the War Poetry of the Twentieth Century* (New York: John Day, 1945), 115.
11. Randall Jarrell, *Randall Jarrell's Letters*, 74.
12. Ibid., 77.
13. Ibid., 82.
14. Ibid., 121.
15. Ibid., 120.
16. Ibid., 106.
17. Ibid., 150–1.
18. Ibid., 128.
19. Karl Shapiro, "The Death of Randall Jarrell," in Karl Shapiro, *Cre-*

ative Glut: Selected Essays of Karl Shapiro, ed. Robert Phillips (Chicago: Ivan R. Dee, 2004), 172.

20. The texts of all poems referred to are those of Randall Jarrell, *The Complete Poems* (New York: Farrar, Straus and Giroux, 1969), 402.

21. Randall Jarrell, *The Complete Poems*, 120.

22. Ibid., 400.

23. Ibid., 8. Unfortunately, Jarrell's notes to the poem are not always included in modern anthologies or texts. Where they are included, the details are sometimes incorrect; one recent text, for instance, states in a note that the ball turret gunner is positioned "upside down in a plexiglass sphere in the belly of a fighter plane." The gunner was not upside down and the plane was a bomber, not a fighter. And the turret is much more metal than plexiglass.

24. Richard Flynn, *Randall Jarrell and the Lost World of Childhood* (Athens: University of Georgia Press, 1990), 29, 33–4.

25. Adam Kirsch, *The Wounded Surgeon: Confession and Transformation in Six American Poets* (New York: W. W. Norton, 2005), 160.

26. Randall Jarrell, *Randall Jarrell's Letters*, 116.

27. Randall Jarrell, *The Complete Poems*, 191.

28. Suzanne Ferguson, *The Poetry of Randall Jarrell* (Baton Rouge: Louisiana State University Press, 1971), 56.

29. Randall Jarrell, *Randall Jarrell's Letters*, 134.

30. Richard Fein, "Randall Jarrell's World of War," in Suzanne Ferguson, ed., *Critical Essays on Randall Jarrell* (Boston: G. K. Hall, 1983), 152.

31. James Dickey made a similar (and often-cited) observation about Jarrell's poems: "I don't think there are really any people in the war poems. There are only The Ball Turret Gunner, A Pilot from the Carrier, The Wingman, and assorted faceless types in uniform. They are just collective Objects, or Attitudes, or Killable Puppets. You care very little what happens to them, and that is terrible." Dickey's comment could have originated in his sense of aerial combatants as real people, the kind he knew from his own wartime experiences. James Dickey, "Randall Jarrell," in Robert Lowell, Peter Taylor, and Robert Penn Warren, eds., *Randall Jarrell 1914–1965* (New York: Farrar, Straus and Giroux, 1967), 44.

32. William Pritchard, *Randall Jarrell: A Literary Life* (New York: Farrar, Straus and Giroux, 1990), 20–1.

33. Cleanth Brooks, "Jarrell's 'Eighth Air Force,'" in Robert Lowell, Peter Taylor, and Robert Penn Warren, eds., *Randall Jarrell 1914–1965*, 27.

34. Randall Jarrell, *The Complete Poems*, 143.

35. This note is found in *The Complete Poems*, 8, greatly expanded over the note provided earlier, in *Losses* (New York: Harcourt Brace, 1948), 66.

Chapter 3

1. John Ciardi, "About Being Born, and Surviving It," in John Ciardi, *John Ciardi: The Measure of the Man*, ed. Vince Clemente (Fayetteville: University of Arkansas Press, 1987), 12.

2. Ibid.

3. Edward Cifelli, *John Ciardi: A Biography* (Fayetteville: University of Arkansas Press, 1997), 73–6.

4. John Ciardi, "About Being Born, and Surviving It," 12.

5. John Ciardi, *Manner of Speaking* (New Brunswick: Rutgers University Press, 1972), 148.

6. John Ciardi, *The Collected Poems of John Ciardi*, ed. Edward M. Cifelli (Fayetteville: University of Arkansas Press, 1997), 26.

7. John Ciardi, *Other Skies* (Boston: Little, Brown, 1947), 26.

8. Ibid., 10.

9. Ibid., 28–9.

10. Edward Krickel, *John Ciardi* (Boston: Twayne, 1980), 43.

11. John Ciardi, *Saipan: The War*

Diary of John Ciardi (Fayetteville: University of Arkansas Press, 1988), 39.
  12. *Ibid*, 24–7.
  13. *Ibid.*, 35.
  14. *Ibid.*, 40.
  15. *Ibid.*, 58.
  16. *Ibid.*, 66.
  17. *Ibid.*, 85.
  18. John Ciardi, "About Being Born, and Surviving It," 18.
  19. John Ciardi, *The Collected Poems*, 135.
  20. *Ibid.*, 47.
  21. *Ibid.*, 42.
  22. *Ibid.*, 48.
  23. John Ciardi, *Other Skies*, 45–7. The version printed in *The Collected Poems* differs from that of *Other Skies*.
  24. John Ciardi, *Saipan*, 99–100.
  25. *Ibid.*
  26. *Ibid.*, 90.
  27. Quoted in Studs Terkel, *The Good War: An Oral History of World War Two* (New York: Pantheon, 1984), 199.
  28. John Ciardi, *The Collected Poems*, 54–3.
  29. *Ibid.*, 57.
  30. "V-J Day" underwent numerous revisions. In the original version, published in *Other Skies*, the final line reads, "Wheels up and flaming on a metal sea." When the poem appeared in *As If*, published eight years later, the final line is "Wheels jammed, and flaming, on a metal sea." The phrase "wheels up" would normally signify an aircraft that had just taken off from its field and was about to depart on a mission; the phrase "wheels jammed" indicates that the wheels cannot be lowered and thus there is no possibility of a safe landing, clearly Ciardi's intent in this poem. The addition of the comma after "flaming" emphasizes the apocalyptic quality of the image. In *As If* Ciardi also modified the second stanza: in *Other Skies*, the stanza reads:
Half way past Iwo we jettisoned to sea
Our cherished bombs like tears and
  tears like bombs
To spring a frolic fountain daintily
Out of the blue metallic seas of doom.

In *As If* the final three lines are totally changed:
Half way past Iwo we jettisoned to sea
Ten tons of arrows from the Eagle's
  claws.
They fell and followed. Half nostalgi-
  cally
We watched them spout a fountain
  from the troughs.

The revision emphasizes the destructive power of the bombs carried by the B-29s, clarifying any ambiguity in the original version. The changes in the later version of the poem, so uncharacteristic of Ciardi, indicate how important personally this poem was to him. The version printed in *The Collected Poems*, assembled and edited by Edward Cifelli after Ciardi's death, retains the original version of the second stanza, includes the "wheels jammed" final line, but omits the comma after "flaming."
  31. John Ciardi, *The Collected Poems*, 50–2.
  32. John Ciardi, *Other Skies*, 78–9.
  33. John Ciardi, *The Collected Poems*, 61.
  34. *Ibid.*, 220.

Chapter 4

  1. Corey Ford, *Short Cut to Tokyo: The Battle for the Aleutians* (New York: Scribner's, 1943), 31–2.
  2. Letter dated 3 October 1943, in Dashiell Hammett, *The Selected Letters of Dashiell Hammett 1921–1960*, ed. Richard Laymen and Julie M. Rivett (Washington DC: Counterpoint, 2001), 234.
  3. Information found in William Meredith's military files, kept in the Charles E. Shain Library, Connecticut College, New London, Connecticut.
  4. Information found on the Kodiak Alaska Military History web site, http://209.165.152.119/vs/vs49.html, accessed 14 September 2004.
  5. William Meredith, *Love Letter from an Impossible Land* (New Haven: Yale University Press, 1944), 9.

6. *Ibid.*, 38–40.
7. Letter dated 7 October 1943, in Dashiell Hammett, *The Selected Letters of Dashiell Hammett 1921–1960*, 237–8.
8. Guy Rotella, *Three Contemporary Poets of New England: William Meredith, Philip Booth, and Peter Davidson* (Boston: Twayne, 1983), 9.
9. Meredith quoted in *Ibid.*, 13.
10. Courtland W. Matthews, *Aleutian Interval* (Seattle: Frank McCaffrey, 1949), 15–6.
11. William Meredith, *Effort at Speech: New and Selected Poems* (Evanston: TriQuarterly, 1997), 12–3.
12. *Ibid.*, 3.
13. William Meredith, *Love Letter from an Impossible Land*, 44.
14. William Meredith, *Effort at Speech*, 15.
15. *Ibid.*, 4.
16. *Ibid.*, 10–1.
17. William Meredith, *Ships and Other Figures* (Princeton: Princeton University Press, 1948), 13.
18. *Ibid.*, 14.
19. *Ibid.*, 11.
20. *Ibid.*, 20.
21. William Meredith, *Effort at Speech*, 19.
22. *Ibid.*, 20.
23. William Meredith, *Ships and Other Figures*, 38.
24. *Ibid.*
25. *Ibid.*, 10.
26. *Ibid.*, 18.
27. *Ibid.*, 39.
28. William Meredith, *Earth Walk: New and Selected Poems* (New York: Alfred A. Knopf, 1970), 25–6.

Chapter 5

1. Howard Nemerov, *The Howard Nemerov Reader* (Columbia: University of Missouri Press, 1991), 306.
2. *Ibid.*
3. Howard Nemerov, *Journal of the Fictive Life* (New Brunswick: Rutgers University Press, 1965), 89.
4. Ross Labrie, *Howard Nemerov* (Boston: Twayne, 1980), 71.
5. Howard Nemerov, *The Collected Poems of Howard Nemerov* (Chicago: University of Chicago Press, 1977), 61.
6. *Ibid.*, 178–9.
7. *Ibid.*, 122.
8. *Ibid.*, 63.
9. A similar reference to a gun as a "toy" can be found, for instance, in the comments of Robert Button, in a letter he wrote home in May of 1941: "Our latest toy ... is what's known as a 155-millimeter cannon that shoots a shell weighing 100 lbs twelve miles." Robert E. Button, *Enigma in Many Keys* (New York: iUniverse, 2004), 21.
10. Howard Nemerov, *The Collected Poems of Howard Nemerov*, 123–4.
11. *Ibid.*, 150.
12. *Ibid.*, 151–2.
13. *Ibid.*, 463–4.
14. Howard Nemerov, *Journal of the Fictive Life*, 89–90.
15. Howard Nemerov, *The Collected Poems*, 35–6.
16. Roy Conyers Nesbit, *The Strike Wings: Special Anti-Shipping Squadrons, 1942–1945* (London: William Kimber, 1984), 32.
17. Stanley Robert Simpson, "An Autobiography," http://www.randpersonnel.co.za/autofour.htm, accessed August 18, 2005.
18. Roy Conyers Nesbit, *The Strike Wings*, 43–51.
19. Howard Nemerov, *The Collected Poems*, 36.
20. Howard Nemerov, *War Stories: Poems about Long Ago and Now* (Chicago: University of Chicago Press, 1987), 25–6.
21. *Ibid.*, 31.
22. *Ibid.*, 28.
23. "The Bristol Beaufighter," http://www.burmabeaufighters.com/pages/beaufighters.php, accessed August 7, 2004.
24. Roy Conyers Nesbit, *The Strike Wings*, 28.
25. "The Bristol Beaufighter."

26. Stanley Robert Simpson, "An Autobiography"
27. Howard Nemerov, *War Stories*, 29–30.
28. Stanley Robert Simpson, "An Autobiography."
29. Howard Nemerov, *Journal of the Fictive Life*, 178.
30. Howard Nemerov, *War Stories*, 34.
31. Stanley Robert Simpson, "An Autobiography."
32. Howard Nemerov, *War Stories*, 32–3.
33. *Ibid.*, 36.
34. Howard Nemerov, *The Collected Poems*, 464.

Chapter 6

1. Louis Simpson, "On Line," in Louis Simpson, *Selected Prose* (New York: Paragon House, 1989), 79.
2. *Ibid.*, 83.
3. *Ibid.*, 120.
4. *Ibid.*, 121.
5. Letter to his mother, written in July 1944, *Ibid.*, 91.
6. *Ibid.*, 155.
7. *Ibid.*, 157.
8. Louis Simpson, *The Owner of the House* (Rochester NY: BOA, 2003), 121.
9. Louis Simpson, *Collected Poems* (New York: Paragon House, 1988), 124.
10. Louis Simpson, "On Line," 157.
11. Louis Simpson, *Owner of the House*, 103.
12. Louis Simpson, "On Line," 121.
13. Louis Simpson, *Owner of the House*, 99.
14. *Ibid.*, 112.
15. Louis Simpson, "On Line," 130.
16. Louis Simpson, *Owner of the House*, 114.
17. Louis Simpson, "On Line," 132.
18. *Ibid.*
19. Louis Simpson, *Owner of the House*, 133.
20. *Ibid.*, 136.
21. *Ibid.*, 138.
22. *Ibid.*, 139–40.
23. *Ibid.*, 141.
24. *Ibid.*, 142.
25. *Ibid.*, 144–5.
26. *Ibid.*, 145–6.
27. *Ibid.*, 147–8.
28. *Ibid.*, 149–53.
29. *Ibid.*, 156–7.
30. *Ibid.*, 158–9.
31. Louis Simpson, "On Line," 139.
32. Vernon Scannell, *Not Without Glory: Poets of the Second World War* (London: Woburn, 1976), 215.
33. Louis Simpson, *The King My Father's Wreck* (Brownsville OR: Story Line Press, 1995), 62.
34. Louis Simpson, *Owner of the House*, 161.
35. Louis Simpson, "On Line," 142.
36. Louis Simpson, "Views from a Window," in Louis Simpson, *Selected Prose* (New York: Paragon House, 1989), 158.
37. Louis Simpson, "On Line," 146–7.
38. Louis Simpson, *Owner of the House*, 113.

Chapter 7

1. William Meredith, *Poems Are Hard to Read* (Ann Arbor: University of Michigan Press, 1991), 205–6.
2. Gordon Van Ness, *The One Voice of James Dickey: His Letters and Life, 1942–1969* (Columbia: University of Missouri Press), 2.
3. James Dickey, *Crux: The Letters of James Dickey*, ed. Matthew J. Bruccoli and Judith S. Baughman (New York: Alfred A. Knopf, 1999), 3.
4. *AAF: The Official Guide to the Army Air Forces* (New York: Scribner's, 1944), 104–5.
5. Gordon Van Ness, *The One Voice of James Dickey*, 9.
6. James Dickey, *Crux: The Letters of James Dickey*, 7.
7. *AAF: The Official Guide to the Army Air Forces*, 107, 111.
8. Gordon Van Ness, *The One Voice of James Dickey*, 17.

9. *Ibid.*, 22.

10. See, for instance, Karl Malkoff's incorrect assertion that during "both World War II and the Korean War [Dickey] was a night-fighter pilot, decorated three times for bravery," in *Crowell's Handbook of Contemporary American Poetry* (New York: Thomas Crowell, 1973), 100.

11. Henry Hart, *James Dickey: The World as Lie* (New York: Picador, 2000), 107–8.

12. James Dickey, *The Whole Motion: Collected Poems, 1945-1992* (Hanover: Wesleyan University Press, 1992), 57–8.

13. *Ibid.*, 55–7.

14. Henry Hart, *James Dickey: The World as Lie*, 97–8.

15. James Dickey, *The Whole Motion*, 58–9.

16. James Dickey, "Metaphor as Pure Adventure," *Sorties: Journals and New Essays* (New York: Doubleday, 1971), 173.

17. James Dickey, *The Whole Motion*, 225–6.

18. *Ibid.*, 10.

19. *Ibid.*, 250–8.

20. James Dickey, *Self-Interviews* (New York: Doubleday, 1970), 163–4.

21. Robert Kirschten, *James Dickey and the Gentle Ecstasy of Earth: A Reading of the Poems* (Baton Rouge: Louisiana State University Press, 1988), 45.

22. *Ibid.*, 30.

23. Henry Hart, *James Dickey: The World as Lie*, 76.

24. James Dickey, *Alnilam* (New York: Doubleday, 1987), 209–10.

25. *Ibid.*, 206.

26. *Ibid.*, 214.

27. *Ibid.*, 213.

28. Henry Hart, *James Dickey: The World as Lie*, 109–10.

29. James Dickey, *The Whole Motion*, 193–200.

30. Quoted in Henry Hart, *James Dickey: The World as Lie*, 110.

31. Henry Hart, *James Dickey: The World as Lie*, 344.

32. James Dickey, *Self-Interviews*, 137.

33. Henry Hart, *James Dickey: The World as Lie*, 102. For some reason, this letter is not reprinted in Dickey, *Crux: The Letters of James Dickey*, or Van Ness, *The One Voice of James Dickey*.

34. Gordon Van Ness, *The One Voice of James Dickey*, 2.

35. James Dickey, *The Whole Motion*, 182–3.

Chapter 8

1. Richard Hugo, "Catch-22, Addendum," in Richard Hugo, *The Real West Marginal Way: A Poet's Autobiography*, ed. Ripley S. Hugo, Lois M. Welch, and James Welch (New York: W. W. Norton, 1986), 98–99.

2. Internet account written by Gerry Smith, pilot, 765th Squadron, http://blogs.salon.com/00002608/categories/myFather, accessed 24 December 2005.

3. Richard Hugo, "Ci Vediamo," in Richard Hugo, *The Real West Marginal Way*, 124.

4. Richard Hugo, "Catch-22, Addendum," 99.

5. Richard Hugo, "Ci Vediamo," 107.

6. Richard Hugo, "Catch-22, Addendum," 97.

7. Richard Hugo, *Making Certain It Goes On: The Collected Poems of Richard Hugo* (New York: W. W. Norton, 1984), 121.

8. Richard Hugo, "Catch-22, Addendum," 103.

9. *Ibid.*

10. *Ibid.*, 105.

11. Richard Hugo, *Making Certain It Goes On*, 81.

12. Richard Hugo, "Catch-22, Addendum," 98.

13. Donna Gerstenberger, *Richard Hugo* (Boise ID: Boise State University, 1983), 8.

14. Richard Hugo, *Making Certain It Goes On*, 105.

15. *Ibid.*, 106.

16. *Ibid.*, 115.

17. Ibid., 118.
18. Ibid., 120.
19. Ibid., 121.
20. Richard Hugo, "Ci Vediamo," 114.
21. Ibid., 115.
22. Richard Hugo, Making Certain It Goes On, 124.
23. Ibid., 126.
24. Ibid., 126–7.
25. Ibid., 129–30.
26. Ibid., 139.
27. Ibid., 232.
28. Sanford Pinsker, Three Pacific Northwest Poets: William Stafford, Richard Hugo, and David Wagoner (Boston: Twayne, 1987), 86.
29. Richard Hugo, Making Certain It Goes On, 281.
30. Ibid., 435.

Chapter 9

1. Lincoln Kirstein, "Afterword," Flesh Is Heir (Carbondale: Southern Illinois State University, 1975), 322.
2. Ibid., 315.
3. Ibid., 317.
4. Lincoln Kirstein, "Notes," Rhymes of a Pfc (Boston: David R. Godine, 1981), 243.
5. Ibid., 241–2.
6. Ibid., 242.
7. Martin Duberman, The Worlds of Lincoln Kirstein (New York: Alfred A. Knopf, 2007), 359–86.
8. Letter from Lincoln Kirstein to A. E. Hamilton of New York City, undated, sent from Fort Belvoir, Virginia. Letter in author's possession.
9. Letter from Lincoln Kirstein to A. E. Hamilton, dated April 13, 1943, sent from Fort Belvoir, Virginia. Letter in author's possession.
10. Letter from Lincoln Kirstein to A. E. Hamilton, undated, sent from Fort Belvoir, Virginia. Letter in author's possession.
11. David Leddick, Intimate Companions: A Triography of George Platt Lynes, Paul Cadmus, Lincoln Kirstein, and Their Circle (New York: St. Martin's, 2001), 189.
12. Martin Duberman, The World of Lincoln Kirstein, 389–90.
13. Lincoln Kirstein, "Notes," Rhymes of a Pfc, 243.
14. David Leddick, Intimate Companions, 169.
15. Vernon Scannell, Not Without Glory: Poets of the Second World War (London: Woburn, 1976), 174.
16. Ibid., 177–8.
17. Lincoln Kirstein, Rhymes of a Pfc, 4.
18. Vernon Scannell, Not Without Glory, 181–2.
19. Lincoln Kirstein, Rhymes of a Pfc, 64.
20. Ibid., 69
21. Martin Duberman, The World of Lincoln Kirstein, 395.
22. Lincoln Kirstein, Rhymes of a Pfc, 88.
23. Ibid., 107–8.
24. Ibid., 100.
25. Ibid., 96.
26. Ibid., 176–7.
27. Ibid., 242.
28. Ibid., 190.
29. Martin Duberman, The World of Lincoln Kirstein, 401.
30. Lincoln Kirstein, Rhymes of a Pfc, 259.
31. Ibid., 184.
32. Ibid., 185.

Chapter 10

1. Harvey Shapiro, ed., Poets of World War II (New York: Library of America, 2003), xxii.
2. "News Notes," Poetry: A Magazine of Verse, June 1945 (66:3), 173. The reviewer was probably Peter De Vries, editor of Poetry.
3. Howard Nemerov, "Models," War Stories: Poems about Long Ago and Now (Chicago: University of Chicago Press, 1987), 21.

Bibliography

AAF: *The Official Guide to the Army Air Forces.* New York: Scribner's, 1944.
"Bristol Beaufighter." http://www.burmabeaufighters.com/pages/beaufighters.php. Accessed August 7, 2004.
Button, Robert E. *Enigma in Many Keys.* New York: iUniverse, 2004.
Calhoun, Richard J., and Robert W. Hill. *James Dickey.* Boston: Twayne, 1983.
Carruth, Hayden. *Reluctantly.* Port Townsend WA: Copper Canyon, 1998.
Ciardi, John. *The Collected Poems of John Ciardi.* Fayetteville: University of Arkansas Press, 1997.
____. *From Time to Time.* New York: Twayne, 1951.
____. *John Ciardi: Measure of the Man.* Ed. Vince Clemente. Fayetteville: University of Arkansas Press, 1987. 3–19.
____. *Manner of Speaking.* New Brunswick: Rutgers University Press, 1972.
____. *Other Skies.* Boston: Little, Brown, 1947.
____. *Saipan: The War Diary of John Ciardi.* Ed. Edward M. Cifelli. Fayetteville: University of Arkansas Press, 1988.
____. *39 Poems.* New Brunswick: Rutgers University Press, 1959.
Cifelli, Edward. *John Ciardi: A Biography.* Fayetteville: University of Arkansas Press, 1997.
Dickey, James. *Alnilam.* New York: Doubleday, 1987.
____. *Crux: The Letters of James Dickey.* Ed. Matthew J. Bruccoli and Judith S. Baughman. New York: Alfred A. Knopf, 1999.
____. *Self-Interviews.* New York: Doubleday, 1970.
____. *Sorties: Journals and New Essays.* Garden City NY: Doubleday, 1971.
____. *The Whole Motion: Collected Poems, 1945–1992.* Hanover NH: Wesleyan University Press, 1992.
Duberman, Martin. *The Worlds of Lincoln Kirstein.* New York: Alfred A. Knopf, 2007.
Ferguson, Suzanne. *The Poetry of Randall Jarrell.* Baton Rouge: Louisiana State University Press, 1971.
____, ed. *Critical Essays on Randall Jarrell.* Boston: G. K. Hall, 1983.
Flynn, Richard. *Randall Jarrell and the Lost World of Childhood.* Athens: University of Georgia Press, 1990.
Ford, Corey. *Short Cut to Tokyo: The Battle for the Aleutians.* New York: Scribner's, 1943.
Gerstenberger, Donna. *Richard Hugo.* Boise ID: Boise State University Press, 1983.
Goldensohn, Lorrie. *Dismantling Glory: Twentieth Century Soldier Poetry.* New York: Columbia University Press, 2003.

Hammett, Dashiell. *The Selected Letters of Dashiell Hammett 1921–1960.* Ed. Richard Laymen and Julie M. Rivett. Washington DC: Counterpoint, 2001.
Hart, Henry. *James Dickey: The World as a Lie.* New York: Picador, 2000.
Hugo, Richard. *Making Certain It Goes On: The Collected Poems of Richard Hugo.* New York: W. W. Norton, 1984.
____. *The Real West Marginal Way: A Poet's Autobiography.* Ed. Ripley S. Hugo, Lois M. Welch, and James Welch. New York: W. W. Norton, 1986.
Jarrell, Randall. *The Complete Poems.* New York: Farrar, Straus and Giroux, 1969.
____. *Little Friend, Little Friend.* New York: Dial, 1945.
____. *Losses.* New York: Harcourt, Brace, 1948.
____. *Randall Jarrell's Letters.* Ed. Mary Jarrell. Boston: Houghton Mifflin, 1985.
Kirsch, Adam. *The Wounded Surgeon: Confession and Transformation in Six American Poets.* New York: W. W. Norton, 2005.
Kirschten, Robert. *James Dickey and the Gentle Ecstasy of Earth: A Reading of the Poems.* Baton Rouge: Louisiana State University Press, 1988.
Kirstein, Lincoln. *Flesh Is Heir.* Carbondale: Southern Illinois State University Press, 1975.
____. *The Poems of Lincoln Kirstein.* New York: Atheneum, 1987.
____. *Rhymes of a Pfc.* Boston: David Godine, 1981.
"Kodiak Alaska Military History." http://209.165.152.119/vs/vs49.html. Accessed September 14, 2004.
Krickel, Edward. *John Ciardi.* Boston: Twayne, 1980.
LaBrie, Ross. *Howard Nemerov.* Boston: Twayne, 1980.
Leddick, David. *Intimate Companions: A Triography of George Platt Lynes, Paul Cadmus, Lincoln Kirstein, and Their Circle.* New York: St. Martin's, 2001.
Lowell, Robert, Peter Taylor, and Robert Penn Warren, eds. *Randall Jarrell, 1914–1965.* New York: Farrar, Straus and Giroux, 1967.
Malkoff, Karl, ed. *Crowell's Handbook of Contemporary American Poetry.* New York: Thomas Crowell, 1973.
Matthews, Courtland W. *Aleutian Interval.* Seattle: Frank McCaffrey, 1949.
Meredith, William. *Earth Walk: New and Selected Poems.* New York: Alfred A. Knopf, 1970.
____. *Love Letter from an Impossible Land.* New Haven: Yale University Press, 1944.
____. *Poems Are Hard to Read.* Ann Arbor: University of Michigan Press, 1991.
____. *Ships and Other Figures.* Princeton: Princeton University Press, 1948.
Nemerov, Howard. *The Collected Poems of Howard Nemerov.* Chicago: University of Chicago Press, 1977.
____. *A Howard Nemerov Reader.* Columbia: University of Missouri Press, 1991.
____. *A Journal of the Fictive Life.* New Brunswick: Rutgers University Press, 1965.
____. *War Stories: Poems about Long Ago and Now.* Chicago: University of Chicago Press, 1987.
Nesbit, Roy Conyers. *The Strike Wings: Special Anti-Shipping Squadrons, 1942–1945.* London: William Kimber, 1984.
Pinsker, Sanford. *Three Pacific Northwest Poets: William Stafford, Richard Hugo, and David Wagoner.* Boston: Twayne, 1987.
Poetry: A Magazine of Verse. Various issues, 1943, 1945.
Pritchard, William H. *Randall Jarrell: A Literary Life.* New York: Farrar, Straus and Giroux, 1990.
Roache, Joel. *Richard Eberhart: The Progress of an American Poet.* New York: Oxford University Press, 1971.
Rosenthal, M. L. *Randall Jarrell.* Minneapolis: University of Minnesota Press, 1972.

Rotella, Guy. *Three Contemporary Poets of New England: William Meredith, Philip Booth, and Peter Davidson.* Boston: Twayne, 1983.
Scannell, Vernon. *Not Without Glory: Poets of the Second World War.* London: Woburn, 1976.
Schweik, Susan. *A Gulf So Deeply Felt: American Women Poets and the Second World War.* Madison: University of Wisconsin Press, 1991.
Shapiro, Harvey, ed. *Poets of World War II.* New York: Library of America, 2003.
Shapiro, Karl. *Creative Glut: Selected Essays of Karl Shapiro.* Ed. Robert Phillips. Chicago: Ivan R. Dee, 2004.
____. *Karl Shapiro: Selected Poems.* Ed. John Updike. New York: Library of America, 2003.
____. *Poems 1940–1953.* New York: Random House, 1953.
____. *Reports of My Death.* Chapel Hill: Algonquin, 1990.
____. *V-Letter and Other Poems.* New York: Reynal & Hitchcock, 1944.
____. *The Younger Son: The Youth and War Years of a Distinguished Poet.* Chapel Hill: Algonquin, 1988.
Simpson, Louis. *Collected Poems.* New York: Paragon House, 1988.
____. *The King My Father's Wreck.* Brownsville OR: Story Line, 1995.
____. *The Owner of the House.* Rochester NY: BOA, 2003.
____. *Selected Prose.* New York: Paragon House, 1989.
Simpson, Stanley Robert. "An Autobiography." http://randpersonnel.co.za/autofour.htm. Accessed August 18, 2005.
Smith, Gerry (Pilot, 765th Squadron). Personal account. http://blogs.salon.com/00002608/categories/myFather. Accessed December 24, 2005.
Terkel, Studs. *The Good War: An Oral History of World War Two.* New York: Pantheon, 1984.
Van Ness, Gordon. *The One Voice of James Dickey: His Letters and Life, 1942–1969.* Columbia: University of Missouri Press, 2003.
Williams, Oscar, ed. *The War Poets: An Anthology of the War Poetry of the Twentieth Century.* New York: John Day, 1945.

Index

Abrams, Gen. Creighton 111
"Absent with Official Leave" 39–40
Adak, AK 66
Adriatic Sea 143
Afognak, AK 66
"Against Excess of Sea or Sun or Reason" 76
Agee, James 152–3, 159
"Air Strike" 161
Aircraft: AT-11 136; AT-23 116; B-17 40, 44, 49, 129, 139; B-24 9, 44, 49, 68, 136; B-25 86, 139; B-26 116; B-29 9, 14, 38, 40, 49, 130; Bristol Beaufighter 83, 91–92; Bristol Blenheim 87; C-47 47, 116; Curtiss Helldiver 74; Douglas Dauntless 74; FW-190 138; Grumman Goose 67; JRF 67; ME-109 138; North American Texan 67; OS2U 66, 74; P-61 9, 116–119; P-70 116; SNJ 67
"Airman's Virtue" 73
Aleutian Islands, AK 65
Alnilam 128–30
"Altitude: 15,000" 72–3
America First Committee 4
"Angels at Hamburg" 42–3
Ardennes Forest, Belgium 105, 109
"Arm in Arm" 102
"Armistice" 84, 163
Armstrong, Donald 116, 123–5
Arnhem, Holland 98–9, 105
Ashcroft, Peggy 159
Atka, Alaska 66
Atlanta Naval Air Station 80
Atlantic Monthly 57
Attu, AK 65
Auden, W.H. 5, 76, 153, 163–5

Baltimore, MD 15
Bastonge, Belgium 98–9, 103, 105, 109, 138, 162
"The Battle" 103
"Battlewagon" 77
Bennington College 97
Benton, Walter 14
Berchtesgaden, Germany 98, 113
Berryman, John 3
Biak, Dutch New Guinea 28
Bishop, Elizabeth 3
Bishop, John Peale 4
Blunden, Edmund 4, 5, 16
Bly, Robert 132–4, 144
Boca Raton, FL 116
Boeing Aircraft Company 145
Bonaparte, Napoleon 3
Boston, MA 48, 152
Bourne, David 7
Bradley, Earl (crewmember) 116, 132
Brandeis University 97
Brisbane, Australia 22
Brooke, Rupert 16
Brooks, Cleanth 44
Browning, Robert 153
Brueghel, Pieter 72
Buckingham Field, Fort Myers, FL 115
Budapest, Romania 137
Burke, Kenneth 94
"Burning the Letters" 43–4
Burns, John Horne 149

Camden, SC 114–5
Campbell, Roy 116
Cape Town, South Africa 19
Capri, Italy 148
Carentan, France 101

191

Index

"Carentan O Carentan" 100–2
Carruth, Hayden 13
"Carrier" 77
Cartwright, Anthony 137
Celestial Navigation Trainer (CNT) 35
"Centuries Near Spinazzola" 147
Cerignola, Italy 137, 146
Chagall, Marc 121
Chanute Army Air Field, Rantoul, IL 34–6
Christensen, Stratton 73
Ciardi, John: 3, 7, 9, 12, 14, 41, 48–64, 90, 148, 151, 171–2; "Elegy" 56; "Elegy Just in Case" 56–7; "Expendability" 56; "I Meet the Motion of Summer Thinking Guns" 63; "Massive Retaliation" 64; "On a Photo of Sgt. Ciardi One Year Later" 63–4; "On Sending Home My Civilian Clothes" 50–1; "Poem for My Twenty-Ninth Birthday" 62; "Reflections While Oiling a Machine Gun" 51–3; "Reveille for My Twenty-Eighth Birthday" 51; "Ritual for Singing Bat" 56; "Suddenly While Squadrons Turn" 51; "Two Songs for a Gunner" 56; "V-J Day" 59–62; "Wafflebutt" 58–9
"Civil Twilight" 76
Civilian Pilot Training Program 33
Clay, Gen. Lucius 155
Clough, Arthur Hugh 153
Columbia University 98, 113
"Confrontation of the Hero" 126–7
Connecticut College 81
"Conscription Camp" 16–7
Corpus Christi Naval Air Station 65
Corsellis, Timothy 7, 14
Cowden, Roy 48
Cox, Denyer 7
Creekmore, Hubert 14
cummings, e. e. 4

"D-Day + All the Years" 95–6
Dam Neck, Virginia 13
Davis, Lambert 33
Davis-Monthan Army Air Field, Tucson, AZ 35, 40
"A Day on the Big Branch" 85
"Death of the Ball Turret Gunner" 40–2
de Blasio, Amy Breyer 33, 42
Deming Army Air Field, Deming, NM 136
De Vries, Peter 7, 170n.

Dickey, James: 9, 11, 12, 114–135, 136, 144, 151, 174–5; *Alnilam* 128–30; "Confrontation of the Hero" 126–7; "The Driver" 134–5; "The Enclosure" 121–3; "The Firebombing" 130–4; "The Jewel" 119–21; "The Performance" 123–5; "Reincarnation (II)" 127–8; "The War Wound" 126
Dies, Martin 49
Dillon, George 7
"Do Not Embrace Your Mind's New Negro Friend" 80
"Double Negative" 93–4
"The Driver" 134–5
Durrell, Lawrence 7
Dutch Harbor, AK 65–6
Dutch New Guinea 22, 24, 28

Eberhart, Richard 7, 13, 14, 53, 88, 169
"Eighth Air Force" 44–7
Eisenhower, Gen. Dwight 161
"Elegy" 56
"Elegy for a Dead Soldier" 24–7
"Elegy Just in Case" 56–7
El Greco 152
Eliot, T.S. 5, 146, 153
"The Emancipators" 38
"The Enclosure" 121–3
"Envoi" to *Ships and Other Figures* 76
Evans, Patrick 7
Evans, Walker 152–3
Ewart, Gavin 14
"Expendability" 56

"The Faith" 94–5
"Fall In" 157–8
Fein, Richard 44
Ferguson, Suzanne 43
Finschhafen, Germany 22
"The Firebombing" 130–4
"The Fly" 17
"Flying, Reflying, Farming" 150
Flynn, Richard 42
"For the Squadron (236th Coastal Command, Royal Air Force)" 87–8
"For W—, Who Commanded Well" 88–9
Ford, Corey 66, 68
Formosa (Taiwan) 117
Fort Belvoir, VA 154
Fort Dix, NJ 19
Fort Hood, TX 98
Fort Lee, VA 15

Fort Leonard Wood, MO 99
"4th Armored" 162–3
Fraser, G.S. 7
Freud, Sigmund 125–6
"Full Moon: New Guinea" 24
Fuller, Roy 7, 14

Galileo 38
Gielgud, John 159
Goldensohn, Lorrie 32–3
Good Luck in Cracked Italian 145–50
Göring, Hermann 154–5
Graves, Robert 4, 16
El Greco 152
"Gunner" 39

Hamburg, Germany 42–3
Hamilton College 97
Hamilton Standard Propellers 142
Hammer Army Air Field, Fresno, CA 116
Hammett, Dashiell 66, 68–9
Hansell, Gen. Heywood 55
Hart, Henry 128
Harvard University 82, 152, 159
Heligoland Island 95
Heller, Joseph 90, 139
Hellman, Lillian 66, 69
"The Heroes" 113
High Point, NC 114
Hollandia, New Guinea 116
"Homecoming" 29–30
"Homeric Simile" 78–80
Hopwood Poetry Award 48
Honig, Edwin 7
Hopkins, Gerard Manley 153
Hugo, Richard 9, 12, 136–50, 176; "Centuries Near Spinazzola" 147; "Flying, Reflying, Farming" 150; *Good Luck in Cracked Italian* 145–50; "In Your Big Dream" 150; "In Your War Dream" 150; "Mission to Linz" 142–5; "Note from Capri to Richard Ryan on the Adriatic Floor" 149; "Spinazzola: Quella Cantina La" 147–8; "Tretitoli, Where the Bomb Group Was" 146–7; "Where We Crashed" 140–1

"I Dreamed That in a City Dark as Paris" 100
"I Meet the Motion of Summer Thinking Guns" 63
"IFF" 92–3
"In Memoriam Stratton Christensen" 73

"In Your Big Dream" 150
"In Your War Dream" 150
Innsbruck, Vienna 141
"Instructions for the Use of This Toy" 84–5
"Inter-Service" 161
Isley Army Air Field, Saipan 13, 53–4
Iwo Jima 54

James, Henry 153
Jarrell, Randall 3, 8, 9, 11, 12, 32–36, 98–113, 136, 175; "Absent with Official Leave" 39–40; "Angels at Hamburg" 42–3; "Burning the Letters" 43–4; "Death of the Ball Turret Gunner" 40–2; "Eighth Air Force" 44–7; "The Emancipators" 38; "Gunner" 39; "Pilot from the Carrier" 39; "2nd Air Force" 39; "Siegfried" 40; "The Soldier" 38; "Soldier [T.P.]" 39; "The State" 38–9
"The Jewel" 119–21
Jones, David 16, 161
"June: Dutch Harbor" 71–2

Kaneohe Bay, HI 74
Katz, Evalyn 28–30
Keyes, Sidney 14
Kipling, Rudyard 5, 153
Kirsch, Adam 42
Kirschten, Robert 128
Kirstein, Lincoln 5, 6, 8, 9, 11, 12, 151–166, 176–7; "Air Strike" 161; "Armistice" 163; "Fall In" 157–8; "4th Armored" 162–3; "Inter-Service" 161; "Patton" 160; "Red Cross" 160; "Siegfriedslage" 163–5; "Tudoresque" 159–60
Kiska, AK 65
Klamath Falls, OR 140
Knapp (crewmember) 137, 141
Kodiak Island, AK 65, 67
"A Kodiak Poem" 72
Korean War 81, 86, 128
Kunitz, Stanley 3, 7, 13–4

LaBrie, Ross 83
Lally, James (crewmember) 116, 123–5, 133
Lawrence of Arabia 5
Leddick, David 154–5
"The Leg" 22–4
LeMay, Gen. Curtis 55–7
Lewis, Alun 7, 14
Lindbergh, Charles 4, 83

"Lines Written but Never Mailed from Hawaii" 74–5
Link Trainer 34–5
Linz, Austria 137, 142
Litvinoff, Emanuel 14
"Lord I Have Seen Too Much" 20
Los Angeles, CA 140
"Love Letter from an Impossible Land" 68–70
Lowell, Robert 3, 36–7
Lowes, John Livingston 152
Lowry Army Air Field, Denver, CO 49
Luce, Henry 158

M-1 Rifle 24, 110
MacLeish, Archibald 4, 68, 70, 72
Mallalieu, H.B. 14
Manifold, John 7, 14
Manila, Philippine Islands 116
Marshall, Margaret 43
"Massive Retaliation" 64
Masters, Edgar Lee 41
Matthews, Courtland 71
Mauldin, William ("Bill") 163
Maxwell Army Air Field, Montgomery, AL 114
McGrath, Thomas 7, 13
Melbourne, Australia 21–2
"Memories of a Lost War" 102–3
"A Memory of the War" 97
Meredith, William 7, 8, 12, 14, 65–81, 136, 151, 172–3; "Against Excess of Sea or Sun or Reason" 76; "Airman's Virtue" 73; "Altitude: 15,000" 72–3; "Battlewagon" 77; "Carrier" 77; "Civil Twilight" 76; "Do Not Embrace Your Mind's New Negro Friend" 80; "Envoi" to *Ships and Other Figures* 76; "Homeric Simile" 78–80; "In Memoriam Stratton Christensen" 73; "June: Dutch Harbor" 71–2; "A Kodiak Poem" 72; "Lines Written but Never Mailed from Hawaii" 74–5; "Love Letter from an Impossible Land" 68–70; "Middle Flight" 77–8; "Notes for an Elegy" 73; "Reading My Poems from World War II" 80; "Reconversion Sonnet" 80; "Transport" 77
Miami Beach, FL 114
"Middle Flight" 77–8
Military organizations and units: 4th Armored Division 162; 20th Bomber Command 59; 36th Infantry Division 13; 36th Signal Company 13; 73rd Bomb Wing 54, 57; 101st Airborne Division 98–9; 143 Squadron, Coastal Command 87–8; 236 Squadron, Coastal Command 83, 87; 254 Squadron, Coastal Command 87–8; 418th Night Fighter Squadron 116–118; 455th Heavy Bombardment Squadron 13; 484th Bomb Group 137; 500th Bomb Group 54; 825th Bomb Squadron 137; 882nd Bomb Squadron 53–4; Arts and Monuments Commission 154–5, 163; Office of Chief of Naval Operations 80; Office of Strategic Services (OSS) 30; Officer Candidate School 34; Scouting Squadron 46 (VS-46) 74; Scouting Squadron 49 (VS-49) 65–7; Scouting Squadron 69 (VS-69) 74; Scouting Squadron 70 (VS-70) 67
Milton, John 76–8
Mindoro, Philippine Islands 116
"Mission to Linz" 142–5
"Models" 89–90, 173–4
Moore, Marianne 153
Munich, Germany 137

Naples, Italy 146, 149
Napoleon 3
Nashville, TN 49, 114
The Nation 43
Nemerov, Howard 3, 9, 11, 12, 14, 82–97, 173–4; "Armistice" 84; "D-Day + All the Years" 95–6; "A Day on the Big Branch" 85; "Double Negative" 93–4; "The Faith" 94–5; "For the Squadron (236th Coastal Command, Royal Air Force)" 87–8; "For W—, Who Commanded Well" 88–9; "IFF" 92–3; "Instructions for the Use of This Toy" 84–5; "A Memory of the War" 97; "Models" 89–90, 173–4; "Night Operations, Coastal Command" 90–2; "The Old Soldiers' Home" 83; "An Old Warplane" 85–6; "Redeployment" 83; "The War in the Air" 90; "The Western Approaches" 86–7
New York State University at Stony Brook 113
New York Times 65
Newton, Isaac 38
Niemoller, Martin 163–4
"Night Operations, Coastal Command" 90–2

Norden Bomb Sight 142
Normandy Peninsula, France 95, 102, 154
North Coates, England 87–8
"Nostalgia" 19–20
"Note from Capri to Richard Ryan on the Adriatic Floor" 149
"Notes for an Elegy" 73
Number 2 Service School, Uplands, Canada 82

Oates, Joyce Carol 130
O'Brien, Ryan (crewmember) 137, 140
Odertal, Germany 137
O'Donnell, Gen. Emmett ("Rosie") 37
Okinawa 116, 131
"Old Soldier" 100
"The Old Soldiers' Home" 83
"An Old Warplane" 85–6
"On a Photo of Sgt. Ciardi One Year Later" 63–4
"On Sending Home My Civilian Clothes" 50–1
Orion (constellation) 24
Otter Point, AK 66
Owen, Wilfrid 4–7, 16, 191, 164

Padua, Italy 146
Palermo, Sicily 145
"Patton" 160
Patton, Gen. George 155, 160
Pavlof Volcano, Alaska 69
Pearl Harbor 5–6, 15, 17, 19, 33, 133
"The Performance" 123–5
Perth, Australia 19
Pilate, Pontius 45–6
"Pilot from the Carrier" 39
Plato 51–2
Plautus 44
Ploesti, Romania 137
"Poem for My Twenty-Ninth Birthday" 62
Poetry: A Magazine of Verse 6–7, 31, 170
Porjescz, Kurt (crewmember) 56
Pound, Exra 5
Pratt and Whitney (engines) 142
Princeton University 65
Pritchard, William 44
Proust, Marcel 82
Pudney, John 14

Queen Mary (ship) 19–20

Rago, Henry 7
"Reading My Poems from World War II" 80

"Recapitulations VIII" 30
"Reconversion Sonnet" 80
"Red Cross" 160
"Redeployment" 83
Reed, Henry 53
"Reflections While Oiling a Machine Gun" 51–3
"Reincarnation (II)" 127–8
"Reveille for My Twenty-Eighth Birthday" 51
Rheims, France 108–9
Rhys, Keidrich 7, 14
Rio de Janeiro, Brazil 19
"Ritual for Singing Bat" 56
Rockefeller, Nelson 154
Rodman, Selden 14
Roethke, Theodore 3, 145
Rome, Italy 146
Roosevelt Field, San Pedro, CA 74
Rosenberg, Isaac 4, 5
Rosenthal, M.L. 6
"The Runner" 104–12
Ryan, Richard (crewmember) 148–9

Salzburg, Germany 163
Sand Point, AK 66
Sarah Lawrence College 47
Sarajevo 149
Sardis, Greece 147
Sassoon, Siegfried 4–6, 16, 161
Saturday Review of Literature 64
Scannell, Vernon 4, 32, 110–1, 155, 158
Schwartz, Delmore 3
"Scyros" 15–6
Seattle, WA 136
"2nd Air Force" 39
Seeger, Alan 4
Self, Ed (crewmember) 137
Selman Army Air Field, LA 49
Shakespeare, William 76, 159
Shapiro, Harvey 4, 14, 167
Shapiro, Karl 3, 7, 9, 10, 12, 13, 14, 15–31, 37, 151, 170; "Conscription Camp" 16–7; "Elegy for a Dead Soldier" 24–7; "The Fly" 17; "Full Moon: New Guinea" 24; "Homecoming" 29–30; "The Leg" 22–4; "Lord I Have Seen Too Much" 20; "Nostalgia" 19–20; "Recapitulations VIII" 30; "Scyros" 15–6; "Troop Train" 21–2; "V-Letter" 27–8
Sheppard Army Air Field, Wichita Falls, TX 33–4

Shishaldin Volcano, AK 69
"Siegfried" 40
"Siegfriedslage" 163–5
Simpson, Louis 8, 9, 11, 12, 98–113, 136, 175; "Arm in Arm" 102; "The Battle" 103; "Carentan O Carentan" 100–2; "The Heroes" 113; "I Dreamed That in a City Dark as Paris" 100; "Memories of a Lost War" 102–3; "Old Soldier" 100; "The Runner" 104–12
Sister Pavlof Volcano, AK 69
Skegness, England 87
Smith, William Jay 7, 14
Snodgrass, W.D. 13
"The Soldier" 38
"Soldier [T.P.]" 39
Southern Cross (constellation) 24
Spender, Stephen 76
Spinazzola, Italy 147
"Spinazzola: Quella Cantina La" 147–8
Stalingrad (Battle of) 29
"The State" 38–9
Stauffer, Donald 14
Steinberg, Howard (crewmember) 137, 141
Stendahl (Marie-Henry Beyle) 3
Stepanchev, Stephen 7
Stewart (crewmember) 137, 140
Stewart, Gervase 7, 14
Strategic Bombing Survey 163
Strobel, Marion 7
"Suddenly While Squadrons Turn" 51
Swanson, Robert (crewmember) 137
Symons, Julian 14

Tate, Allen 35–6
Tennyson, Alfred Lord 153
Tergensee, Germany 163–4
Terkel, Studs 57, 90
Thomson, Dunstan 14
Tokyo, Japan 54
Toretta, Italy 137
"Transport" 77
Treece, Henry 9, 14
Tretitoli, Italy 146
"Tretitoli, Where the Bomb Group Was" 146–7
Trilling, Lionel 98
Triobrand Islands 22
"Troop Train" 21–2
"Tudoresque" 159–60
Tufts University 48
"Two Songs for a Gunner" 56

Unalaska Island, AK 66
Unimak Island, AK 69
University of Iowa 150
University of Kansas City 48
University of Michigan 48
University of Montana 145
University of South Carolina 135
University of Texas (Austin) 33
University of Washington 145
Updike, John 17

"V-J Day" 59–62
"V-Letter" 27–8
USS *Valley Forge* (ship) 81
Vanderbilt University 135
Van Doren, Mark 98
Van Eyck, Hubert 163
Van Eyck, Jan 163
Van Ness, Gordon 115, 133
Venice, Italy 146
Vienna, Austria 137, 141
Vietnam War 132, 149

"Wafflebutt" 58–9
Wagner, Richard 164
Walker Army Air Field, Kansas 49
"The War in the Air" 90
"The War Wound" 126
Washington University 97
Watkins, Vernon 14
Weir, Nigel 7
Weismiller, Edward 14
"The Western Approaches" 86–7
"Where We Crashed" 140–1
Whitehead, Alfred North 152
Whitman, Walt 5, 153
Whittemore, Reed 3
Wilbur, Richard 3, 13
Wildwood, NJ 13
Williams, Oscar 14, 34
Wilson, Edmund 33
Women's College of the University of North Carolina 47
Wordsworth, William 76
World War I 6, 38, 84, 100, 103, 149, 150, 153

Xerxes (Persian king) 147

Yeats, W.B. 5, 76

Zodiac (constellations group) 127

www.ingramcontent.com/pod-product-compliance
Ingram Content Group UK Ltd.
Pitfield, Milton Keynes, MK11 3LW, UK
UKHW042009140426
5217IPUK00015B/1074